Andrei Tarkovsky (1932-1986) is one of the most fascinating of filmmakers. He is supremely romantic, an old-fashioned, traditional artist – at home in the company of Leonardo da Vinci, Pieter Brueghel, Aleksandr Pushkin, Fyodor Dostoievsky, Byzantine icon painters and Romantics such as Johann Wolfgang von Goethe. Tarkovsky is a magician. His films are full of magical events, dreams, memory sequences, multiple viewpoints, multiple time-scales and bizarre occurrences. He is a marvellous filmmaker, a creator of miracles, a poet.

MEDIA, FEMINISM, CULTURAL STUDIES

FROM CRESCENT MOON PUBLISHING

Arseny Tarkovsky: *Life, Life: Selected Poems*
translated by Virginia Rounding

Stepping Forward: Essays, Lectures and Interviews
by Wolfgang Iser

Wild Zones: Pornography, Art and Feminism
by Kelly Ives

Global Media Warning: Explorations of Radio, Television and the Press
by Oliver Whitehorne

'Cosmo Woman': The World of Women's Magazines
by Oliver Whitehorne

Andrea Dworkin
by Jeremy Mark Robinson

Cixous, Irigaray, Kristeva: The Jouissance *of French Feminism*
by Kelly Ives

Sex in Art: Pornography and Pleasure in Painting and Sculpture
by Cassidy Hughes

*The Erotic Object: Sexuality in Sculpture
From Prehistory to the Present Day*
by Susan Quinnell

Women in Pop Music
by Helen Challis

Detonation Britain: Nuclear War in the UK
by Jeremy Mark Robinson

Julia Kristeva: Art, Love, Melancholy, Philosophy, Semiotics and Psychoanalysis
by Kelly Ives

Luce Irigaray: Lips, Kissing, and the Politics of Sexual Difference
by Kelly Ives

Helene Cixous I Love You: The Jouissance *of Writing*
by Kelly Ives

The Poetry of Cinema
by John Madden

Disney Business, Disney Films, Disney Lands
Daniel Cerruti

Feminism and Shakespeare
by B.D. Barnacle

Andrei Tarkovsky
Pocket Guide

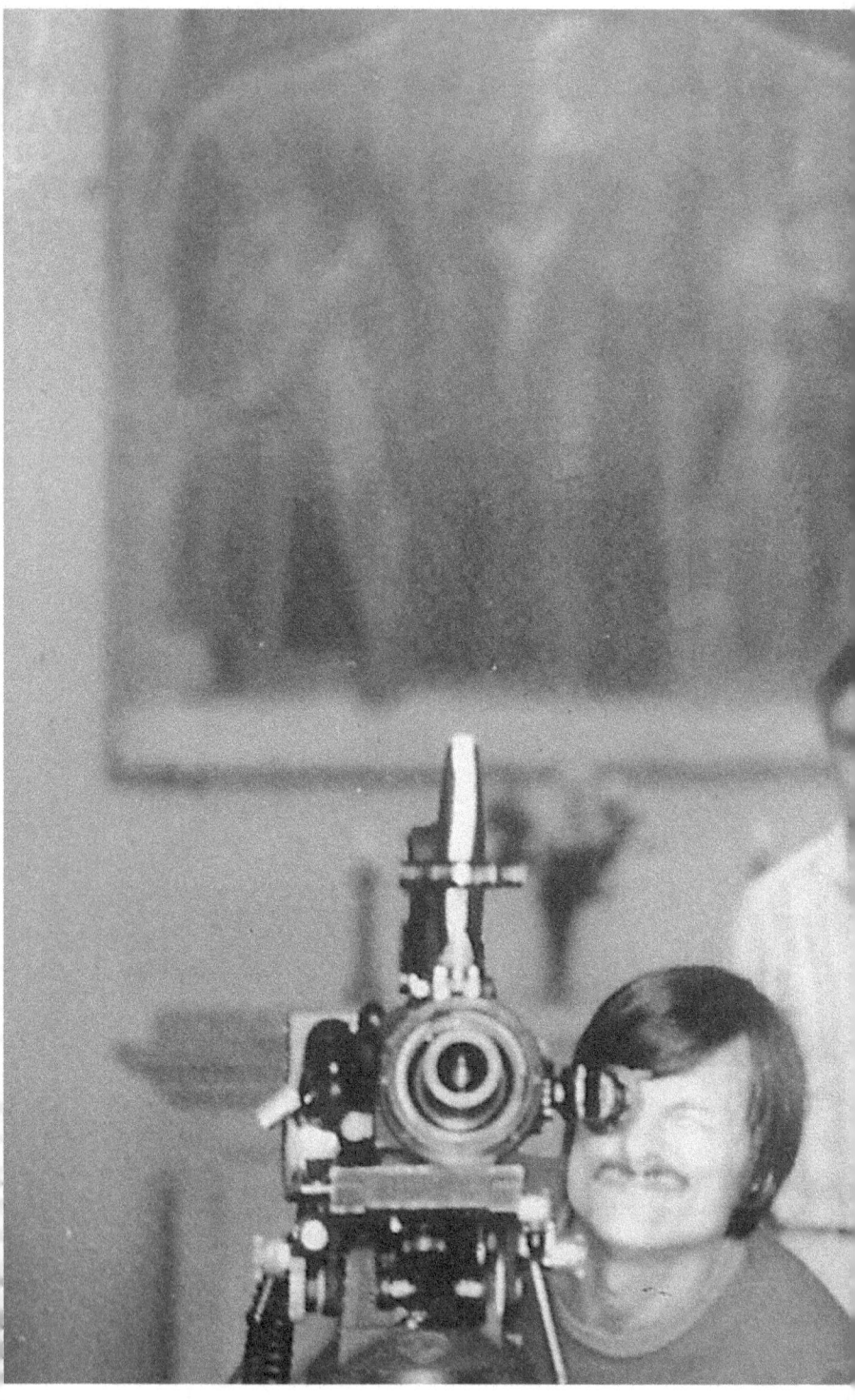

Andrei Tarkovsky
Pocket Guide

Jeremy Mark Robinson

CRESCENT MOON

CRESCENT MOON PUBLISHING
P.O. Box 1312, Maidstone
Kent, ME14 5XU
Great Britain
www.crmoon.com

First published 2010. Second edition 2013.
© Jeremy Mark Robinson 2013.

Printed and bound in the U.S.A.
Set in Helvetica Neue Condensed, 9 on 11pt.
Designed by Radiance Graphics.

The right of Jeremy Mark Robinson to be identified as the author of *Andrei Tarkovsky* has been asserted generally in accordance with sections 77 and 78 of the Copyright, Designs and Patents Act 1988.

All rights reserved. No part of this book may be reprinted or reproduced, stored in a retrieval system, or transmitted, in any form or by any means, electronic, mechanical, photocopying, recording or otherwise, without permission from the publisher.

British Library Cataloguing in Publication data

Andrei Tarkovsky: Pocket Guide
1. Tarkovskii, Andrei Arsenevich, 1932-1986
— Criticism and interpretation
1. Title
791.4'3'0233'092

ISBN 9781861714336 (Pbk)
ISBN 9781861713834 (Hbk)

Contents

Acknowledgements *11*
Abbreviations *11*
Illustrations *13*
Introduction *17*

PART ONE: THE ARTIST

1 *The Poetry of Cinema* *36*
2 *The Film Image* *44*
3 *The Mysteries of Space and Time* *54*
4 *Symbols and Motifs* *66*
5 *The Worlds of Andrei Tarkovsky* *81*
6 *Sound and Music* *91*
7 *Production* *102*
8 *Andrei Tarkovsky and Painting* *124*
9 *Philosophy and Religion in Andrei Tarkovsky's Cinema* *133*
10 *Structure and Narration* *148*
11 *Childhood, Family and Character* *157*
12 *Love, Gender and Sexuality* *165*

Illustrations *171*

PART TWO: THE FILMS

13	*Ivan's Childhood*	*200*
14	*The Passion According To Andrei Roublyov*	*208*
15	*Solaris*	*216*
16	*Mirror*	*224*
17	*Stalker*	*233*
18	*Nostalghia*	*244*
19	*The Sacrifice*	*250*
20	*Critical Responses to Andrei Tarkovsky's Cinema*	*257*

Ten Best Moments In Andrei Tarkovsky's Movies   *267*
Notes   *268*
Filmography   *273*
Availability   *275*
Bibliography   *276*

Acknowledgements

Thanks to: Danny Rivers, Nick Shaddick, Mark Tompkins, Tony Maestri, Chris Fassnidge, Cath Richmond, Ruth Herbert, Artificial Eye, British Film Institute Library, University College for the Creative Arts Library, Kent County Library, West Kent College Library.

Acknowledgements to authors quoted and their publishers: British Film Institute. Faber & Faber. Indiana University Press. Oxford University Press. Seagull Books, Calcutta. Prentice-Hall. Penguin. Thames & Hudson. *Iskusstvo kino. Sight and Sound. Positif.* McGraw-Hill. Russian Cinema Council. Routledge.

Picture credits:
Museum of Modern Art Film Stills Archive. Films Incorporated. Jerry Ohlinger's Movie Material Store. Evgeny Tsimbal. National Film Archive, London. Swedish Film Institute. Artificial Eye. Contemporary Films.

Every effort has been made to contact copyright owners of the illustrations. No copyright infringement is intended. We welcome enquiries about any copyright issues for future editions of this book.

Abbreviations

ST *Sculpting in Time*, by Andrei Tarkovsky
D   *Time Within Time: The Diaries 1970-1986* by Andrei Tarkovsky
CS *Collected Screenplays*, by Andrei Tarkovsky
JP *The Films of Andrei Tarkovsky* by Vida T. Johnson and Graham Petrie

Tarkovsky on the set of The Sacrifice

Andrei Roublyov

One of the original posters for Stalker

Japanese DVD artwork for Mirror

Introduction

LIFE

Andrei Tarkovsky (April 4, 1932, Zavrazhye – December 29, 1986, Paris) is one of the most fascinating of filmmakers. He is supremely romantic, an old-fashioned, traditional artist – at home in the company of Leonardo da Vinci, Pieter Brueghel, Aleksandr Pushkin, Fyodor Dostoievsky, Byzantine icon painters and Romantics such as Johann Wolfgang von Goethe. Tarkovsky is a magician, no question, but argues for demystification (even while his films celebrate mystery). He speaks endlessly of the 'truth', of 'spirit', of 'faith'. He talks in Christian, Platonic, Neoplatonic, Romantic, metaphysical and religious terms. He is a purist, always aiming for the essence of things. His movies are full of magical events, dreams, memory sequences, multiple viewpoints, multiple time-scales and bizarre occurrences. He is a marvellous filmmaker, a creator of miracles, a 'maker', a poet (the Greek word *poeitas* means 'maker').

Few contemporary movie-makers have even a millionth of the mystery and depth of Andrei Tarkovsky's art. Tarkovsky has an extraordinary feeling for sensuous experiences. *The Sacrifice* is surely one of the most voluptuous movies ever made. It has a præternatural feeling for surfaces, for texture and light and space. And yet, although Tarkovsky is a master of the presentation of surfaces – all that glass and water and polished wood and metal – his images also contain such depth. It is a depth only attained by directors such as Robert Bresson, Pier Paolo Pasolini and Werner Herzog. Tarkovsky has a deeply subtle sense of space. Contemporary Hollywood directors can create spaces very quickly and dynamically in films – with their over-determined, self-conscious use of the camera, point-of-view, motion and editing. But Hollywood's filmic spaces can appear as mainly superficial gloss, and the characters are too often cardboard cut-outs. Tarkovsky's cinema, meanwhile, achieves a sense of depth on every level: the visual, temporal, symbolic, kinetic, personal, social, narrative and spiritual.

Critic Herbert Marshall located Andrei Tarkovsky's movies as part of a number which appeared in the Soviet Union following Sergei Paradjanov:

Tengiz Abuladze's *Prayer*, L. Osyka's *The Stone Cross*, Georgi Shengelaia's *Pirosmani*, Ivan Drach and Iuri Ilenko's *On the Eve of Ivan Kupala*, and Paradjanov's *The Colour of Pomegranates*. These 'New Wave' movies were seen as 'difficult', poetic, abstract, painterly, drawing on folk and fairy tales, religion, history and poetics.

> In these films every shot represents a self-contained part of the total composition; every shot is a painting in itself; every shot, even if it has an inner movement, freezes in its graphic expressiveness. At the same time speech and commentary also disappear.[1]

Andrei Tarkovsky studied film at VGIK (the All-Union State Cinema Institute, formerly GTK and GIK), founded in 1919 by Vladimir Gardin, Lev Kuleshov and others. At VGIK Tarkovsky made a short TV film (*Segodnya uvol'neniya ne budget/ There Will Be No Leave Today* [1959]) and his graduation diploma piece, *The Steamroller and the Violin* (1961).

Many of the great names of Soviet cinema studied or taught at VGIK, including: Sergei Bondarchuk, Nikolai Batalov, Alexander Dovzhenko, Mikhail Romm (one of Andrei Tarkovsky's teachers), Sergei Yutkevich, Marlen Khutsiev, Sergei Eisenstein, Vsevolod Pudovkin and Grigori Kotzintsev. At film school (VGIK), Tarkovsky saw many movies as part of his course: *Citizen Kane, The Little Foxes*, Jean Renoir, Jean Vigo, John Ford, the Italian Neorealists, Andrzej Wajda and Andrzej Munk. When Tarkovsky was offering advice to young filmmakers about which filmmakers to study, he suggested five masters: Dovzhenko, Luis Buñuel, Ingmar Bergman, Michelangelo Antonioni and Carl Theodor Dreyer (D, 361). At film school, students should watch lots of movies, Tarkovsky recommended, and should also read lots of books (and not just the set texts).

Andrei Tarkovsky sometimes discussed fellow Russian movie-makers who had gone to Hollywood. Though wary, he must have been tempted. After all, one of Tarkovsky's important collaborators, Andrei Mikhalkov-Konchalovsky, went to Hollywood and made some terrific movies: *Runaway Train* is a film any filmmaker would have been proud to have produced, and *The Odyssey* (1997) is a superb reinvention of Homer.

Andrei Tarkovsky was born in Zavrazhye, near Yuryevets, on the River Volga. His early life was spent in the country, when his parents moved out of Moscow (but the Tarkovskys moved back to the city fairly soon). Tarkovsky would later poeticize his early life near Yuryevets in *Mirror*, but he spent far less time there than in Moscow. During WW2, the family moved into the countryside around Yuryevets while Arseny Tarkovsky fought in the war. Vida Johnson and Graham Petrie call the 'major trauma' of Tarkovsky's youth the break-up of the family and Tarkovsky's father being absent (JP, 18).

In his youth, Andrei Tarkovsky worked in the far east of Russia, in the Turukhansky region and the Kureika river, making sketches and conducting research for a scientific institute. The year he spent exploring the *taiga* in Turukhansky was an important time for Tarkovsky. A lesser-known fact about Tarkovsky's career is that he worked in the mid-Sixties at the All-Soviet radio station. He directed a radio play based on a William Faulkner short story.

Andrei Tarkovsky's mother worked at the First State Publishing House in Moscow as an editor (some of that life finds its way into *Mirror*). Maria Ivanovna was a major force in inspiring Tarkovsky to become an artist; she was also 'a very strict disciplinarian' (JP, 19). Tarkovsky said that his mother 'obviously had a very strong influence on me – influence is not even the right word – simply the whole world is for me connected with my mother'.

Andrei Tarkovsky's first wife, Irma Rauch, had been his class mate at VGIK; they wed in 1957. Tarkovsky's first son, Arseny, was born in 1962. (Commentators have noted how Tarkovsky junior followed his father in leaving his first wife and child.) As echoed in *Mirror*, Tarkovsky grew up surrounded by women. Tarkovsky found the emotional environment oppressive as well as inspiring.

Andrei Tarkovsky married Larissa Pavlovna Yegorkina, his second wife, in 1970 (they had met and romanced during the shooting of *Andrei Roublyov*). They had a son, Andrei (born in 1970). Larissa worked on Tarkovsky's movies on set (she was assistant director on *Mirror*, for instance). Since Tarkovsky's death in 1986, Larissa was increasingly the guardian of Tarkovsky's flame. She helped to edit Tarkovsky's diaries, which were published in 1991 as *Time Within Time* (*Martylog* in Germany). Much of Tarkovsky's private life was excised from the diaries, as well as his personal comments on his contemporaries and friends. By most accounts, Larissa Tarkovskaya was a formidable personality, and was keen to shape the Tarkovsky cult as it grew after the director's demise. Larissa in particular fell out with Tarkovsky's sister Marina (and she often fought with Tarkovsky too). Tarkovsky didn't know he had cancer while he was shooting *The Sacrifice*; he was diagnosed in December, 1985, when the movie had already been shot.

After *Nostalghia*, Andrei Tarkovsky wasn't granted permission to continue to work outside Russia, and in 1984 he announced his decision to stay in the West. His wife, Larissa, had been allowed to join him in Europe, but not his son Andrei. While he lived in the West, Tarkovsky attended film festivals (such as Telluride), directed operas (*Boris Godunov*), and gave lectures.

Too old to be a hippy, really (he was 28 at the start of the Sixties), Andrei Tarkovsky's movies do exhibit some of the traits of hippy culture. An obvious one is the exaltation of the natural world, and the urge to escape the city for nature. Like J.R.R. Tolkien and Thomas Hardy, Tarkovsky is a bit of a tree-hugger (people embrace trees in his films: Masha in *Ivan's Childhood*, Alexander in *The Sacrifice*, and trees play a significant role in every Tarkovsky movie).

Layla Garrett remarked that Andrei Tarkovsky 'was a very complex, difficult man'. Lesser-known aspects of Andrei Tarkovsky's personality include his bisexuality, and his sadomasochism. (Few critics have approached Tarkovsky's films from a gay, lesbian or queer perspective. The sexuality in his movies appears to be resolutely heterosexual (but open displays of homoeroticism are still rare in Russian cinema – and society). Though if one wanted to approach Tarkovsky's *œuvre* using gay and queer theory, it would be easy (consider the brotherhoods in *Andrei Roublyov* or *Stalker*, for instance, the groups of men travelling together. The Stalker, for example, seems to have a more significant relationship with the Writer and the Professor than his own wife and daughter).

There's a disturbing element of the lecherous old man and voyeur in Andrei Tarkovsky's cinema, too. The eroticized red-haired girl with the chapped lip in *Mirror,* for instance, is a teenage object of sexual desire for both the middle-aged military instructor and the middle-aged narrator (and she was played by Tarkovsky's own step-daughter). Then there's the young woman Martha in *The Sacrifice*, seen naked in Alexander's dreams (with hints of incestuous desires); and Alex sleeps with a much younger woman. G. Petrie and V. Johnson see the lovemaking between Alex and the 'witch' as 'devoid of all eroticism' (JP, 249). True, it does seem somewhat chaste, and it is meant to be a spiritual union, a life-affirming act. But it is also presented specifically as lovemaking. In his diaries, Tarkovsky contemplated a movie about an old man and a young woman. While art movies of the 1960s and 1970s regularly featured gorgeous young women in relationships with far older men, some of those films now take on a creepy, dubious edge (*Last Tango In Paris,* Woody Allen's *Manhattan, The Story of O,* and anything by Walerian Borowczyk are obvious examples that come to mind).

THE TARKOVSKY INDUSTRY

There's already a wealth of information about Andrei Tarkovsky. Documentaries on Tarkovsky include *Andrei Tarkovsky Directs Nostalghia*, a.k.a. *Un Poeta nel Cinema* (Donatella Baglivo, 1983, CIAK, Italy), *Moscow Elegy* (Alexander Sokurov, 1987, USSR), *Directed By Tarkovsky* (Michal Leszcylowski, 1988, Sweden), and *In Remembrance of Things Past: The Exile and Death of Andrei Tarkovsky* (Ebbo Demant, 1987, Germany).

Chris Marker directed a 55 minute documentary on Andrei Tarkovsky, entitled *One Day in the Life of Andrei Arsenevich* in 2000. Donatella Baglivo also produced *Il cinema è un mosaico fatto di tempo* (*Cinema Is A Mosaic Made Up Of Time*) for CIAK (Italy) in 1984, and *Andrey Tarkovsky: A Poet in the Cinema* (1984).

Then there's a Russian documentary on *Andrei Roublyov* (*Andrei Rublov: How it Came into Being*, 2000), including interviews with many of the cast and crew. A BBC *Arena* programme about Andrei Tarkovsky (*Tarkovsky's Cinema*, 1987). A Channel Four documentary on *The Sacrifice* (*Behind the Scenes on The Sacrifice*, Jeremy Isaacs, 1987). *Stalker's Dreams* (1998, Evgenii Tsymbal) was a Russian documentary about actor Alexander Kaidanovsky. *After Tarkovsky* (2003) was a Russian documentary made by Peter Shepotinnik, and included interviews with people who had worked with Tarkovsky. A Japanese documentary, *Tarkovsky: A Journey to His Beginning*, appeared in 1996. *The Recall* (1996) was a 25 minute documentary made by Tarkovsky's son.

Other documentaries and movies which discuss Andrei Tarkovsky include: a documentary on Tarkovsky's father: *Arseny Tarkovsky: Eternal Presence* (Viatcheslav Amirkhanian, 2004, Russia). *Student Andrei Tarkovsky* (Galina Leontieva, 2003). *Remembering Andrei Tarkovsky* (1987, Moscow). *At the shooting of the film Andrei Rublov* (1965, USSR). *The Three Andreis* (Dina Musatova, 1966, USSR). *Group of Friends* (M. Lakhovetsky, 1988, USSR). *Paradjanov: The Last Spring* (2004) has a section on Sergei Paradjanov and Andrei Tarkovsky. *The Reflected Time* (1998, Eugene Borzo, Russia). *Screenshot: 1: Lighting* (Kerstin Eriksdotter, 1988, Sweden), which featured Sven Nykvist shooting *The Sacrifice*. Tarkovsky had appeared in a Dutch TV documentary on Robert Bresson (*The Road To Bresson*, 1984).

There is a Friends of the Andrei Tarkovsky Institute, which produces a newsletter. A book of Tarkovsky's polaroids (*Instant Light*) which also toured as an exhibition. A concert tour, *Imaginary Offering* (2005), inspired by Tarkovsky's movies. A play of *Solaris* was directed by Martin Wuttke in 2004. There were 'Tarkovsky committees' campaigning on Tarkovsky's behalf in Iceland, Italy, France and England.

Andrei Tarkovsky and computer games? Yes. The video game *Stalker: Oblivion Lost* (designed by Ukranian Sergiy Grygorovych) was based on Tarkovsky's *Stalker*, as well as the Strugatskys' book *Roadside Picnic*, and the Chernobyl disaster. Erland Josephson wrote a play about shooting *The Sacrifice*, *A Night in the Swedish Summer*, which was staged in Sweden in 2002.

Andrei Tarkovsky's version of the opera *Boris Gudunov* was revived three times in London by 1994; it was part of the repertory of the Kirov Theater in St Petersburg, and was performed by Vienna Opera in 1991.[1] A stage play of Tarkovsky's script *Hoffmanniana* was performed in Paris in 2003. A radio programme, *Andrei Tarkovski ou le son de la terre*, was co-produced by the Tarkovsky Institute and Atelier création radiophonique.

There is a Museum of Tarkovsky, opened in 1996, situated 315 miles from Moscow, in Yuryevets (it was Tarkovsky's mother's home during WW2). There are also various websites on the internet devoted to various aspects of Tarkovsky's œuvre, some with links to other sites, such as *2001: A Space Odyssey* and sci-fi films. Some websites do come and go all too rapidly. For years the Tarkovsky site at www.skywalking.com was excellent. Probably the best site for research material is: www.nostalghia.com.

There is also a Czech site (www.nostalgia.cz), a Hungarian site (www.tarkovszkj.hu), a Korean site (www.nostalgiya.com) and a Spanish site (www.andreitarkovski.org). Pages can be found in many of the cinema websites (such as at Senses of Cinema: www.sensesofcinema.com). There are also websites dedicated to Sergei Paradjanov: www.parajanov.com.

Manufacturers and distributors of Andrei Tarkovsky's movies on DVD and video include the Russian Cinema Council (Ruscico), Kino Video, Artificial Eye, Fox Lober, Criterion, Image Entertainment, and Facets Video. Home DVD and video distribution have brought new problems in Tarkovsky studies – with the quality of prints, of transfers, of audio quality, of soundtracks, and 'restoration'. Issues such as the director's 'intentions', 'director's cuts', and sound remixes are confronted yet again.

Sculpting In Time (1986 and 1989) is the major prose work Andrei Tarkovsky produced. It contains his thoughts on a wide variety of subjects, and is referred to throughout this study. Tarkovsky collaborated with Olga Surkova on the book *Sculpting In Time*. She was a fellow student at VGIK, and had worked on *Andrei Roublyov*. *Sculpting In Time* started out as a series of interviews between Surkova and Tarkovsky, but when it was eventually published in the West, Surkova's contribution was largely cut out. Thus, *Sculpting In Time* is not wholly Tarkovsky's work, though it looks that way (Surkova doesn't share a credit on the cover or title page, and isn't mentioned on the copyright page of the revised British edition from Faber & Faber).

The *Diaries* and the screenplays Andrei Tarkovsky wrote are further secondary sources for this book. (Perhaps the book Tarkovsky fans and critics would most like to see is an edition of his letters. A book of annotated scripts, storyboards and notes on production would also be nice).

In criticism, most of the work on Andrei Tarkovsky has appeared in essays and articles, published in the expected film studies arenas (*Cahiers du Cinéma, Positif, Iskusstvo kino, Journal of Religion and Film, American Film,* etc). Special numbers of journals have also been dedicated to Tarkovsky, as well collections of essays. Full-length studies have appeared by Maya Turovskaya, Mark Le Fanu, F. Borin, Tatyana Elmanovits, Balint Anrdás Kovács and Akos Szilágyi, V.I. Mikhalkovich, M. Zak, Peter Green, Vida T. Johnson and Graham Petrie (Johnson's and Petrie's *The Films of Andrei Tarkovsky* is undoubtedly the best of the bunch in Tarkovsky studies that's available in the West). But the primary texts employed in this study are the movies.

The seven features are available on video and DVD in the West, though you may have to hunt around a bit to find them, even in big stores. Andrei Tarkovsky seems to have a dedicated but relatively small following. One can't imagine his films being consumed in large quantities in the home entertainment sector like mainstream movies coming out of Hong Kong, Bollywood, Paris, Rome or Hollywood. On the plus side, it's not too difficult obtaining the collected works on home entertainment formats: there are only seven features and two shorts to buy (*The Steamroller and the Violin* and *There Will Be No Leave Today*). The documentary by Michal Leszczylowski about the making of *The Sacrifice* is a must-have, as is the documentary Tarkovsky made in Italy, *Tempo di Viaggio*. (Some other documentaries are also available, including one on the making of *Nostalghia*). But there are no different editions or 'director's cuts' of the movies to collect (though the different versions of *Andrei Roublyov* would be great to have, though it's highly unlikely they'll appear, given Tarkovsky's relatively small sales). Some of the DVDs and videos of Tarkovsky's movies come with documentaries, some specially shot (valuable interviews with, for instance, Tarkovsky's cameramen, Vadim Yusov and A. Knyazhinsky, production designer R. Safiullin, composer Vyacheslav Ovchinnikov, or actors E. Zharikov and Natalia Bondarchuk).

In global cinema terms, Andrei Tarkovsky's movies are a difficult sell.

They have none of the selling points or marketability of entertainment cinema: no stars (and few well-known actors), no recognizable source material, and they're not in English (or French, or German, or Spanish, or Chinese, or Japanese, but the more 'difficult' languages, Russian and Swedish). They're known as 'difficult', long, tedious and pretentious (Tarkovsky recognized that poetic cinema could turn into pretentiousness; it was a pitfall he was conscious of (though plenty of viewers and critics have felt that Tarkovsky's films are pretentious).)

Even among passionate film students and fans, Andrei Tarkovsky's movies are not to everyone's taste. Many viewers don't seem to 'get' Tarkovsky; his movies aren't as approachable as, say a Jackie Chan or Jet Li martial arts flick, or a Hollywood actioner. Tarkovsky is popular among some filmmakers and critics – he's a 'filmmaker's filmmaker' in that respect. But it's hard to imagine Tarkovsky's movies increasing the size of their audience, despite the development since his death of the newer home entertainment formats like DVD, or the increase in the number of cinema screens globally.

Herb Slocomb, from Miami, reviewed *Andrei Roublyov* on the internet (in 2002) as 'one of the worst best movies ever made':

> slow moving, ponderous, little character development, with chaotic plot detours to what little plot there is, and the final payoff after 3 hours of this is that you get the "reward" of viewing some static images of Russian orthodox icon art.

Stuart Hancock's account of the first time he saw an Andrei Tarkovsky movie reads like something out of a Woody Allen film:

> I will never forget the first time I saw *Andrei Rublev*. A friend had told me about a Tarkovsky retrospective at the Film Forum, which at the time was just off Varick Street in lower Manhattan. I had never heard of Tarkovsky, and when I arrived at the theater, I was surprised to find hundreds of Soho types lined up around the block, all dressed in black, smoking Egyptian cigarettes and looking like extras from a Fellini film. It was then that my friend informed me, 'The movie is in black and white, is three-and-a-half hours long, and in Russian with subtitles.' I entered the theater expecting the worst... Thirty minutes into the film, I was hopelessly lost. (1986)

Another obstacle is that Andrei Tarkovsky doesn't offer an easy way-in for audiences. There isn't one Tarkovsky movie one could recommend as being representative and easy to watch. The obvious choice would be *Mirror* (being 106 minutes long and not one of the two-and-a-half-hour-plus films). But *Mirror* has a complex structure, three time zones, and the same actors playing characters in different historical periods. Maybe *Ivan's Childhood* or *The Sacrifice* would be good starting-points (*Ivan's Childhood* has a strong through-line and a character that's easy to identify with; *The Sacrifice*, while Tarkovsky's most accomplished work in many respects, is probably too dense, too intense and too downbeat to recommend as the First Tarkovsky Film). Not *Solaris* (probably too slow for some contemporary audiences – like the remake, which was wrongly marketed as a sci-fi flick when it's really a psychodrama about marital breakdown). Perhaps *Andrei Roublyov*, although a masterpiece in every possible respect, is too complicated, too long, and too obscure (and it's a period piece in black-and-white about a painter little-known in the West). Maybe if *Andrei Roublyov* had Kirk Douglas, Charlton Heston or Yul Brenner in it audiences might find it amenable. *Stalker* was the first Tarkovsky movie for many Tarkovsky fans and, in a way, it might just be the one to put forward (if only it was half the length for the impatient folk!).

But it's just not the same as considering a film director like, say, Orson Welles. With Welles, you just say: look at *Citizen Kane* and *The Magnificent Ambersons* and the genius should be fairly clear. Even a movie-maker like Werner Herzog, who can be as obscure and 'difficult' as Andrei Tarkovsky, has approachable movies: Dracula remakes (*Nosferatu*), megalomaniacs in the Amazon (*Fitzcarraldo*), crazy Klaus Kinski chewing the scenery (*Aguirre: Wrath of God*), and dwarves running riot in *Even Dwarves Started Small* (1969), which even Bart Simpson, with the attention span of an average TV viewer, might find amusing.

But Werner Herzog can be wilfully obtuse too: *Heart of Glass* (1976) is a truly strange movie: set in rural Germany in perhaps the 18th century, the actors were hyptnozied (by Herzog himself) before shooting, resulting in bizarre, s-l-o-w, somnambulistic performances. Dreamy and mystery, yes, but far more eccentric than any of Andrei Tarkovsky's films. Indeed, every movie viewer can probably remember movies far weirder or more unwatchable than a Tarkovsky film. (Personally, I find plenty of stuff in cinema and TV that's excruciatingly difficult to watch. I'd rather watch a three hour Tarkovsky film than even five minutes of a Ken Loach, Mike Leigh, James Cameron or Guy Ritchie movie).

NEGATIVE CRITICISMS OF ANDREI TARKOVSKY'S CINEMA

These are some of the common criticisms that are levelled against Andrei Tarkovsky and his films.

(1) *The films are obscure.* True, they can be very obscure, and also *deliberately* obscure and 'difficult'. Andrei Tarkovsky doesn't have any problem with making audiences look deep.

(2) *They are vulgar and over-bold.* True, but not vulgar or bold enough to be glaringly obvious to everybody. There are still plenty of viewers who come aware confused – if they manage to reach the end of one of his movies at all.

(3) *They are élitist.* Yes, Andrei Tarkovsky's movies are undoubtedly designed for minority audiences. This is clear from the stories (no dinosaurs, aliens or space battles for him), the choice of actors (the avoidance of stars), the music (no market-friendly soundtracks), the narrative techniques (lengthy takes), the subjects (a poet adrift in Italy, for instance), the allusions, and the cultural references (to Renaissance painting, say).

The élitism is also reflected in the marketing of the films, and in the way in which they are consumed (consider the video and DVD packaging – by Artificial Eye and Criterion in the UK). The home entertainment audiences for Andrei Tarkovsky's movies are likely to be highly educated, culturally sophisticated and affluent. They probably consume opera and classical music, visit cinemas and art galleries, read literary and current affairs magazines, and so on. Or consider the way Tarkovsky's films are presented on television (Channel Four's 1989 Tarkovsky movie season emulated the auteurist approach taken by the repertory cinemas such as the National Film Theatre in London).

(4) *The movies are self-indulgent.* But take many great films – *Intolerance, Citizen Kane, Vertigo, City Lights, Greed* – or most great filmmakers – Orson Welles, Jean-Luc Godard, Carl Theodor Dreyer, Buster Keaton, Luchino Visconti – they are also 'self-indulgent'. The same goes for great artists such as Sappho, Homer, Friedrich Hölderlin, Leonardo da Vinci, William Shakespeare or Emily Dickinson. In fact, it is a way of becoming critically acclaimed: the more self-indulgent the better (think of James Joyce's endless *Ulysses*, Francesco Petrarch's over-the-top romanticism in the *Rime Sparse* or Marcel Proust's epic soap opera *Remembrance of Things Past,* to name a few examples from literature).

The view of the greatest animator in the world, Hayao Miyazaki, is worth quoting here:

> I think it's impossible to do everything you want. You have to make such

a movie in a different place from a movie which one or two million people pay to see and get satisfied. When I watch a movie such as Tarkovsky's *Stalker*, I feel 'this SOB is doing as he pleases!' I think he is such a talented guy.

(5) *Andrei Tarkovsky the man was pompous, arrogant, difficult, blinkered, too idealistic, and a control freak.* Definitely – all of those. Here was a man with a spiritual mission to fulfil. The slide (ascent?) into pomposity is inevitable (even in the humblest religious teachers, such as Lao-tzu or Buddha), or the humblest of movies (such as Robert Bresson's *The Diary of a Country Priest*). Certainly Tarkovsky's views could be too idealistic – and simplistic. He could be difficult. And nobody could doubt that, when it came to making movies, Tarkovsky was a classic control freak.

(6) *Andrei Tarkovsky's movies are too long.* True, he could've pruned his films and still achieved everything he aimed for. *Mirror*, at 106 minutes, is beautifully judged and doesn't feel at all rushed; *Solaris*, meanwhile, at 165 minutes, may be too long for some viewers. But because he only completed seven movies, every minute is precious.

Perhaps he should have tried to make a movie in one continuous 90-minute shot, to really drive the critics crazy. (Alexander Sokurov, sometimes dubbed Tarkovsky's successor, did just that in *The Russian Ark*, and critics loved it).

(7) *The movies are too slow.* Yes, but the slowness was inextricably enmeshed with Andrei Tarkovsky's sense of style and the sacred. Speeding up the pace of his movies would be impossible without turning them into something very different.

(8) *His films are manipulative.* Yes, but all movies (all artworks) are manipulations, from the obvious ones (mainstream international cinema) to the most decentred and deliberately open or vague.

(9) *Andrei Tarkovsky's characters are cyphers, one-dimensional, vehicles for his obsessions.* Yes, his characters can appear too flat, too one-sided, too schematic. That's a fault of scriptwriting – and the script is where movies fail more than in any other single aspect of filmmaking.

(10) *His movies are boring.* Undoubtedly, set next to *The Terminator, Jurassic Park 2: The Lost World, Star Wars 3 (Return of the Jedi), Jaws IV, Rocky V, Police Academy 6: City Under Siege, Hallowe'en H20 (a.k.a. Hallowe'en 7)*, and *Friday the Thirteenth Part VIII: Jason Takes Manhattan*. Actually, compared to many of those films, Tarkovsky's movies are not boring at all.

(11) *Andrei Tarkovsky's approaches are limited and repetitive.* True,

Tarkovsky did confine himself to a very channelled approach, making the same film (or a very similar one) again and again. But he also showed he could create any cinematic effect there is, if required, from pornography to science fiction visual effects to epic historical spectacle involving a cast of thousands.

(12) *Andrei Tarkovsky and his movies are humourless.* Yes, and this is a serious failing, even in films dealing with 'serious' issues such as religious quests and moral crises. There aren't many laughs in Tarkovsky's films, that's true. Yet *Mirror* was emotionally warm and tender. And his movies can have profoundly uplifting effects.

(13) *Andrei Tarkovsky was pretentious.* Not at all. Tarkovsky didn't 'pretend'. He was *doing it*, for real. He was the real thing, no question. He wasn't pretending to tackle big themes. Perhaps that's what some people dislike about Tarkovsky: such sincerity and artistic committment can be off-putting to non-artists, especially when it is not leavened by postmodern irony and self-deprecation. Filmmakers such as Orson Welles, Federico Fellini and Peter Greenaway still suffer the same attacks of being pretentious. It's one of film critics' lazy labels.

(14) *Over-ambitious?* Yes, but beautifully so. Maybe Andrei Tarkovsky's movies might have been improved had he been less ambitious. But it's just not in his artistic make-up to produce modest films.

(15) *Andrei Tarkovsky's films display a lack of humanity.* Yes and no. In the later works he wanted to strip everything away, to leave just the individual and the problem with nothing cluttering up the movie or things getting in the way: a film of clarity and transparency, luminous as clear water in sunlight. This is a dream of Stendhal, Gustave Flaubert, André Gide and Samuel Beckett among writers (which can lead to an abstraction which some viewers might find obscure).

(16) *Andrei Tarkovsky's movies are sexist and biased towards masculinism.* True, Tarkovsky didn't explore female characters, the feminine, identity or gender issues deeply enough for some critics. Other filmmakers (such as Pedro Almodóvar, Bette Gordon, Susan Seidelman, Ingmar Bergman, and Krzysztof Kieslowski) went far beyond Tarkovsky in this respect. Also, as a Christian believer, and a conservative reactionary, politically, Tarkovsky was not so much scared of challenging the patriarchal socio-political establishment, as not interested in such an exploration: he was unpolitical (or apolitical) because it suited his spiritual investigations (although the context in which he produced his movies was highly politicized, with politics often thrust into the foreground).

THIS BOOK

This present study concentrates on Andrei Tarkovsky's seven feature movies, with a more detailed reading of *Mirror, Nostalghia* and *The Sacrifice*, which illuminate Tarkovsky's art. This is a compressed edition of my full-length study of Tarkovsky, *The Sacred Cinema of Andrei Tarkovsky* (2006).

Vida Johnson and Graham Petrie have reminded readers that it's easy to misinterpret Andrei Tarkovsky's films, to miss what's going on in the movies, or recall them incorrectly (JP, xiv). Tarkovsky's films do demand careful readings – their ambiguity and complexity can confuse viewers, and some movie critics have invented events and images that do not occur in Tarkovsky's films.

Andrei Tarkovsky's movies are placed within the 'art cinema' tradition here – that is, a (mainly European) tradition (of Ingmar Bergman, Luis Buñuel, Werner Herzog, Federico Fellini and Robert Bresson) rather than a Russian or Soviet film tradition. It is with the (European) art cinema tradition that Tarkovsky identified himself (throughout, for example, his major written text, S*culpting in Time*).

Some of the hallmarks of European art cinema – most of which can apply to Andrei Tarkovsky's movies – are: (1) Open forms, (2) Ambiguity, (3) Expressionism, (4) Non-linearity, (5) Psychology, (6) Digressions, (7) Subjectivity and (8) Revision of genre. All through the *Diaries* and *Sculpting in Time*, Tarkovsky mentions a group of filmmakers he admires, and they are all art cinema *auteurs*: Ingmar Bergman, Robert Bresson, Federico Fellini, Alexander Dovzhenko, Akira Kurosawa, Luis Buñuel, Kenji Mizoguchi and Michelangelo Antonioni.[1] This is the central group in the Tarkovsky pantheon of cinematic gods. Other directors Tarkovsky admired included Jean Cocteau, Charlie Chaplin, Jean Vigo, John Ford, Jean Renoir and nearly every filmmaker's favourite, Orson Welles. Tarkovsky was impressed by Andrzej Wajda, Andrzej Munk, and the Polish school, which he had seen at film school in the Fifties. Tarkovsky said that *Ashes and Diamonds* had been a revelation.

These were the movie-makers who didn't work in any particular genre. As Andrei Tarkovsky put it in *Sculpting in Time*: 'Bresson is Bresson. He is a genre in himself'. These directors were one-offs, as Tarkovsky remarked of Charlie Chaplin: 'he is Chaplin, pure and simple; a unique phenomenon, never to be repeated' (*Sculpting In Time*; hereafter as ST, 150). Bresson amazed Tarkovsky: he was 'serious, profound, noble', 'his concentration was extraordinary', all of his movies were high art (ST, 189).

> When I am working, it helps me a lot to think of Bresson [Tarkovsky confessed]. Only the thought of Bresson! I don't remember any of his works concretely. I remember only his supremely ascetic manner. His simplicity. His clarity. The thought of Bresson helps me to concentrate on the central idea of the film.

Robert Bresson was perhaps the only filmmaker whose finished films corresponded closely with the script, Andrei Tarkovsky maintained (ST, 94). For Tarkovsky, 'in the poetry of film, Bresson, more than anyone else, has united theory and practice in his work with a singleness of purpose, consistently and uniformly' (95). I think you could also add Bergman and Kurosawa.

Andrei Tarkovsky admired Federico Fellini's *8 1/2*, and *Casanova*, and the *Toby Dammit* section of *Spirits of the Dead*. It wasn't the story of *Casanova* Tarkovsky appreciated so much as the formal qualities. *Casanova* is an eccentric, sometimes wilfully obscure movie, with a highly stylized performance from Donald Sutherland, but for Tarkovsky 'the formal aspect is of an extremely high level, its plasticity is incredibly profound'. However, Tarkovsky was dismissive of Fellini's *Roma*, which was shown at Cannes in 1973. Tarkovsky remarked at Cannes that *Roma* pandered too much to the audience. The inner rhythm of a film, which Tarkovsky regarded as vital, was rejected in *Roma* in favour of a commercial product. As Tarkovsky put it, 'the editorial rhythm is so slick that one feels offended on behalf of Fellini'.

Most of the filmmakers Tarkovsky admired were European, or from the Far East (and Japan in particular). Few American directors were regularly cited by Andrei Tarkovsky, and hardly ever an American director working after Orson Welles. None of the 'movie brats' or filmmakers of the 'New Hollywood' were mentioned (Martin Scorsese, Peter Bogdanovitch, Francis Coppola, Brian de Palma, John Carpenter, Steven Spielberg, George Lucas *et al*. Spielberg was noted once or twice by Tarkovsky).

Note the omission of Sergei Eisenstein, perhaps the most influential Soviet movie-maker of the 20th century, from Andrei Tarkovsky's favourites. Tarkovsky disliked the intellectual flavour of Eisenstein's movies, but, whether he was aware of it or not, Tarkovsky used some of Eisenstein's ideas (such as Eisenstein's 'dynamization of space', and theory of montage). Eisenstein's historical epics, *Alexander Nevsky* and *Ivan the Terrible*, inevitably influenced Tarkovsky's films, in particular *Andrei Roublyov*, which covers similar late mediæval periods in Russian history. Personally, I'm with Tarkovsky on Eisenstein: his movies are extraordinary on many levels (formally, socially, politically), and are classics of world cinema, but they're not films to return to many times.

(And the ideological aspect of Eisenstein's cinema – its alignment with Stalin and the Soviet regime – is problematic. Tarkovsky's cinema is also compromised by its links with the Russian authorities, but nowhere near as much as Eisenstein's work).

A questionnaire published in Andrei Tarkovsky's *Diaries* lists Aleksandr Pushkin, Fyodor Dostoievsky, Thomas Mann and Guy de Maupassant among writers; Robert Bresson among directors; Johann Sebastian Bach among composers; and 'dawn, summer, mist' as his favourite landscape (D, 89). There's also an answer to 'what is a woman's driving-force?' which feminists won't like at all: 'submission, humiliation in the name of love'.

If, as some critics have suggested, that Tarkovsky didn't really like the sci-fi genre, he spent a significant part of his film career on sci-fi projects: two feature movies (and *The Sacrifice*, with its nuclear war scenario, has affinities with sci-fi). The musician Eduard Artemiev remembered that Tarkovsky had a box of sci-fi books at his home.

As genre films, Andrei Tarkovsky's are some of the most accomplished in cinema. As science fiction movies, *Stalker* and *Solaris* have no superiors, and very few peers. Only the greatest sci-fi films can match them: *Metropolis, King Kong, Ghost In the Shell, Akira, Close Encounters of the Third Kind* and *2001: A Space Odyssey*. Tarkovsky happily and methodically rewrote the rules of sci-fi genre: *Stalker* and *Solaris* are definitely not routine genre outings. They don't have the monsters, the aliens, the visual effects, the space battles, the laser guns, the stunts and action set-pieces of regular science fiction movies. No one could deny that *Andrei Roublyov* is one of the greatest historical films to explore the Middle Ages, up there with *The Seventh Seal, El Cid, The Navigator* and Pier Paolo Pasolini's 'Life' trilogy. If you judge *Andrei Roublyov* in terms of historical accuracy, epic spectacle, serious themes, or cinematic poetry, it comes out at the top.

Finally, in the religious movie genre, *The Sacrifice* and *Nostalghia* are among the finest in cinema, the equals of the best of Ingmar Bergman, Buñuel, Robert Bresson and Carl Theodor Dreyer. (In a way, it was partly the *timing* of the release of Tarkovsky's religious films that has made them appear as anomalies: had *The Sacrifice* and *Nostalghia* been released during the 1950s and 1960s, they'd be regarded as instant classics, and placed beside the great religious films of the era: *The Seventh Seal, Gertrud, Viridiana, Diary of a Country Priest* and *The Gospel According To Matthew*. But by the time of the 1980s, with the 'Hollywood Renaissance' of the 1970s and the European New Wave over, movies like *The Sacrifice* and *Nostalghia* seemed out of step with the drift of contemporary cinema.)

'The cinema does not just present images, it surrounds them with a world', wrote Gilles Deleuze in 1985.2 In an interview in *Directed By Andrei Tarkovsky*, shot during *The Sacrifice*, Andrei Tarkovsky said there were two kinds of filmmaker: those who try to imitate their world, and those who create a world. The latter kind, Tarkovsky said, are poets. As examples, Tarkovsky cited 'Bresson above all', and also Mizoguchi, Buñuel, Akira Kurosawa and Bergman. It's clear that Tarkovsky identifies himself with the filmmaker-as-poet. Ivor Montagu called Tarkovsky a *'realist poet in images'*, who digs underneath the narrative structure of his movies to layer it with 'overtones and undertones, hints, symbols suggestive of and reflecting on the theme' (1973, 92).

In some ways, Andrei Tarkovsky is one of the last of the *auteurs*, the last of those movie-makers who were formed in (and by) the Sixties, like Michelangelo Antonioni, Jean-Luc Godard, Bernardo Bertolucci and Rainer Werner Fassbinder, who made large-scale personal movies, films full of big ideas and passions, in the art cinema tradition. Tarkovsky lamented the passing of the 'greats': on June 6, 1980 he wrote in his diary (while in Italy):

> In the evening I watched Cocteau's *The Return of Orpheus* [*Le Testament d'Orphée*, 1960, France], on television.
> Where have all the great ones gone?
> Where are Rossellini, Cocteau, Renoir, Vigo? The great – who are poor in spirit? Where has poetry gone? Money, money, money and fear...
> Fellini is afraid, Antonioni is afraid... the only one who is afraid of nothing is Bresson. (D, 256)

Feminist Camille Paglia would have agreed with Andrei Tarkovsky in lamenting the decline in cinema since the New Wave days: '[o]n the whole, film has fallen off in artistic quality from the high point of European art film in the late fifties and sixties'.3 Krysztof Kieslowski, a filmmaker with many affinities with Tarkovsky, said that all the great film personalities and movies were in the past, were dead or retired (1993, 33). For some critics, cinema is dying if not dead. How so? Tarkovsky asked 'where are the cinema greats?' Where is the great cinema being made in the years since the 1980s?

My first encounter with Andrei Tarkovsky's art was seeing *Mirror*, when it was broadcast on British television in 1982. I was struck by the image of the trees blowing in the wind at night. This is intensely poetic – about as deeply poetic as cinema ever gets. It is one of the starting points for the film, for the childhood scenes. It is scene four: the boy is in bed; night noises are heard – a bird; cut to some trees and bushes: the camera tracks slowly, laterally, to the left; a breeze rustles the trees; cut back to the boy; he leans up in the bed and says 'Papa'. The yearning in this sequence is immense. It's so simple: just a shot of a boy in a bed and some trees. Yet Tarkovsky's sacred cinema manages to imbue it with such richness, such power, such mystery. One is not sure exactly how he does it. The elements appear mundane, viewed individually. One can recognize the language, the signs and symbols, and so on, but none of this knowledge explains the mystery. Tarkovsky's art transcends ordinary cinematic approaches.

Few filmmaker's works are so sparse, so economical, yet so rich and subtle (one thinks of Ingmar Bergman, Yasujiro Ozu, and Robert Bresson). Andrei Tarkovsky's movies contain many elements the hungry devotee demand from a film: (1) intensely sensuous images; (2) great acting; (3) subtlety; (4) religious and mythic themes and allusions; (5) poetic treatment and subject matter; (6) use of classical and folk music; (7) singular (natural) sounds; (8) magic and mystery; (9) clarity *and* complexity; (10) multiple layers; (11) multiple viewpoints; (12) eidetic details; (13) acknowledgement of the past (personal, historical and cultural); (14) use of the history of art and painting; (15) use of symbols; (16) non-linear narration; (17) a deep sense of the family, of childhood and parents; and (18) an extraordinary sense of space, design, props and colour.[4]

But Andrei Tarkovsky's cinema is also in another realm from Western European (British, Italian, Spanish, French and German) cinema. It has perhaps more affinities with what used to be called East European cinema. In Andrei Tarkovsky's art, the European art movie is fused with the majesty, tragedy and infinity of Eastern European and Russian culture (why is that phrase *Mother Russia* so potent, even if ideologically, politically and culturally suspect?). Tarkovsky's sacred cinema is suggestive; he shows things, but not completely; Tarkovsky is didactic, but not analytical or comprehensive (sometimes he's wilfully intellectually anti-intellectual); his cinema shows the viewer events, but doesn't give them only one interpretation. One sees things, but mystery is still there. In Hollywood/ international (dominant) entertainment cinema, with its stolid camerawork, incessant swelling music underlining every gesture, routine dialogue, by-numbers plots, rampant materialism, pro-militaristic ideology, and immovable (monoscopic) viewpoints, the viewer always knows exactly where they are. There is no room to manœuvre, no ambiguity. In Tarkovsky's cinema, one can move about, because his films are *spacious*.

Andrei Tarkovsky's images excite enormously: an angel under clear running water; a room full of rain; a glass bottle; a Leonardo da Vinci or

Piero della Francesca painting; a house on fire (the *whole house*, not just the roof or a window, as in conventional movies, but the *whole structure*). These images can be seen as rapturous and radiant. An image from a Tarkovsky film is easily identified as a Tarkovsky image, although the production crew, the script, the setting, and the actors are different. As an example of Tarkovsky's stunning imagery, take the birds flying out of the Madonna's body at the beginning of *Nostalghia*, for example. Many other filmmakers have excelled at slowly and carefully establishing a seemingly ordinary scene and having something bizarre happen in the middle of it to stun the viewer. Tarkovsky achieves cinematic wonder without all the technological wizardry mainstream cinema can muster. And there are still many more and more surprises with every viewing of a Tarkovsky movie.

Ingmar Bergman was reported to have seen *Andrei Roublyov* ten times (D, 248). Andrei Tarkovsky was one of Bergman's favourites: the Swede saw *Andrei Roublyov* at Svensk Filmindustri in 1971, in a print without subtitles. It made a big impression on Bergman. Bergman said that he had spent his 'entire life knocking at the door leading to the space where he moves with such obvious naturalness'.[5] Of Tarkovsky, Bergman said he was 'the greatest, the one who invented a new language'.[6]

PART ONE
THE ARTIST

ONE

The Poetry of Cinema

EMOTION AND SPECTACLE: VISCERAL CINEMA

In Jean-Luc Godard's wonderful film *Pierrot le fou* (1965, France), director Sam Fuller defines cinema in 'one word... Emotion'. Emotion (feeling, desire, affect) is important to the success of most artforms – whether painting, music, dance or drama. Or, to put it another way, at its best cinema works on a number of levels, of which the emotional is perhaps the most powerful. It is this gut-response that Hollywood cinema exploits, from D.W. Griffith to Steven Spielberg. In postmodern, post-everything philosophy, the search for meaning has been replaced by experience; no authorship, just effect. Not 'what does it mean?' or 'who's the author?' but 'what does it feel like?' or 'does it feel good?' A cinema of spectacle, visceral thrill, sensory overload.

Art's effect is emotional, Andrei Tarkovsky always said. It works first on a person's emotions, not their intellect, their mind, their thoughts (ST, 165). A movie is an 'emotional reality', Tarkovsky claimed, and the audiences perceives it as a '*second reality*' (ST, 176). The audience of a film, for Tarkovsky, always thinks of the events being depicted on the screen as something real, something truly there; whereas a painting, say, was always taken as an '*image* of reality', a construct (ST, 178).

The most successful religious movie-makers – Ingmar Bergman, Robert Bresson, Luis Buñuel and Pier Paolo Pasolini – have made smaller scale movies which are characterized by intense, lyrical moments. Andrei Tarkovsky is of the Robert Bresson School of Sacred Cinema – quiet, introspective, controlled (why shout when you can whisper just as effectively?). Yet both Tarkovsky's and Bresson's films are highly emotional, and as manipulative as Cecil B. DeMille or Steven Spielberg (but all art is manipulation: great art is just better at hiding how much it's manipulating the audience).

In its grander moments it's easy to see how Andrei Tarkovsky's cinema echoes the gestures of High Romanticism – its Blakean, Wordsworthian, Goethean, Turnerian gestures. The marks of late 18th / early 19th century European Romanticism include: exalting nature; going to extremes; the cult of solitude; the predominance of subjectivity; rebellion; the artist as outsider; infinity; the sublime, and so on.

Andrei Tarkovsky and his cinema embodies so many of the marks of High Romantic culture: (1) the cult of the artist as sacred creator (something Tarkovsky and most of the Romantics believed in); (2) the sovereignty of the artist; (3) the holy aloneness of the artist (the artist as outsider, marginal, apart, different); (4) the artist as rebel and romantic rebellion (the artist or individual versus the mob or establishment, such as Percy Bysshe Shelley, or Mary Shelley's Dr Frankenstein; one recalls Tarkovsky's long-running disputations with the Soviet authorities); (5) the Romantics' awe of the natural world (Friedrich Hölderlin's beloved Swiss Alps or William Worthsworth's Lake District); (6) going to extremes; (7) nostalgia and romanticizing the past (a recurring passion for Tarkovsky); (8) a love of the exotic, the far-off, the Oriental; (9) wildernesses, deserts, oceans, forests, mountains; (10) beauty and heightened sensuality; (11) synæsthesia and magical correspondences (*à la* Charles Baudelaire); (12) magic and the occult (as in Novalis or Johann Wolfgang von Goethe); (13) shamanism and religion; (14) mythology and history; (15) intensity; (16) horror and the Gothic (Romanticism has many links with Gothic literature, and there's a strong Gothic strain in Tarkovsky's cinema – not least in his *Hoffmanniana* script); (16) the urge towards the infinite and the eternal; (17) the visionary, spectacular and sublime; and (18) barely disguised spiritual longing and mysticism.

Andrei Tarkovsky's debt to or links with Romantic culture are no surprise, really, because the Romantic definition of the artist pretty much describes the modern artist. Tarkovsky and Tarkovsky's cinema would disagree, however, with postmodern and contemporary artists who exalt playfulness; irony, coolness and distance; surface not depth; objectivity not subjectivity; and the death of the author.

THE POETICS OF CINEMA

Cinema poeticizes reality and the real. The filmmaker may not intend poetry, but, as in Sergei Eisensteinian montage, the effect, as far as the viewer is concerned, can be poetic. The images, the colours, the textures, the manipulation of time, the multiple viewpoints, the metaphors and connections made – all these can be made poetic. Certainly the movies of Charlie Chaplin, Milos Forman, Atom Egoyam, Ermanno Olmi, Douglas Sirk and Li Shaohong, six very different filmmakers, contain moments of intense poetry. When the subject is bleak, such as poverty-stricken childhood (as in Bill Douglas's trilogy), or cannibalism (as in Jean-Luc Godard's *Weekend* [1967, France] or in Marco Ferreri's *Blow Out* [*La Grande Boufe*, 1973, Italy]), the results can still be very poetic. If lyricism is in the perception of the beholder, then any (and every) movie can be poetic. Often it is the films that strive self-consciously to be lyrical that fail: the mythopœic experience can be elusive.

Like poetry, cinema is full of rhymes, of dissonances, assonances, cross-references, plots and sub-plots. Like poetry, cinema uses images, motifs, metaphors, allusions, allegories, repetitions, fables, refrains, subjective viewpoints, lyricism and so on. Many moviemakers, like most poets, have their own vocabulary, full of their own words (or shots), their own phrases (or camera movements, lighting styles) and their own quotes (or *hommages*, as the French New Wave filmmakers called them). A platitude of the academy is that writers have to establish their own 'voice', that the most successful artists have personal vision. Each of cinema's *auteurs* has her/ his own 'voice' – Tarkovsky has his long water-filled takes; Ingmar Bergman has his ensemble playing, Expressionist camera and alienated winterscapes; Sergei Eisenstein has his montage, and so on.

In a 1964 essay, Andrei Tarkovsky said he wanted cinema to fuse the subjective and the objective, to be both facts and feelings, to have its own poetic logic, to have its own form, separate from literature or theatre, and to express the 'poetic concreteness' of dreams. Poetry, Tarkovsky asserted in *Sculpting In Time* (21), is 'an awareness of the world, a particular way of relating to reality. So poetry becomes a philosophy to guide a man throughout his life'. For Tarkovsky, poetic thinking (intuitive, subjective, associative) may be closer to life, and to thought itself, than the narrative logic of traditional drama (and cinema), which was the only model used for expressing dramatic conflict. It was cinema's task, Tarkovsky reckoned, to convey some of the impressions, the associations, the memories and subjective states of life (ST, 23).

Poetic moments are central fo Andrei Tarkovsky's cinema (a shot of trees rustling in the wind at night, from *Mirror*, or the snow falling at the end of *Nostalghia*). Tarkovsky made such suddenly thrilling evocations one of his specialities. The Tarkovsky shock moment was a set-piece that often revelled in the self-conscious fakery of cinema. But it is the images that do the talking, that stay in the mind, that creep in under the mundane architecture of dialogue, characters, action and plot.

Andrei Tarkovsky's religious cinema goes beyond the poetic cinema of Alexander Dovzhenko and Lev Kuleshov: Tarkovsky says, repeatedly (in *Sculpting in Time*), how he hates the manipulative and artificial effects of Eisensteinian montage cinema ('I am radically opposed to the way Sergei Eisenstein used the frame to codify intellectual formulæ... Eisenstein makes thought into a despot' are two typical Tarkovskyan criticisms of Eisenstein [ST, 183]). Yet Tarkovsky employs poetic montage many times – in *Mirror*, for example, which is (really) one long poetic montage. There are sequences of montage in Tarkovsky's poetic cinema as manipulative (or overly 'intellectual') as anything in Eisenstein or Dziga Vertov, or in Russian 'poetic cinema', abstract and formal movie, and American 1940s *avant garde* cinema.

Andrei Tarkovsky is not a filmmaker who employs movie references in his movies. Indeed, he studiously avoids any shot or sequence that looks like the work of another movie-maker.[1] Some filmmakers load many allusions to the history of cinema into their movies. Jean-Luc Godard is always discussing cinema in his films, either through his characters, his voiceovers, his *mise-en-scène*, or his quotations. Some filmmakers delight in producing *hommages* to movies or filmmakers (Woody Allen to Ingmar Bergman, for instance, or Francis Coppola to Orson Welles or Akira Kurosawa, or Peter Bogdanovitch to John Ford), while others can't resist spoofing movies (Mel Brooks, Jim Abrahams, the Marx Brothers). Some movie franchises are built almost entirely on references to movies and popular culture: *Shrek, Scary Movie, Scream, Indiana Jones, Star Wars*, and don't seem have any 'centre' or 'substance' if you take away the quotes, allusions and jokes.

Andrei Tarkovsky's movies are the polar opposite of that kind of playful, multi-allusive postmodernity. Tarkovsky's films *never* wink at the audience. Tarkovsky really means it, *maaan*. A movie is never 'just a movie' for Tarkovsky, as it is for so many filmmakers. *Just* a movie! The idea is absurd in the Tarkovsky universe. And Tarkovsky's films haven't yet entered popular culture in the West like, say, the figure of Death in Ingmar Bergman's *The Seventh Seal*, who crops up in *Monty Python, The Simpsons* and *Bill & Ted* movies.

ANDREI TARKOVSKY AS POET

For Andrei Tarkovsky, poetic cinema is subjective, intuitive, non-rational, non-literary. It begins and ends with an individual's perception (ST, 20). For Tarkovsky, ever the Renaissance philosopher, the individual is the measure of everything. Thus, Tarkovsky rejects logic, classical drama, cause-and-effect and simplistic notions of narration. Tarkovsky exalts dream-logic (what Elisabeth Sewell in *The Orphic Voice* called 'post-logic'), poetic associations, non-linearity, and the primacy of the individual response. 'Poetic cinema' is the best term for his kind of cinema. He defines it thus:

> I find poetic links, the logic of poetry in cinema, extraordinarily pleasing. They seem to me perfectly appropriate to the potential of cinema as the most truthful and poetic of art forms. (ST, 18)

Andrei Tarkovsky's concept of poetic cinema is the same as his concept of art: he exalts the spiritual, the search for 'truth', subjectivity and so on. Tarkovsky forces cinema to become increasingly dreamlike. Tarkovsky blurs the boundaries of dream and actuality. As Robert Bresson put it: '[y]our film must resemble what you see on shutting your eyes' (50). For Ingmar Bergman, Tarkovsky was the master of dream films: 'Tarkovsky is the greatest of them all. He moves with such naturalness in the room of dreams...'[1]

For Barthelemy Amengual, Andrei Tarkovsky's cinema is like Byzantine icons: 'the icon transposes the spiritual into physical space; Tarkovsky transposes it into physical time'.[2] Try considering what it *does* not what it *means*: instead of trying to decipher the rain, smoke, horses and other Tarkovsky motifs and symbols, turning them into categories of written or verbal language, accept them as experiences or effects. That is, of course, the overriding project of one strain of contemporary cultural theory which reckons that questions like 'what does it mean?' are no longer valid. More to the point is: 'what does it feel like?', and: 'what is its effect?' And Tarkovsky's films work elegantly on both these levels, on the levels of meaning and doing (and on other levels too).

Andrei Tarkovsky speaks of cinema in terms of poetry and music. Like music, he says, cinema needs no mediating language: it deals with reality (ST, 176-7). 'I classify cinema and music among the *immediate* artforms since they need no mediating language' (ST, 176). Any passage taken at random from *Sculpting in Time* gives a clear sense of Tarkovsky's notions of art: '[a]rt is born and takes hold wherever there is a timeless and insatiable longing for the spiritual' (ST, 38). Tarkovsky saw himself within Alexandre Astruc's *camera-stylo/ auteur* theory tradition. Tarkovsky is a *ciné*-poet *par excellence*, a movie-maker who takes Dziga Vertov's *kino-glaz* ('cinema-eye') and theory of *kino-pravda* ('cinema-truth') to the point of mysticism. Tarkovsky's cinema is more mystical than most, in the true sense of the word. Not 'mystical' because it is strange, unreal, poetic or even religious, in the traditional sense, but 'mystical' because his cinema constantly strives, like authentic mysticism, for something wholly other, for the numinous, the divine, the beyond.

Authentic mysticism lies at the heart of religion (such as Sufic mysticism within Islam). In the same way, the mystical cinema of Carl Theodor Dreyer, Ingmar Bergman, Yasujiro Ozu and Andrei Tarkovsky lies at the centre of world cinema. The advances that people such as Bergman, Ozu and Tarkovsky have made are not in the mundane realm of visual effects, box office receipts or synergetic distribution, but in explorations of the human condition. For Andrei Tarkovsky, art, religion, cinema and poetry are all part of the same thing: a mysticism of cinema. 'Pictures must be miraculous', said the tragic painter Mark Rothko,[3] and Tarkovsky's images aim to be similarly thaumaturgic. The cinematic (or poetic) and the sacred are (or should be) equivalent for Tarkovsky. As Georges Bataille put it: 'all that is sacred is poetic and all that is poetic is sacred'.[4] Tarkovsky's mode of cinema is to construct the conditions in which an exploration of the sacred can occur. The long take, the slow tracking shot, bleached-out colour, Johann Sebastian Bach music – these are mechanisms by which Tarkovsky's cinema can evoke the numinous. As in all mysticism, the search for the sacred in Tarkovsky's cinema is a process doomed to failure: the would-be mystic can only carry on dauntlessly, trying to find the transcendent in the immanent, trying to nurture such delicate notions (or illusions) as hope and faith. There are no technical problems in cinema, Tarkovsky stated, 'once you know exactly what to say' (ST, 110).

ANDREI TARKOVSKY AND THE HISTORY OF POETRY

In his movies Andrei Tarkovsky quoted Aleksandr Pushkin, Fyodor Tyutchev, William Shakespeare and, above all, his father, Arseny Tarkovsky (not to be confused with Aleksandr Tvardovsky, 1910-71). Ironically, the general public in Russia knew about Tarkovsky and his films before Tarkovsky senior and his poetry (so that Arseny Tarkovsky was known as the father of Tarkovsky the movie director, not the other way around).[1]

Arseny Tarkovsky (who died in 1989), was a poet who remained unpublished during Andrei Tarkovsky's childhood. Today, Tarkovsky senior is regarded as a significant poet, though definitely not to be classed among the greats like, say, Aleksandr Pushkin, Alexander Blok or Yevgeny Yvetushenko. Tarkovsky's poetry is essentially lyrical – poetry in the classical sense: impressionistic experiences of the world. It does not have a self-conscious ideological or political agenda, for instance. But it was hugely important for his son's films: when Andrei Tarkovsky quotes from a poet, it is from Arseny Tarkovsky more than any other (though he does quote from Pushkin and Fyodor Tyuchev. Pushkin is one of Tarkovsky's poetry gods: Pushkin's poem 'The Prophet' was one of Tarkovsky's key poetic inspirations). A school friend (Yuri Kochevrin) recalled that Tarkovsky carried a book of Tarkovsky senior's poetry with him all the time (JP, 19).

Andrei Tarkovsky's father's poetry influenced much of Tarkovsky's cinema. It's easy to spot the influence of the conservative, classical, musical and metaphysical style of Tarkovsky senior in his son's movies. Tarkovsky not only incorporated his father's poetry into the background and tone of his films, he also included them in the soundtrack and dialogue, most prominently in *Mirror* and *Nostalghia*. The first poem in *Zerkalo* (read by his father) is probably the best, most moving Arseny Tarkovsky poem appearing in a Tarkovsky movie: 'First Meeting' (published in 1962):

> Every moment that we were together
> Was a celebration, like Epiphany,
> In all the world the two of us alone,
> You were bolder, lighter than a bird-wing,
> Heady as vertigo you ran downstairs
> Two steps at a time, and led me
> Through damp lilac, into your domain
> On the other side, beyond the mirror. (ST, 101)

The movie goes on to trace the life led 'beyond the mirror'. After his father Arseny, Aleksandr Pushkin is Andrei Tarkovsky's main poetic influence (or most often cited). In poems such as 'Autumn', Pushkin created the dream of a mythical, snowbound Russia:

> O mournful season! How enchanting to the eye! Your beauty with its message of farewell delights me: I love nature's sumptuous fading, the woods clothed in purple and gold, the noise of the wind and the fresh

breeze in the tree-tops, the skies covered with rolling mist, the infrequent sun-ray, the first frost, and the distant threat of hoary winter.2

This is the mist-soaked Russia Andrei Tarkovsky portrays in *Andrei Roublyov*, *Mirror* and *Nostalghia*. In *Mirror* the boy quotes Aleksandr Pushkin's letter of October 19, 1836 to Piotr Chadayev on the founding of Russia (ST, 195). Tarkovsky's poetic cinema is part of the Russian poetic tradition, and Pushkin is the spirit and apotheosis of Russian poetry. Tarkovsky worked in that Russian lyrical tradition, which runs from Pushkin and Fyodor Tyutchev through Alexander Blok, Anna Akhmatova, Boris Pasternak, Osip Mandelstam and Sergei Esenin, to Arseny Tarkovsky and Yevgeny Yvetushenko.

One can see similarities between Andrei Tarkovsky's art and the cosmological visions of Dante in his *Divina Commedia*; with William Shakespeare's tragic humanism; with the religious fervour of the British Metaphysical poets (John Donne, George Herbert, Richard Crashaw and Henry Vaughan); with the nature-loving pantheism of Romantics such as Novalis, Friedrich Hölderlin, Johann Wolfgang von Goethe and William Wordsworth; with the musicality and linguistic philosophies of the French Symbolists (Paul Verlaine, Stephane Mallarmé, Paul Valéry and Stefan George); and with modern European poets such as St-John Perse, Paul Celan and Georg Trakl.

One of the key works of literature that Andrei Tarkovsky quotes from in his movies is the *Bible*. After the *Bible*, William Shakespeare, Aleksandr Pushkin and Fyodor Mikhaylovich Dostoievsky are favourites. *Don Quixote* is referenced in *Solaris*; Fyodor Tyuchev in *Stalker*; Anton Chekhov, Dante Alighieri (the *Inferno*), Dostoievsky (*The Devils*), Arseny Tarkovsky and Pushkin in *Mirror*. In his book on cinema, *Sculpting In Time*, Tarkovsky frequently refers to literary figures: apart from the ones cited above are Boris Pasternak, Osip Mandelstham, Nikolai Gogol, Ivan Bunin, Alexander Herzen, Alexander Blok, Vyacheslav Ivanov and Nikolai Gumilyov among Russian writers and poets, and Hermann Hesse, G.W.F. Hegel, Paul Valéry, Ernest Hemingway, Emile Zola, Gustave Flaubert, Johann Wolfgang von Goethe, Dante Alighieri, Thomas Mann, Franz Kafka, and Marcel Proust among international writers.

TWO

The Film Image

CAMERAWORK

Andrei Tarkovsky's film image is incredibly beautiful. His film image is apparently so simple and so concrete: the faded stone, the water, the wood and trees. Real beauty in the texture, the light, the form, concrete and plastic. Such presence, such simplicity – the simplest of elements, yet so *sensuous*. Not like the remoteness or abstraction of Johann Sebastian Bach's music at all, but sensuous, like Franz von Liszt or Ottorino Respighi. Graham Petrie spoke of Tarkovsky's films' 'intense moral seriousness'. Tarkovsky used the poetry of dreams in cinema to 'speak directly to the receptive viewer by means of images whose beauty and suggestive power resonate with a forcefulness unmatched by almost any other filmmaker' (1996, 647). The sense of the beautiful is something Tarkovsky emphasized time and again in *Sculpting In Time* (38, 40, 42, *passim*). 'Truth' and the 'absolute' were central elements in Tarkovsky's poetics, but the insistence on the apprehension of beauty should never be forgotten (it's a much more problematic issue deciding what is beauty and the beautiful – a vast area in theology and philosophy, and beyond the scope of this book).

Andrei Tarkovsky is a modernist in his use of the camera (in the sense of the relation of the camera to the narration, to the themes, to the image, to the artist wielding it): the camera tracks through the printing works in *Mirror* as if through a maze – down corridors, around machines, following people. This labyrinthine motion recalls the camera of Rainer Werner Fassbinder's *Despair* (1977, West Germany), Bernardo Bertolucci's *The Spider's Stratagem* (1970, Italy) and Jean-Luc Godard's *Breathless* (1960, France). It's the familiar dollying camera of modernist, New Wave cinema, the elaborate post-Wellesian camera moves which draw attention to themselves. Bertolucci spoke of the 'unmotivated camera', where the camera moves independently of the dramatic action:

> The camera has a dialectical relationship to the actors and is not merely recording the event, but is an invisible participant with its own soul. Sometimes the camera even enters into competition with the actor – while the actor moves, the camera moves independently. (1976b, 8)

Andrei Tarkovsky's camera often drifts on its own, as an independent participant in the movie. Commenting on the action, reframing it, reworking the blocking of the actors against the background. Creating the film as it comments upon it. Tarkovsky's framing is often of the decentred, centrifugal kind (D. Cook, 796).

Andrei Tarkovsky uses crane or boom shots, but not in the style of Hollywood Westerns, or the vertiginous manner of D.W. Griffith, Alfred Hitchcock or Orson Welles (classic self-conscious movie-makers). In *Andrei Roublyov* there are epic-style crane shots to capture the crowd scenes, as well as the ecstasy of the opening flying sequence. But more typical is the slow crane shot in *The Sacrifice*, up the tree, at the end of the film. This very obviously represents spiritual rebirth, psychological renewal. It is a shot with a precise narrative function, and fits in exactly with the structure of the movie. The way Janet Leigh describes Alfred Hitchcock's cinematic technique while making *Psycho* could apply to many filmmakers (though not necessarily a favourite style with actors or crew): there was *no* collaboration, *no* discussion. Hitch knew exactly what he wanted: 'his camera was absolute', in every scene, Leigh remarked, and there was no way someone on set could suggest doing it differently. 'Hitchcock's camera was the most important thing in his mind'.[1] This sense of visual precision could apply to Orson Welles, Bernardo Bertolucci and Andrei Tarkovsky, and other *auteurs* who were precious and precise with their cameras.

Andrei Tarkovsky's hero Robert Bresson said that one of the movie director's tasks was to find not just the *right* way of doing a shot, but the *only* way of doing it. One can see in their films *auteurs* such as Tarkovsky, Orson Welles, Alfred Hitchcock and Bergman looking for the single best way of making a shot. It is a kind of artistic asceticism and purism, an inability to compromise. Tarkovsky was certainly an adherent of such an approach.

Andrei Tarkovsky sometimes operated the camera on parts of his movies, but he didn't (couldn't) do everything: there were always camera operators, grips, assistants, sparks, gaffers and, of course, cinematographers. Tarkovsky said he regarded his DPs as the co-authors of his films (ST, 135). While we're discussing photography, the DPs and camera operators should be mentioned: Vadim Yusov (who shot all Tarkovsky's movies through to *Solaris*), Georgy Rerberg, A. Nikolayev and I. Shtanko (*Mirror*), Alexander Knyazhinsky, N. Fudim, S. Naugolnikh, G. Verkhovsky, L. Kazmin and T. Maslennikova (*Stalker*; Rerberg also shot the first version of *Stalker*), Giuseppe Lanci and Giuseppe De Crisanti (*Nostalghia*), Sven Nykvist, Lasse Karlsson and Dan Myhrman (*The Sacrifice*).

THE TRACKING SHOT

Andrei Tarkovsky's typical movement of the camera is the slow tracking shot, often crabwise (i.e., parallel to the subject). Tarkovsky uses tracking shots that last longer than, say, Jean-Luc Godard's famous traffic jam shot in *Weekend* (1967, France), or Orson Welles' crane shot in *Touch of Evil* (1957, U.S.A.), or the brothel sequence in Max Ophüls' *Le Plaisir* (1952, France). Tarkovsky's tracking shots, like Theo Angelopoulos's, are some of the longest in cinema (in time if not in space). Each one could be regarded as a short film in themselves. Bernardo Bertolucci said precisely this: 'I want each take to be a film in itself'.[1] The candle-carrying scene in *Nostalghia*, for instance, is conceived as a complete sequence, in three acts, with a beginning (he lights the candle), tension (will he make it across the pool?), high and low points (he gets quite far – but the candle goes out and he has to go back) and an ending (he sets the candle, alight, down on the far side). Music fades in. He dies.

The tracking shot requires a careful orchestration of movement, timing, blocking, props, practical effects, lighting, dialogue and sound – it is a carefully controlled, very artificial cinematographic technique. Andrei Tarkovsky's enhances the artificiality – and unreality – of tracking shots sometimes, by building in actions or beats which draw attention to time expanding within the frame.

DISTANCE AND VIEWPOINT

As for the distance between camera and subject, Andrei Tarkovsky uses many long shots. He favours a cool objectivity, even though at times he can be highly contrived and self-conscious in his choice of angles, compositions and distance. He does not go in for Expressionist close-ups, like Carl-Theodor Dreyer, Charlie Chaplin, Ingmar Bergman or Orson Welles. He often uses cutaways and inserts – shots of objects, photographed lovingly in close-up. He often shoots people from slightly above – in *The Sacrifice* the camera tracks in and bears down upon the kneeling, praying figure of Alexander (as it does in *Stalker*, when the three men rest by the pool).

In a number of movies the camera, in close-up, cranes down the body of a figure, emphasizing the stature, vulnerability and physiology of the person. *Behold the Man*, this kind of shot could be saying, as it travels over the landscape of the body (as at the beginning of *Nostalghia*), much as sculptor's gaze might, or a painter turning the body into a landscape, or a series of forms.

Sometimes a bird's-eye view is deployed, as of Kelvin in bed in *Solaris*, or the artisans in the wood before they are blinded in *Andrei Roublyov*. One sort of tracking shot – looking down on a tiny portion of a landscape – seems exclusive to Andrei Tarkovsky. It is used to great effect to illustrate (or to embody) the Stalker's dream: the camera tracks in close-up over a series of objects under some water. The same shot is used in *The Sacrifice*, across a snowbound chunk of earth, and in *Nostalghia*, over the model landscape at Domenico's home.

These high angle viewpoints are some of the most unreal in cinema – the world is rarely experienced by people in everyday life in this way. It is like flying slowly and gently over the Earth – an image from a flying dream. Alfred Hitchcock asserted that the chase is best suited to film (or cinema was the best at depicting a chase: 'the chase seems to me the final expression of the motion picture medium,' Hitch remarked in 1950; 'it's the time factor in movement that makes the chase').[1] In the same way, flying is well suited to cinema – and vice versa; cinema is well suited to depicting flight. Form and content fuse seamlessly.

SLOW MOTION

Andrei Tarkovsky's use of slow motion is not like Sam Peckinpah's, or as it is used in horror movies – to stretch out moments of blood, guts and extreme violence, producing a cinema that is existentially visceral (eviscerating). But Tarkovsky does have a slow motion death: it's in *Andrei Roublyov*, as Roublyov's assistant Foma is pierced by an arrow and falls into the river. The ancestor of Tarkovsky's use of slow motion is Akira Kurosawa's cinema, and Foma's demise is a definite *hommage* to Kurosawa, and to the peerless *The Seven Samurai* in particular. The way that Tarkovsky cuts together slow motion, in his montages of dreams or heightened moments, is also inspired by the *sensei* of Japanese cinema. (As well as Peckinpah and Tarkovsky, Kurosawa's influence is acknowledged by John Woo, Ingmar Bergman, John Milius, George Lucas and Paul Verhoeven, among many others).

Andrei Tarkovsky's slow motion is softly poetic, stemming from his lyrical view of life. There is a great deal of slow motion in Tarkovsky's cinema – mostly of the gentle kind, where actions are filmed in slight slow motion. In *Mirror* objects fall to the ground, people walk or run, fires flicker and the mother turns to stare into the camera in slow motion. The result is to alter perception, to re-organize reality, and take the film into another world. Often slow motion means an experience of the past, as in *Nostalghia*. But in *Mirror* slow motion is used to re-write, and represent, many aspects of life. It does not, as it does in mainstream cinema, extend, elastically, some violent moment (a car crash, a bullet wound); rather, it poeticizes everyday reality. It is a lyrical device. (Slight slow motion has become far more common in Hollywood cinema, as well as TV advertizing, although the influence there comes from the speed ramping available on computers and in digital editing, and cameras which can switch film speeds within the same shot. Martin Scorsese is a particular fan of the in-camera technique).

No realist he, Andrei Tarkovsky is not a fantasist either. He used slow motion to imbue screen moments with the lucidity, the magnitude and the utter rightness of a dream. One of the most extraordinary and deeply poetic uses of slow motion occurs in Jean-Luc Godard's *Sauve qui peut la vie* (*Slow Motion*, 1980, France). A woman riding a bike is freeze-framed, and caught in very slow slow motion, to the sound of classical piano music. The effect is like projecting a movie at a very slow speed (a technique used in Derek Jarman's *The Angelic Conversation*, 1985, GB). Films such as *The Matrix*, *GoodFellas* and *Casino* have employed freeze frames within shots, and speed ramping, familiar to audiences. Where slow motion might once have been employed by only a few film directors, with many more traditional directors too conventional to go near it, it's commonplace nowadays.

THE MYSTERIES OF BLACK-AND-WHITE AND COLOUR

Andrei Tarkovsky's use of alternating colour and black-and-white is essentially no different from that of *The Wizard of Oz* (Victor Fleming, 1939, U.S.A.). Changing from colour to black-and-white (as in *Mirror* and *Nostalghia*) indicates a movement from one world, one mental state, one perception, to another. Sometimes Tarkovsky uses black-and-white to portray the past (in *Mirror* and *Nostalghia*), whereas in *Nostalghia* sepia-and-white images are part of Domenico's past and Gorchakov's Russian dreams. In a 1966 interview, Tarkovsky said he preferred black-and-white movies over colour films, because black-and-white seemed closer, he asserted, to how perception works in real life, how colour isn't really noticed in real life, but colour films artificially attract attention to themselves (D, 356). Although the world is in colour, Tarkovsky reckoned that black-and-white movie somehow came closer to the psychology of art (ST, 139).

Andrei Tarkovsky's restrained use of colour produced colours that were naturalistic, muted, often optically washed-out. For the desaturated look of *The Sacrifice*, Sven Nykvist employed a photographic technique which combined colour and a black-and-white dupes, made from a colour negative. An optical printer is used to blend them together until the right mix is achieved. About fifty of the night shots in *The Sacrifice* were treated optically to give them the right 'magical, mystical' effect. Nykvist said that he found out about the technique from *Moby Dick* (which had been shot by Ossie Morris and Freddie Francis). Tarkovsky preferred to 'neutralize' the colour in a film, to make it subservient to the drama or expression. Tarkovsky was particularly suspicious of movies that featured bold colours which fought against the expressivity of the image (ST, 138).

The near-monochrome look became popular with filmmakers in the Nineties (particularly those who aren't allowed by distributors and studios to use total black-and-white – chiefly because executives think it puts audiences off – but who can have something approximating it instead). Steven Spielberg and Janusz Kaminski used it in *Minority Report, Saving Private Ryan* and *Amistad*; Tim Burton employed it in *Batman* (shot by Roger Pratt) and *Sleepy Hollow* (shot by Emmanuel Lubezki); and it was the speciality of DP Darius Khondji (*Seven, Alien 4, City of Lost Children*). The bleach bypass process was combined with treated filters and lenses. Probably the most famous usage in modern cinema occurred in *The Godfather* films, shot by the 'prince of darkness', Gordon Willis (who provided the same look for Woody Allen's Bergmanesque *Interiors*).

Andrei Tarkovsky also liked, along with so many filmmakers, to shoot at the magic hour (some of the great magic hour movies include *The Black*

Stallion; one of the very best is *Days of Heaven* [Terence Malick, 1978, U.S.A.], shot by Nestor Almendros and Haskell Wexler). On *The Sacrifice*, the dawn light meant shooting at two in the morning (in May in Gotland). Tarkovsky sometimes set-dressed the natural world to achieve particular effects (such as spray painting vegetation in *Stalker*, spraying trees with water in *The Sacrifice* to make them look darker, or, for *Mirror*, painting leaves gold).

There isn't a particular scheme to the use of black-and-white, sepia and colour in *Mirror*: while other movies might employ colour for dreams and black-and-white for 'reality' (as in the most famous case, *The Wizard of Oz*), *Mirror* doesn't abide by a strict pattern.

Sometimes it seems as if the different hues of black-and-white film stock in Andrei Tarkovsky's movies (as in *Mirror* or *Stalker*) was deliberate, and sometimes it appears rather arbitrary, not part of a premeditated pattern (and simply the result of how the celluloid was processed at the labs).

Andrei Tarkovsky often treats the colours in post-production (collaborating with his DP and the laboratories). The colours of *Nostalghia* are deliberately held-back, beaten-out, pale. *Nostalghia* uses black-and-white, sepia-and-white, muted colour, and full colour.

Andrei Tarkovsky's use of colour is, in general, very restrained, tending towards browns, greys, whites, blacks, greens and blues, usually in desaturated hues or a *chiaroscuro* style. Tarkovsky did not go for the excessive colour artificiality of, say, Vincente Minnelli in his MGM musicals, or Jacques Demy in *The Umbrellas of Cherbourg* (1964). The move into full colour was inevitable for Tarkovsky in the commercial world of feature filmmaking. Fewer filmmakers are allowed to use straight black-and-white than ever before (even for prestigious or art films). Tarkovsky compromised by employing selective black-and-white sequences inside colour films, and for combining muted colours with black-and-white and sepia.

In *Stalker*, the Zone is a vividly green and abundant place in a post-industrial, post-apocayptic world of greys, blacks and browns. The summery, green growths of the Zone contrast boldly with the black-and-white world that surrounds it. The Zone, though a dangerous and perhaps radiated space, is in fact more alive than the rest of the world.

Andrei Tarkovsky's unusual in one key respect, however: while many filmmakers employ transformations between colour to black-and-white from time to time, or just the once, for Tarkovsky it's a recurring technique, employed up to and including his last film.

As for his lighting, Andrei Tarkovsky favours natural light effects, hence his interiors are often very dim (the houses in *Mirror* and *The Sacrifice*). One reason that *Solaris* looks so odd in the Tarkovsky pantheon is all that bright, shadowless lighting. In *Nostalghia* and *Stalker*, and especially in *The Sacrifice*, characters lurk in deep shadows, as if in the dark recesses of Leonardo's *sfumato* lighting. Not as extreme as *film noir*, Tarkovsky's lighting is nevertheless full of dark zones. The exteriors too feature diffuse light, as if filmed under thin cloud cover. Tarkovsky's Italy is a mist-ridden pastoral landscape – every scene seems to have been filmed at dawn or in the magic hour.

The later movies in particular are filled with a soft light, a glow which is emphasized by the candles, bonfires and domestic lamps. These are a feature of every movie. The soft lighting brings out the texture of stone and wood, while the back-lighting makes rain shine (so many classic Andrei Tarkovsky images are carefully back-lit, emphasizing the translucency and fluidity of water).

SURFACES

Andrei Tarkovsky has an unparalleled sense of surfaces in cinema – of wooden, tiled or stone floors; of the texture of hair, cloth and tree trunks; of the reflections on water; and of the untouchable presence of fire. The Tarkovskyan wall must rank as one of his major motifs. Look at the walls in *Mirror*, *Andrei Roublyov* or *Stalker*. They are battered, weathered, pitted, with peeling paint and plaster. The camera tracks along a cracked wall or bank of earth at the beginning of *Ivan's Childhood*. In *Mirror*, the walls fall apart on camera. (Irma Rausch, Tarkovsky's first wife, recalled that Tarkovsky used to point out particularly interesting old, textured walls when they were walking around Moscow [JP, 230]. You know you're with someone unusual when, of the things to notice, they notice old walls). However, intricately art-directed wall appear in the cinemas of Walerian Borowczyk, Jan Svankmajer and Sergei Paradjanov.

The last four Andrei Tarkovsky movies in particular have an extraordinary sense of surface. One thinks again of Michelangelo Antonioni, but Tarkovsky goes beyond him. There is the table top in *Mirror*, with the drying condensation mark on it. There are the battered walls of Domenico's house, the polished wooden floor of *The Sacrifice*, and so on. The bare, weather-beaten walls recall Leonardo da Vinci, who used to look at walls in a Zen-like meditation, and see fantastic things in them. When he painted *The Last Supper* in S. Maria delle Grazie, Milan, in 1497, it was reported by

Matteo Bandello that Leonardo sat for hours staring at his painting, not doing anything:

> ...from sunrise to dusk he never laid aside his brushes and went on painting, forgetting about food and drink. Then it so happened that he did not touch his brushes for two, three or even four days running, and yet he would often sit for one or two hours at a stretch examining his work only; he would look at his figures and think and appraise them.[1]

This is nothing unusual, though – many artists do this. The viewer is encouraged to sit and contemplate Tarkovsky's movies in the same way. Tarkovsky's decayed walls are also similar in feel to the oil and wax textures of Jasper Johns and Robert Ryman, or Jean Dubuffet's mixed media canvases. Leonardo experimented with oil instead of fresco on *The Last Supper,* but his tests proved fatal, and 'the painting was already a wreck in his own lifetime'.[2] The fate of Leonardo's Milan painting offers an interesting parallel with Tarkovsky's career in movies.

The emphasis on texture, glass, surface, mirrors, rain, back-lighting, *chiaroscuro* and *sfumato* light make Andrei Tarkovsky's movie image very painterly. Although he admired the Early Renaissance painters, such as Fra Angelico and Sandro Botticelli, his film image looks more like Rembrandt van Rijn or Diego Velásquez. The end of *Solaris*, for example, when the father lays his hands on the shoulders of his kneeling son, exactly mirrors Rembrandt's *The Return of the Prodigal Son* (c. 1669, Hermitage Museum, St Petersburg). There are other directors who enjoy filming surfaces and the psychology behind them, who like exploring the ontology of frames, glass and mirrors: Borowczyk, Kubrick, Fassbinder, Bresson, Michelangelo Antonioni and Cocteau.

DECAY AND TRASH

Andrei Tarkovsky's floors and landscapes are full of trash, bits and pieces of junk, old machines, newspapers, chunks of wood, soggy cardboard, and all sorts of objects. His images look lived in, and old – not ancient, but severely humanized. Roublyov, Ivan, Domenico and the Stalker live in dilapidated places. The landscape of *The Sacrifice* looks post-Apocalyptic even before the bombers approach. The spaceship in *Solaris* is littered with defunct technology, a sci-fi 'look' not found in *2,001: A Space Odyssey* but in *Alien* (Ridley Scott, 1979), the *Mad Max* series (George Miller, 1979-1985, Australia) and other post-*Star Wars* post-punk post-holocaust movies. For Tarkovsky the world is a messy place, and although his movies are spiritual investigations, they are set in sometimes filthy worlds. This is part of Tarkovsky's filmic 'realism'. The real world *is* chaotic (but humans are a lot messier than nature, with their vast, industrial pollution).

Films that try to present the world as a clinically clean place sometimes tend to look artificial. This kind of artificiality Andrei Tarkovsky hates, being a searcher for 'the truth'. In this sense, his wet, dark, dirty images seem truer than most of movie and television. There is a conflict between the worlds of shit and spirit in Tarkovsky's sacred cinema, as there is in Samuel Beckett's fiction. But as writers such as Arthur Rimbaud, D.H. Lawrence, Georges Bataille, Samuel Beckett and John Cowper Powys show, the anal/ fæcal realm and the spiritual/ ecstatic realm are not so far apart, especially when treated by an imaginative mind that can transform things alchemically.[1]

THREE

The Mysteries of Space and Time

TIMELESS TIME

> *Cinema came into being as a means of recording the very movement of reality: factual, specific, within time and unique; of reproducing again and again the moment, instant by instant, in its fluid mutability. This is what determines the medium of cinema.*
>
> Andrei Tarkovsky, *Sculpting in Time* (94)

Andrei Tarkovsky was opposed to the manipulation of Sergei Eisenstein's *gestalt* theory of dialectical montage. But, like Eisenstein, Tarkovsky understood the possibilities of seeing everything at once. Not shot after shot, or sequences bound by linear time, but an all-at-once experience, a totality. This is what the Abstract Expressionist painters were trying to achieve. Barnett Newman wrote: 'I was concerned constantly in doing a painting that would move in its totality as you see it. You look at it and you see it'.[1] In a similar manner, Tarkovsky spoke of doing a film in a continuous shot. It is a dream of filmic intensity, a dream of cinema as revelation, where one sees (or rather, *feels*) everything at once. This is cinema moving towards Zen Buddhist *satori* or enlightenment, where there is an all-over experience, the James Joycean epiphany, the prime æsthetic experience. There's the object, and one sees it, all at once. It is a dream of every artist: instant and complete communication, inducing instant and complete understanding in the viewer. Tarkovsky wrote in *Sculpting in Time*:

> I think that what a person normally goes to the cinema for is time: for time lost or spent, or not yet had. He goes there for living experience; for cinema, like no other art, widens, enhances and concentrates a person's experience – and not only enhances it but makes it longer, significantly longer. (ST, 63)

Andrei Tarkovsky's claims for cinema could also be made by music, painting and other artforms. This is cinema as Time Refound, Paradise Regained, life enhanced, the sacred re-affirmed. It is the return to the mythic centre of mysticism – of Taoism and modern mystics such as Thomas Merton. The mythic centre is found again, and the initiate can escape from what Mircea Eliade called the 'terror of history':

> The "terror of history", for me, is the feeling experienced by a man who is no longer religious, who therefore has no hope of finding any ultimate meaning in the drama of history, and who must undergo the crimes of history without grasping the meaning of them. (1984, 128)

This, surely, is the state of Existential anguish the Andrei Tarkovskyan anti-hero finds her/ herself enduring: doomed or born into an areligious, ahistorical, apoetic, amusical world. So the Tarkoskian protagonist tries to re-instate the sacred, the divine, the poetic.

Another recurring concern of Andrei Tarkovsky's movies is war and conflict – from the Second World War in *Mirror* and *Ivan's Childhood*, to the Tartar raids in *Andrei Roublyov*, and global nuclear catastrophe in *The Sacrifice*. Those large, social concerns belie the received view that Tarkovsky's cinema only concentrates on subjective, poetic states. Tarkovsky's films are definitely not social and political commentaries like, say, Oliver Stone's explorations of contemporary America, or Jean-Luc Godard's Maoist-Marxist period. But they are concerned with the relation between the artist and her/ his social context, the artist's place within history, and wider, historical events such as the Second World War, or the formation of early modern Russia.

As to time periods and history, Andrei Tarkovsky, like most filmmakers, had his favourite periods: *Nostalghia*, *The Sacrifice*, *Mirror* and *Stalker* take place in the present (*Stalker* may be in the near future). *Mirror* and *Ivan's Childhood* go back to the Second World War (and both contain flashbacks to an idyllic childhood prior to the war). Alone among Tarkovsky's movies, *Solaris* is set in the future. *Andrei Roublyov* goes back in time the furthest in the Tarkovsky canon: to the early 1400s, with a flashback to the Crucifixion (although it's shot as if it were contemporary with the rest of the movie, not A.D. 33).

Having said that, the present day of Andrei Tarkovsky's movies is not the straightforward one of most other films. *Stalker*, for example, could be set in any time since the 1940s to the present. The visual references in *Stalker* are vague enough for it to be 1979, when the film was released, or 1949. Or it maybe some time in the future.

CINEMA OF DEATH

Along with the life-affirming Eternal Now of cinema, there is also the inescapable dimension of mortality and death. Cinema is filmed death, in one sense. It is no surprise that death is one of the main subjects of cinema. There are deaths in Andrei Tarkovsky's movies: slow motion deaths, heroic deaths, brutal murders and pathetic suicides. Death is bound to feature prominently in a filmmaker so bound up with eschatology. As with the Existentialist philosophers, death for Tarkovsky is the ultimate barrier, the absolute test. The main characters in *Stalker, Andrei Roublyov, Nostalghia* and *The Sacrifice* all come close to death. Tarkovsky doesn't go as far as German mediæval painting or the Mexican 'Day of the Dead' festival, and have skeletons wielding scythes as Death prancing about, but death is a strong presence in his cinema, and his characters are often peering over the abyss of their own unconscious, looking at the black depths of the soul below.

TIME IN ANDREI TARKOVSKY'S CINEMA

Some of Andrei Tarkovsky's contemporaries have excelled in the realms of editing. Few filmmakers are as clinically precise as Stanley Kubrick, whose Bible was Vsevolod Pudovkin's book *Film Technique* (1926). Kubrick's *Dr Strangelove* (1963) and *The Killing* (1956, U.S.A.) use parallel action and cross-cutting in a complex and powerful way. Kubrick's narrator gives the impression of having a God-like overview of a whole movie, and all the layers in it. Similarly, Francis Coppola is a master of montage, as the endings of *The Godfather* (1972, U.S.A.), *The Cotton Club* (1984, U.S.A.) and *The Godfather III* (1990) demonstrate.

Andrei Tarkovsky, meanwhile, does not place this overview in his films. He rarely uses cross-cutting or parallel action (the basis of cinema as a chase). He says you have to show one thing after another; there's no other way (ST, 70). And that's what he does that at the climax of *Nostalghia*, where many another editor would have intercut the two climactic events. Tarkovsky doesn't even like reaction shots; he dubs them redundant in *Sculpting In Time* (70). His basic technique is to fill each shot with emotion and time, to achieve his effects with long takes, with the long sequence shot, rather than with the dialectics of Eisensteinian montage.

Andrei Tarkovsky was very much involved with the technical aspects of filmmaking, with preparing a shot, but when he came to shoot it, he preferred one or two takes. That meant a lot of effort went into preparation, rather than, as with perfectionists like Stanley Kubrick or Jackie Chan, repeating the same actions time after time (Tarkovsky was similarly a perfectionist, but not to the point of endless retakes). Sometimes, Tarkovsky might spend two days setting up a difficult shot, and shoot it on the third day. DP on *Stalker*, Alexander Knyazhinsky, explained that once the shot had been set up and rehearsed, it was shot as planned, without deviating from it. (Sometimes, Tarkovsky did inject spontaneity into a shot – such as throwing geese in front of the camera on *Andrei Roublyov* without telling anyone). (On *Stalker*, of course, two days could easily be set aside for camera rehearsals, if the shot ended up being a six minute take that made it into the final cut. An average Hollywood production shoots about 5/8ths of a page of script a day).

The low number of takes also meant editing was usually a lot easier (except on *Mirror*), because there wasn't thousands of feet of takes of each scene to wade through (the *Lord of the Rings* movies [2001-03], for instance, shot over five million feet of 35mm film). Even though the editing of an Andrei Tarkovsky movie often meant simply selecting the order for the scenes, there were still numerous ways the movies could be cut (partly because Tarkovsky's films tended towards poetic, subjective or dream states of mind, which do not act in a linear or logical fashion). There was little waste, too, on a Tarkovsky movie: most of what was shot appeared in the final cut. Tarkovsky rarely shot scenes that didn't make it into the release print. (On *Solaris*, two scenes didn't make it into the finished film: one in a mirrored room (a tiny fragment was left), and a night scene set on Earth).

In *Sculpting In Time*, Andrei Tarkovsky stated that for him editing was 'ultimately no more than the ideal variant of the assembly of the shots, necessarily contained within the material that has been put onto the roll of film' (ST, 116). A lot of movie editors (and directors) would disagree with this. But Tarkovsky reckoned that the editing process was essentially one of finding the intrinsic pattern that already existed in the filmed material (the footage having been shot with the editing style in mind [119]). So that editing was 'simply a question of recognising and following this pattern while joining and cutting' (116). Thus, editing for Tarkovsky didn't mean creating new ideas and themes from the material (as in montage editing), but finding the ones that were already there in the footage.

Many movie editors would say exactly the opposite: that a lot of editing is about discovering ideas, motifs and themes that weren't necessarily in the material as it was conceived or as it was shot. Plenty of editors, for instance, create new scenes or connections between scenes and characters via editing. But Tarkovsky resisted montage editing – at least in theory (in *Mirror*, for instance, there are clearly a series of montages in the dreams, memories and flashbacks which were largely constructed during post-production). So Tarkovsky would resist obvious places where parallel action could occur, as in the twin climaxes of *Nostalghia*, which many another editor would have intertwined them.

Andrei Tarkovsky realized that editing was still an imposition the material, and a coercion of the audience. So the viewer either goes along with the director's manipulation of rhythm and time, or they don't.

Many *auteurs* have carefully controlled the editing of their films (Orson Welles, Charlie Chaplin, Alfred Hitchcock). Andrei Tarkovsky was clearly closely involved in editing each of his movies. His editor on *The Sacrifice*, Michal Leszcylowski, said: 'I knew nothing would go wrong professionally, that I would be working with a genius'.[1] Nevertheless, it was not all Tarkovsky commanding and Leszcylowski obeying: Leszcylowski showed Tarkovsky that he could take out a few seconds from the celebrated climactic single take of the burning house, to cover up a moment where the action was delayed. Henri Colpi was supervising editor. (If Tarkovsky had made *The Sacrifice* in the age of CGI, that shot could have been cleaned up easily – actors could have been erased or replaced, or performed dangerous fire stunts, more smoke or fire could have been added, the sky could have been darkened, or clouds added, practical effects could have been re-timed, and so on. It's just as likely, though, that a movie-maker like Tarkovsky might have insisted on shooting as much of the scene as practically as possible. Besides, the budget of two or three million bucks of *The Sacrifice* wouldn't have run to digital visual effects).

Time and rhythm were vital to movie for Andrei Tarkovsky. As Tarkovsky put it, one could imagine a film without actors, music, settings or even editing, but not without a 'sense of time passing through the shot' (ST, 113). Rhythm wasn't editing, though: it wasn't the length of the shots that determined rhythm, but the 'pressure of time' that ran through the shots (ST, 117). The sense of time for Tarkovsky was a feeling that what you saw on screen was not limited to the visuals alone, but was 'a pointer to something stretching beyond frame and to infinity' (ibid.).

Time and rhythm were one of a director's signatures, Andrei Tarkovsky said – intuitive, a response to a director's 'innate awareness of life' (120). So editing became 'the ultimate embodiment of his philosophy of life'. It was thus easy to identify the editing styles of the great directors – Ingmar Bergman, Kurosawa, Robert Bresson, Michelangelo Antonioni – Tarkovsky reckoned, because their 'perception of time, as expressed in the rhythm of [their] films, is always the same' (121).

A very important person in Andrei Tarkovsky's cinema is editor Lyudmilla Feiginova, who edited all of Tarkovsky's Russian movies (she started out as assistant editor on *Ivan's Childhood*). The editor is often a collaborator overlooked by critics, who are more likely to discuss composers, DPs, producers, production designers, visual effects designers or even stunt co-ordinators, before they get to editors (if they tackle any technical stuff at all; which they rarely do).

But Feiginova is hugely significant in Andrei Tarkovsky's cinema in being a major force in developing Tarkovsky's distinctive editing style. Critics of Tarkovsky's films routinely cite the visuals, but rarely the editing. The rhythm and pace of Tarkovsky's movies, though, is as central as the *mise-en-scène* or the sound. Feiginova, for example, said it was her idea to use the scene with the stutterer as the prologue to *Mirror*. That particular film went through some twenty versions before the final one was chanced upon (Feiginova and Tarkovsky employed a common method of laying out the film – listing the scenes on cards and shuffling them about).

SCULPTING IN TIME

The image becomes authentically cinematic when (among other things) not only does it live within time, but time also lives within it, even within each separate frame.

Andrei Tarkovsky, *Sculpting in Time* (68)

Notable examples of the long take occur in the movies of Alfred Hitchcock, Orson Welles, Kenji Mizoguchi, Bernardo Bertolucci, Carl Theodor Dreyer, Miklós Jancso and Jean Renoir, as well as many *avant garde* filmmakers (Michael Snow's *Wavelength,* for instance, was founded on an endless zoom). The entire shooting style of Andy Warhol and Theo Angelopoulos was built around the long take. The 'sequence shot' is known as the *plan-séquence*: instead of a series of shots, the filmmaker constructs the action so that it can be captured in one take. The long take often employs the mobile frame, via craning, tracking, tilting, panning and zooming, added to complex blocking of actors and props (and, in the celebrated long takes of Hitch and Welles, sliding set walls, repositioned lamps, and large crews manning huge cameras on cranes that lumbered around the studio).

Andrei Konchalovsky remembered Andrei Tarkovsky discussing long takes, saying that a shot that was slightly longer could be boring, but a longer one created a new interest. If a shot was even longer, 'a special intensity of attention' could be generated.1

For Andrei Tarkovsky, the rhythm of a movie came from within a shot, sculpting within the time of the shot, rather than being imposed from outside by editing. Hence Tarkovsky's cinematic technique of long takes, allowing time to fill up the shot. Although the sequence shots were much longer in the later films, Tarkovsky was experimenting with long takes from his first film onwards (in *Ivan's Childhood*, for instance, there are lengthy sequence shots which cover dialogue and action: when Galtsev talks with the doctor in the bunker, for example, the camera tracks back and forth, following the characters, without cutting. And in *Andrei Roublyov* there are many lengthy takes).

Andrei Tarkovsky's extended takes are not always complex tracking shots, like the finale of *The Sacrifice* or the candle-carrying in *Nostalghia*; they often involve one actor talking to camera or another character, while the camera slowly zooms or tracks in.

The number of shots in *Nostalghia* is about the same as in *The Sacrifice*: 115-120, giving an average shot length of about a minute (a very high length). In *The Sacrifice*, it's even higher: an average of one minute twenty-five seconds. Shots of 2, 3, 4 or more minutes are common in Tarkovsky's last three movies. In *Nostalghia*, long takes include Gorchakov's 'dream' in the hotel room, Eugenia berating Gorchakov, and the candle-carrying scene. In *The Sacrifice*, sequence shots include Otto telling Alex to visit Maria (7 mins 12 secs), the house burning, and the opening scene (which's 9 mins and 26 seconds, according to Graham Petrie and Vida Johnson – it's shorter on DVD and video, perhaps due to the way film is transferred – it's irritating the way films are sped up, when they don't have to be). In *Stalker*, the long takes include the telephone room (6m 50s), the Writer's speech in the room of sand dunes, the Stalker's wife's monologue, and the final shot.

But Andrei Tarkovsky's long takes must contain tension. The tension can be suspense, waiting for something to happen. But more usually, the tension must be spiritual. The long take must illustrate, express or be the embodiment of some spiritual state. In the long sequence shot where Gorchakov carries the candle over the pool at Bagno Vignoni in *Nostalghia*, the tension, dramatically, is whether he'll make it without the candle blowing out. But this shot works on other levels; its placement within the structure of the movie makes it a spiritual test and apotheosis. It is Gorchakov's baptism by fire, his Calvary and his martyrdom in *Nostalghia*.

More typical is when Andrei Tarkovsky unbalances the ordinariness of a shot by having something extraordinary happening within it: a door creaks open, a bottle falls off a table. Suddenly, the shot is charged with emotion and expectation. Time must breathe within the shot for Tarkovsky. Hence his use of bizarre occurrences, which kick the shot into suspense, into the unknown. The implication is that anything *might* happen. Tarkovsky displaces normality and lets uncertainty rush in. Strangeness is just around the corner. This unexpectedness, this new, Zen-like wakefulness of living, is best summed up by Lawrence Durrell, who says that the most unexpected things are what is happening in the next room.

Andrei Tarkovsky's cinema actualizes the strangeness of living. The strangeness is here, all around people, but they become immune to it. One of the artist's tasks is therefore to refresh body and soul, so that the incredible beauty and strangeness of life is once again experienced. In poetry the movement is towards the Blakean (and Coleridgean) direct contact with the world stemming from the cleansing of the senses. D.H. Lawrence spoke of the touch of tenderness, the pure touch, which reactivates hidden/ latent/ unconscious feelings. It is this touch, this new relation, that counts, that reactivates livingness. As Lawrence says: '[b]lossoming means the establishing of a pure, *new* relationship with all the cosmos. This is the state of heaven'.[2]

To achieve life breathing through the frame, Tarkovsky movies motion: grass, trees, clothes blowing in the breeze and (so often) running water. The soundtrack emphasizes motion: dripping, creaking, rustling, the noises of nature on the move, a world that never keeps still. Even when Tarkovsky's frame seems to be static, the soundtrack evokes motion. Robert Bresson wrote: '[t]o TRANSLATE the invisible wind by the water it sculpts in passing' (67). This is precisely what Tarkovsky tries to do: to depict the invisible by showing what it touches and moves. The invisible in Tarkovsky's philosophic cinema is the spiritual, the divine, the unknown and unknowable. So he depicts a group of trees and then has the wind rustle the leaves.

Andrei Tarkovsky spoke of editing in terms of rhythm, necessity, sense and unity (ST, 113-121). Each shot must be filled with time, like a glass bottle being filled up (gently but surely) by a stream of water. The aim of editing is unity – to make an organic whole out of all the parts. 'Editing brings together shots which are already filled with time, and organises the unified, living structure inherent in the film', Tarkovsky stated (ST, 114). This recalls Eisensteinian montage again. Each shot has its own 'time-pressure' (ib., 121) and these must be connected carefully.

Editing for Andrei Tarkovsky is a musical process of harmonizing and counter-pointing, of refrains and codas. Editing is highly personal, the stamp of a creative personality. What Tarkovsky dislikes is the imposition of a foreign structure on the material. It should all be one – the planning, shooting, editing and post-production. Tarkovsky edited his films as they were being shot, so that he could rearrange what was still to be shot, and react to material already shot. When he moved to the Western system, he said he had to wait until all of *Nostalghia* was filmed before he could start editing. (Actually, quite a few filmmakers edit as they go along, having their editors start cutting the film as soon as it's been shot).

Gilles Deleuze was critical of Andrei Tarkovsky's insistence on time flowing with a shot, and Tarkovsky's opposition to montage, which he saw as higher up the cinematic hierarchy. Deleuze pointed out that 'montage itself works and lives in time' (1989, 42).

Andrei Tarkovsky's movies are open structures. They could be edited in a number of ways. Tarkovsky proves this himself, when he admits the production team got into a terrible mess over *Mirror*, which was edited into 'some twenty or more variants' (ST, 116). Indeed, *Mirror* could be re-edited *ad infinitum*. Sections could be added, subtracted, re-shuffled. Tarkovsky spoke of working very hard at editing *Zerkalo*: the twenty edited versions were not just subtly different, but were 'major alterations in the actual structure, in the order of the episodes' (ST, 116). When they tried 'one last, desperate rearrangement', the film started to gel. Understandably, it took the director a long time to believe that *Mirror* was working at last. 'For a long time I still couldn't believe the miracle' (ST, 116).

One could re-edit the dreams in *The Sacrifice* or *Nostalghia* again and again. Like Jean-Luc Godard's cinema, Andrei Tarkovsky's cinema can be seen as postmodernist: one could fold all sorts of material into his movies, and, providing it was selected or shot by Tarkovsky, the result would probably be unified (just add the sound of running water).

Having said this, Andrei Tarkovsky's movies are basically narratively linear: they progress (or decay) from one situation to another. Sometimes the order of events can be re-arranged (in *Nostalghia*, for instance), but his films are linear (except for *Mirror*). Works such as *Stalker* and *The Sacrifice* move towards definite endings. Even if the endings are open and ambiguous, they still have many elements of narrative and cinematic closure. (The end of *Nostalghia*, though ambiguous, is a spectacular finale to the film).

Within his narrative structures, Andrei Tarkovsky organizes his sequences meticulously. He thinks in terms of sequences – of dreams, of strange happenings (a family goes outside to watch a neighbour's house burning), of rituals, of memories. This is the standard Tarkovskyan way of making cinema. The set-piece, the elaborate sequence, the best (or most arrogant) of which are done in one shot (Alex's crucifixion by fire in *The Sacrifice* being the most obvious example). Each sequence in Tarkovsky's cinema is joined to the next one (sometimes with linking images or refrains, like the fires in *Mirror*). Sometimes he intercuts a shot from an earlier (dream) sequence into a later sequence, but his basic technique is the long master take expanded to the point of mysticism.

THE SACRALIZATION OF SPACE

Andrei Tarkovsky's sacred cinema has a Renaissance sense of space, in which the individual's subjectivity is paramount. Tarkovsky's cinematic perception recalls Leonardo da Vinci's Vitrivius figure, which embodied the Renaissance view of the individual as the centre of the cosmos. Like most *ciné*-poets, Tarkovsky tries to maintain a continuity of space. But filmic space is not and never was the space of painting. In cinema there is what art historian Erwin Panofsky called a 'dynamization of space' (G. Mast, 154), and what Sergei Eisenstein called 'an impression of spatial dynamics' (ib., 82). In Andrei Tarkovsky's cinema, the tendency is not a dynamicization or temporalization but a *sacralization* of space. That is, the sense of space in Tarkovsky's poetic films tends towards the sacred. The spaces in his movies aim to be landscapes of the soul. The outer world, with its water, glass and run-down appearance, is designed to reflect inner states – of 'soul' and 'truth'. Titus Burckhardt, in his book *Sacred Art in East and West*, said that '"physical space" is always the objectivization of "spiritual space"' (47). In cinema, space has a temporal dimension – '[d]istance is time', said the artist Paul Klee.[1]

SPACE AND ABSTRACTION

In Andrei Tarkovsky's cinema, space has a mystical dimension. As with the Renaissance painter Piero della Francesca, there is a movement in Tarkovsky's cinema towards spatial mysticism and abstraction. Tarkovsky tracks his camera into walls and surfaces. His movies are full of veils, like Bernardo Bertolucci's – layers upon layers of glass, water, wind, shawls, smoke, fog and curtains. As the camera dollies in, it encloses a claustrophobic, ever more abstract space. Tarkovsky's camera drifting into empty, modernist spaces has affinities with the filmic spaces of Jean-Luc Godard, Bertolucci and Michelangelo Antonioni. This abstraction in Tarkovsky's cinema has a mystical dimension. From Kasimir Malevich and Wassily

Kandinsky to Brice Marden and Frank Stella, abstraction has had a mystical edge.

Speaking about his decision to use 3-D – not false-front – sets on *Throne of Blood*, Akira Kurosawa said he wanted to achieve a sense of realism. 'After all, the real life of any film lies just in its being as true as possible to appearances' (D. Richie, 122f), a view that can apply to Andrei Tarkovsky (if possible, Tarkovsky would opt for three dimensional sets. And Steven Spielberg, in the age of CGI, still preferred to build real sets).

Georges Matthieu described the problem like this: '[f]rom the Ideal to the real, from the real to the abstract, from the abstract one moves to the possible'.[1] Whether non-objective or representational, the aim is for what Titus Burckhardt called 'spiritual realism' (150). It is impossible to authentically depict the divine: so religious art is automatically abstract as well as aiming to be spiritually realistic. Realism yes, but not naturalism. Although Andrei Tarkovsky's movies depict the natural world, it is a psychological realism that Tarkovsky was aiming for (his films are definitely not 'naturalistic'). In Edmund Husserl's phenomenological terminology, the 'self-appearance' of the world is a kind of total objectivity, an 'itself there'.[2]

Cinema can never show the world exactly as it is, as 'itself there', as what Jean-Paul Sartre called a 'given'. Cinema always deals in images. Its sense of presence is largely manufactured; it's illusion (everything is a cheat). It is merely coloured shadows on a screen, T.S. Eliot's 'heap of broken images' in Plato's shadowy cave. Andrei Tarkovsky, like Ingmar Bergman, goes for psycho-spiritual truths. Realizing that cinema is a heap of coloured images, which best make sense when mediated through individual experience, Tarkovsky makes psychological cinema. The movement towards syntactic abstraction is countered by a concentration on semantic realism.

Andrei Tarkovsky's cinema (like most cinema) is representational and figurative, but it is non-objective in the sense of being very subjective, and has its moments of abstraction. Tarkovsky's art moves towards sacrality, mystery and interiorization. Cinema as religious contemplation of the sacred.

Andrei Tarkovsky might have profited by looking at Islamic art, with its intricate arabesques which intertwine so beautifully and speak of the unity of Allah. In Islamic non-representational art, mystery is retained and unity is glorified. The equivalent in cinema might be purely formal or abstract film, a field Tarkovsky didn't explore, but he suggested glimpses of it. Imagine *Nostalghia* without Gorchakov or Eugenia or Domenico in it. It would be a series of gentle tracking shots into and along walls, over puddles and streams, and through empty hotel rooms. It would be a new, more abstract Tarkovskyan cinema, more difficult and more boring maybe, but perhaps also more mystical.

FOUR

Symbols and Motifs

> *Of late I have frequently found myself addressing audiences, and I have noticed that whenever I declare that there are no symbols or metaphors in my films, those present express incredulity. They persist in asking again and again, for instance, what rain signifies in my films; why does it figure in film after film; and why the repeated images of wind, fire, water? I really don't know how to deal with such questions.*
>
> Andrei Tarkovsky (*Sculpting in Time*, 212)

ON SYMBOLISM

No other filmmaker uses rain, water, fire or flight in the same, idiosyncratic, hypnotic and profound way as Andrei Tarkovsky. The way these motifs or symbols are used is distinctly Tarkovskyan, setting him apart from other filmmakers. Yet Tarkovsky denies that these elements are 'symbols' – he dislikes symbols, metaphors, parables and fantasies. He acknowledges the power of dreams, the occurrence of miracles, the movement of inanimate objects and the existence of God, but he denies symbols and metaphors. Yet he so deliberately and self-consciously places fire or water in his filmic spaces. Often these 'motifs' appear on cue, timed to make the biggest impact – such as the rain falling at the end of *Stalker*, after the men have stopped fighting. The rain here, at this point in the movie, is the re-affirmation of nature and the natural forces of life. It washes away the delusions of the three seekers, re-aligning their expectations. The rainfall through the smashed roof of the building next to the Room in the Zone makes the water glitter, and it sounds refreshing and calming.

Krzysztof Kieslowski said he didn't film in terms of metaphors, but if viewers wanted to see things in terms of metaphors, that was fine with him. The important thing was to move the audience in some way, to have an effect on them, 'to make people experience something. It doesn't matter if they experience it intellectually or emotionally' (1993, 193). If Kieslowski filmed milk, he said, it was just milk. It didn't symbolize anything more. Very rarely, in cinema, it would mean something more, a miracle. 'Welles achieved that miracle once. Only one director in the world has managed to achieve that miracle in the last few years and that's Tarkovsky. Bergman achieved this miracle a few times. Fellini achieved it a few times' (1993, 195).

Certainly Andrei Tarkovsky's motifs act on the symbolic level, as well as the concrete and the dramatic. The motifs play a part in the dramatic narrative of the movie, but they also work on the symbolic, spiritual, social and ideological levels. Asked if there was any symbolism in *Mirror*, Tarkovsky replied: 'No! The images themselves are like symbols, but unlike accepted symbols they cannot be deciphered. The image is like a clot of life, and even the author may not be able to work out what it means, let alone the audience' (D, 369).

But symbols are not meant to be 'deciphered'. Part of their power is that they go beyond rationalization. Andrei Tarkovsky is digging himself into a hermeneutic hole by claiming there is no symbolism in his movies. There is, masses of it.

Andrei Tarkovsky's intention is to be concrete and realistic, to portray rain as it is because it is part of people's lives, he said in *Sculpting in Time* (212), adding:

> I am therefore puzzled when I am told that people cannot simply enjoy watching nature, when it is lovingly reproduced on the screen, but have to look for some hidden meaning. (ib., 212)

One can simply enjoy seeing rain or fire on the screen. But the rain is *reproduced on the screen*, as Andrei Tarkovsky says: it isn't there of its own accord. It is manufactured firstly, then represented on a screen. Rain is *created* – with hoses, rigs, rain towers, pumps, fire engines. Tarkovsky's rain is as contrived and artificial as the tackiest Hollywood B-movie studio painted backdrop. Tarkovsky's rain has a materiality which is simultaneously sublime and pretentious, both sensual and synthetic, authentic and obsessive.

Probably the director prior to Andrei Tarkovsky who made rain one of his chief motifs was Akira Kurosawa (rain appears in most of his films). Kurosawa's use of rain is clearly the precursor of Tarkovsky's: *Throne of Blood*, *Rashomon* and *The Seven Samurai* come to mind as great rain movies. The *sensei* commented: 'I love all of Tarkovsky's films. I love his personality and all his works. Every cut from his films is a marvelous image in itself'.

Andrei Tarkovsky wanted the spectator to surrender to the cinematic experience, and the experience is of a world created by an *auteur* (ST, 213). Tarkovsky tried to create life itself – as he saw it, that is. It is a personal view, which exalts the unconscious, the intuitive, and is profoundly anti-scientific, anti-political, and anti-rational. Tarkovsky said he grew annoyed by viewers asking what the Zone was in *Stalker*: '[t]he Zone *doesn't symbolize anything, anymore than anything does in my films*: the zone is a zone, it's life' (ST, 200; my italics).

What the Zone definitely was, was a zone. That is, a space divided off from the rest of the world. The Zone was clearly a sacred space in amongst profane space. According to Mircea Eliade, marking out a space in the world is equivalent to creating a sacred space, a mythic centre. Before magicians begin their rituals they sometimes draw a nine-foot magic circle, which becomes a temporary sacred site. The Zone in *Stalker* is clearly of a similar religious nature: it is a goal of the three protagonists for a start, and the Room within the Zone is the end of their quest. Further, the Zone is regarded with religious awe by the Stalker (and Tarkovsky carefully delineates the spaces of the Zone, which are poetically evoked, as well as remaining ultimately ambiguous).

With Andrei Tarkovsky's poetic cinema, one is sure the motifs are there for a purpose, and have a special value, symbolic or concrete or spiritual or otherwise, as may be, for the director. Of *Mirror* Tarkovsky wrote that 'there is no hidden, coded meaning in the film, nothing beyond the desire to tell the truth' (ST, 133). Yet this is the movie with more Tarkovskyan motifs than any other: rain, water, fire, painting, birds, wind and flying.

In *Sculpting in Time*, Andrei Tarkovsky rather lamely tried to explain the contrived ending of *Nostalghia* (213-6), saying that he hoped it was 'free of vulgar symbolism' (216). Well, it is *full* of vulgar symbolism, but it is no less astounding for that. But vulgar or eclectic, the symbolic dimension cannot be denied. Indeed, Tarkovsky displays his lack of knowledge of symbolism, because the really powerful and authentic symbol is the one that is both concrete and spiritual, the one that exists naturally and plastically, while also being highly mystical. Think of the snake, circle, moon, egg or mirror. The mirror motif, one of the most appropriate symbols for cinema itself, is at home in most contexts. Yet the mirror has multiple layers of symbolism (explored so well by movie-makers such as Rainer Werner Fassbinder, or Jean Cocteau in the *Orpheus* films).

Andrei Tarkovsky said he always thought of himself as a poet rather than a filmmaker (ST, 221). The best way to think of Tarkovsky's motifs or emblems is poetically. He uses them as a poet uses images, as pieces of intuitive magic that occur quite logically. A tree, a candle, a lake – these are special effects made special by the gaze of the camera. Really, there is nothing unusual about them. They are distinctly non-urban. Tarkovsky rarely discusses the technological city in his movies. It is inferred from the outside (in *The Sacrifice* and *Mirror*). When the city is filmed, as in *Solaris*, it is as a nightmarish, surreal place, full of strange noises. The establishing shot of Rome, centred on St Peter's Church, in *Nostalghia*, for instance, is accompanied by the whine of a jet.

RAIN

The one emblem that Andrei Tarkovsky probably uses more than any other is rain. Traditionally, rain symbolizes beautitude, purification, fecundity, revelation, divinity, and blessing (J. Cooper, 136). Clearly, rain doesn't 'mean' all these things in Tarkovsky's metaphysical cinema. Yet it is no coincidence that rain presides over much of the childhood *dacha* scenes in *Mirror* (and *Nostalghia*). In *Mirror*, the ruler of the narrator's childhood is his mother. She is deified, shot in a number of glorifying poses and lighting designs which exalt her as a Goddess. In *Mirror*'s opening image, she sits on the fence, presiding over that huge field of buckwheat, and the trees of the Ignatievo forest behind her (lyrically evoked in Andrei's father's poetry). She is an agricultural Goddess, an Earth Mother. So it's only natural that it rains here, for as Aeschlyus says: '[t]he rain, falling from the sky, impregnates the earth, so that she gives birth to plants and grain for man and beast' (in ib., 136).

The first mysterious event in *Mirror*, the house on fire, is framed by the rain dripping from the roof. Later, the mother washes her hair and the room rains; she runs to work through the rain; and at the printing works the water runs out on her in the shower. In this and other movies, rain is a purifying and regenerating element, often associated with childhood, parents and sexuality. In *Solaris*, at the end, rain pours into the father's house, and the self-absorbed patriarch doesn't notice it. In *Stalker*, masculinist/ patriarchal science (the nuclear bomb) is broken up ritually, and thrown into the feminine pool of regeneration; then comes that lengthy rainfall; each protagonist muses on their life and future. In *Andrei Roublyov* and *Ivan's Childhood*, rain seems not to have so much of a symbolic purpose, even though it begins and ends on cue, as it does at the beginning of *Solaris*, when the father steps inside the house to avoid a shower. However, it is raining during Ivan's third dream, on the apple truck (rain heightened the dream's significance). And in *Andrei Roublyov*, rain appears at many key moments: the rain shower with the three monks at the beginning; the flashback Roublyov has; when Boriska finds the right kind of clay; and running down the paintings and the horses in the rain in the epilogue.

WATER

Rain is part of Andrei Tarkovsky's mythology of water. When Tarkovsky's rain slides down the screen it is a personal signature, one of the director's recurring cinematographic devices. Yet the hermeneutics of water in Tarkovsky's cinema is much deeper. Water is the source and grave of all life. J.C. Cooper remarked that '[w]ater is the liquid counterpart of light' (188), which is an interesting point for a filmmaker. Cinema is constructed, materially, from reflected light, and certainly water is very filmic – it looks good. Like D.H. Lawrence in his novels *Sons and Lovers* and *The Rainbow*, Andrei Tarkovsky sets many of his scenes beside water – there are many rivers, for instance. Tarkovsky loves rivers, loves flowing water. Scenes often take place *in* rivers (the boy swimming in *Mirror*, the 'pagan' woman swimming in *Andrei Roublyov*, Gorchakov walking through the stream in *Nostalghia*). Tarkovsky said he preferred rivers and streams to the sea. The ocean was too big (and monotonous) for him.

Contemplating water is often a way back into the past – Kelvin stares at the river in *Solaris*, and the Stalker's dream features a long travelling shot over objects in a flooded building, which are like a tapestry of the lost bits and pieces of history. There are oceans too, in particular the calm sea next to Alex's house in *The Sacrifice*, and the ocean of the unconscious itself in *Solaris*, which spins slowly like a galaxy, and contrasts so vividly with the placid lake of Kelvin's home.

Objects are often sunk under water – the angel and the flooded church in *Nostalghia*, the flooded forest in *Ivan's Childhood*. No doubt, if he had the facilities and budget, Andrei Tarkovsky might have shot a flood in action – sweeping into houses, drenching precious artifacts, the waves rushing down cobbled streets. A flood would have made a useful counterpoint to the burning houses of *Mirror* and *The Sacrifice*.

There are many puddles and pools in Andrei Tarkovsky's cinema – the pool in the Room in *Stalker*, the puddle in front of the *dacha* in *Nostalghia*, and the numerous puddles that surround Alex's house in *The Sacrifice*, as if it is partially an island (which seems to appear from nowhere). The muddy pools that surround the painter and the bell-maker at the end of *Andrei Roublyov*, and the pools the balloonist flies over. In *Stalker*, the Stalker lies down on a tiny island, surrounded by shallow water. The pools look as if there's been a heavy rainfall in between scenes ('there are so many damn puddles, you can't avoid them', the Wrtiter complains to Stalker in the script of *Stalker* [CS, 383]). Rain stops and starts unnaturally in Tarkovsky's movies, and, if it isn't actually raining, it looks as if it has just rained.

These half-soaked landscapes (or half-dry waterscapes) reflect the in-between-worlds nature of the Tarkovskyan protagonist's predicament. These pools obscure reality and also invigorate it. Water runs down roads and – much stranger – down walls. *Mirror* features a whole room of wet walls. The mother (as wife here) has just washed her hair – she stands back and flails her arms mysteriously. Suddenly the room is full of rain and the ceiling starts caving in. Clearly this dream-rain refers to some powers or influences Maria has – powers over her husband, and over her son, who is the implied voyeur (like the viewer) of this bizarre scene (the scene portrays the estranged and erotic relationship between the mother and father). The woman, shaman-like, conjures up this psychic rainfall. In the corner of the room a flame flickers. Fire and water are similarly pointed up in the scene a few minutes earlier, when the neighbour's house burns.

Water on fire – the powerful symbolism is reversed in *Nostalghia*, when Gorchakov carries the candle over the drained pool. This is a patriarchal ending to the movie, in which the two male protagonists both perform rituals of life and death. The woman, Eugenia, has been displaced and decentred. At the end of *Nostalghia*, in her final appearance, she is only an observer of Domenico's suicide, not an active participant (Gorchakov had rejected her sexual advances earlier).

Andei Tarkovsky's most water-drenched movie is *Nostalghia*. Domenico's house is a water-logged building – there's a piece of polythene stretched above his bed, collecting water (wouldn't it make sense for him to move the bed?); it rains continually, even though it's sunny outside; there is the model of the Italian countryside, with a river running through it; Gorchakov wades through a stream to the submerged church; there are the Baths themselves; it rains outside the hotel window; in the Russian dream there is a river and a pool; it snows at the end, and so on.

Nostalghia is one of the wettest of all films. Not just visually, but in the soundtrack too. One doesn't see but one often hears water in Andrei Tarkovsky's movies: sounds recorded in all sorts of contexts: dripping water in a birch forest; running water in a disused warehouse; water running through reeds in a river, and so on. Water noises for every occasion, a vast library of natural sounds.

The Taoist philosophers said 'the sound of water says what I think.' Clearly for Andrei Tarkovsky the sound of water has a meditative, sacral value. Water often has a ritual dimension in Tarkovsky's works – associated with the Christian rites of baptism and purification. Purification by water occurs in *Solaris* and *The Sacrifice,* when hands are ritually washed (in both cases by mother/ Mary Magdalene surrogates). Then there are the wells in *Stalker, Ivan's Childhood* and *Mirror.*

Whereas in many contemporary filmmakers blood features prominently (as bodies are cut or blown up – in the cinemas of Hong Kong and Hollywood), in Andrei Tarkovsky's *œuvre* there is an emphasis on *milk*. The cat in *Mirror* laps at milk; and later on, milk drips on the floor at the doctor's house. A bottle of milk lies on the ground beside the policeman as Domenico's wife bends down to embrace his feet after she is released from her imprisonment in *Nostalghia*. In *Andrei Roublyov,* milk seeps into the stream after the stone masons are blinded (here it might be a stand-in for blood – partly because of censorship, but also because red blood wouldn't show up in dark water in black-and-white). Milk also appears in *Stalker* (in the glass on the table at the end, and the dog licks milk), and in *Solaris.*

Milk is clearly a motif of childhood and innocence (recalling the Orphic formula: *like a kid I have fallen into milk,* and the cauldron of the Celtic Goddess Ceriddwen).[1] Milk also speaks of suckling, mother-child bonding, domesticity and sexuality. In *The Sacrifice,* during the first airstrike, a large bottle of milk, seemingly straight out of *Mirror,* smashes spectacularly, needing no explication as a dramatic moment. The maternal realm is shattered by the Law of the Father, embodied by the over-flying bombers. The spilt milk marks the end of living within the mother-world, the end of calm and nurturance, the end of living within maternal *jouissance.*

FIRE

Like water (but unlike air), fire is very filmic. Like water, it moves, it flows and flickers, it speaks of time flowing within cinema's looking glass. And it is supremely magical, and religious. As Weston La Barre explained, the word for God, *diew* (later *deus*), root of the names Zeus, Jupiter, and Diana, originally meant 'the shining one'. Fire, light, seed, semen, Soma, phallus and gold – all these are part of the same mystery.[1] For ancient Greek philosophers like Heraclitus, all was a flux of fire; with Empodecles the four elements (each of which Andrei Tarkovsky and the teams explores in the movies), were established. Fire, in traditional Western symbolism, represents transformation, purification, renewal, energy, passion, transcendence, and so on. Many Christian mystics (such as Catherine of Genoa, Mechthilde of Magdeburg, Richard of St Victor and Jan van Ruysbroeck) spoke of their ecstatic experiences as like being burned. The fire of love is one of the most common tropes in Christian mysticism. Blood, fire, heart, love and passion are all connected in Christian symbolism.

Andrei Tarkovsky uses fire in an alchemical fashion: he burns it on screen in the hope of alchemically forging another element – preferably the Philosopher's Stone or a magical child, if not some cinematic gold. In *Mirror*, fire – in a field or in a grate – is the image that connects past and present, that binds space and time. The image of a hand warming itself functions like the dog in *Nostalghia*, it jogs the memory and induces the flight from the present into the past. In a number of films Tarkovsky explored how fire eats away at reality, replacing it with a blackened mass. There are the burning houses; the burning book (in *Nostalghia*); Kelvin burns his papers (the bonfire appears later in *Solaris* in the childhood sequence). François Truffaut had heaps of books burning in *Fahrenheit 451* (1966, France), where the message is of ideological violence. But Tarkovsky adds a personal dimension: the book Gorchakov burns is a collection of Tarkovsky's father's poems. Such an image cannot fail to have distinct personal resonance for Tarkovsky. Perhaps here, as he burns a book of Russian poetry, Gorchakov severs his links with the past, and gives up the possibility of returning to his life in Russia as it used to be.

There is an explicit religious dimension to the burning bush in *Mirror* – the narrator and his wife discuss the Biblical source of the burning bush. During this conversation the camera lingers on the narrator's wife: this is significant, because the episode of God talking to Moses through a burning bush (*Exodus*, 3:2) relates to the sacred virginity of the Virgin Mary. The mother in *Mirror* is again likened to the Virgin Mary (as are the mother and Eugenia in *Nostalghia*). Like the burning bush, Mary remained intact (J. Metford, 56). It is another example of the Goddess symbolism in the film.

There is religious continuity here, over five thousand years: Moses sees God in the burning bush, and the camera tracks to the window of a flat in modern Moscow, and outside is a burning bush.

In *Andrei Roublyov*, there is the astonishing imagery of the 'pagan' festival – the naked people flitting through the trees carrying torches. Later, fire will be used in an utterly secular gesture as the Tartars invade Vladimir. But the final use of fire is overtly alchemical: the bell-casting (and later the segue from the bonfire in black-and-white to Roublyov's paintings in colour). In Andrei Tarkovsky's cinema, fire and water are two great principles, both active, both necessary. The hot, dry soul is best, said Heraclitus, but the cold, wet dimension is also needed for life. Thus Tarkovsky often has fire and water in the same shot (in *Nostalghia* there is the Baths and the candle; and the burning book with the sun-dappled water behind it).

Andrei Tarkovsky's last two movies both end with extraordinary fire rituals. Both rituals involve the destruction of a whole world – a human body and a house. Domenico's crucifixion by fire is a tremendously powerful act, a ritual suicide staged for maximum ideological shock. The music goes wrong, the tied-up dog barks, the people stand and stare, mutely – but this adds to the futility of the act. Domenico is consumed by fire, the symbol of Buddha, Zeus, Hermes, Shiva, Kali, Mazda and deities everywhere; yet, tragically, nobody reacts. Everyone is dumb. The police wearily climb the steps – to them it's merely another psychotic, another charred body to clear up, more forms to fill in.

The location is important: it is the Capitoline Hill, the ancient spiritual and political centre of the Eternal City. This is the capital of two dead empires: the Roman Empire and Catholicism. Rome condemned Christ to death. Andrei Tarkovsky chose Rome for its religious associations: the establishing shot of Rome centres on St Peter's Church not, for instance, the Roman Forum, Spanish Steps, the Colosseum, Vittorio Emanuele Monument or the Pantheon. That opening shot says 'Rome', like Big Ben says 'London' or the Eiffel Tower says 'Paris'. But the emphasis on St Peter's Church underlines the religious aspect – of dead religion, loss of spirituality, and martyrdom, all of which are part of Domenico's self-immolation. The flame leaves the body at death, and one sees very clearly the transference of power: Domenico dies, and Gorchakov, at that very moment, lights the candle, which is, on one level, Domenico's soul, but on the highest level, the candle and its carrying ritual represents hope for the future, for the rebirth of life. To light a candle is a tiny act, in the cosmic scheme of things. Yet Tarkovsky gives the gesture a cosmological and spiritual grandeur due to the structure and nature of the film. Suddenly the candle stands for all kinds of rebirth.

SNOW

Snow is part of Andrei Tarkovsky's water symbolism and is also, of course, a part of Russia's landscape. Snow appears in most of the movies, as a naturalistic setting (in *Andrei Roublyov*), or as a psychological background (the dream sequence in *The Sacrifice*), or as an event of sudden beauty (in *Ivan's Childhood*), or as the landscape of childhood (in *Solaris*), or as the final, climactic addition to Gorchakov's Russian/ Italian dream in *Nostalghia*. The snow falling so silently and beautifully here is (partly) a reference to Ingmar Bergman.

In *Solaris* Kelvin and Hari contemplate one of Pieter Brueghel's paintings of peasants at play in the snow (*Hunters in the Snow*, 1565, Kunsthistorisches Museum, Vienna). The camera pans around the many details of the painting, to the stately sounds of Johann Sebastian Bach. This is a long sequence: at the end of it, there is an insert of a boy and a swing in the snow. This is from Kelvin's father's home movie. Later, Kelvin replays this film, in which his mother appears. The viewpoints multiply as in a hall of mirrors (though in a gentle way, utterly different from the famous climax of Orson Welles' *The Lady From Shanghai*).

A similar Brueghel-inspired image (like Brueghel's snowscape) occurs in *Mirror* – anonymous people are dotted about the snowscape with a similar meticulous sense of *mise-en-scène* that informs *Last Year at Marienbad* (Alain Resnais, 1961, France). Tarkovsky condemns setting up scenes taken from paintings, yet here are two examples. It could be that here he is saying no more than 'I remember childhood Winters as if they were from a Brueghel painting.'

WIND AND AIR

With most filmmakers, blowing wind could not be counted as a 'symbol' or 'motif'. Yet a wind machine is usually necessary for an Andrei Tarkovsky production. In *The Sacrifice*, for instance, there is an (imagined?) atomic blast wave that blows away some snow and old doors. There are two gusts of wind at the beginning of *Mirror*, which at first are simply mysterious, simply *there*. But the prologue of *Mirror* features a stutterer being 'cured'; and, after the wind has gone, the mother turns away and the poetry begins. Here the narrative proper begins: and it is the Creative Word through air which has set it in motion: from the stuttering youth, through the title sequence, to the wind in the field to the spoken words of the poetry, the gusts of the creative spirit blow through the movie.

Wind and air is the spirit, the *pneuma*, the breath of life, associated with procreation (in Aristotle), orgasm and the soul. Wind or breath is part of the same holy male mystery of fire. One recalls that in *Mirror* fire suggests the father or the narrator (the son of the present) remembering, and that rain and water relates to the mother (or feminine principle). This fits; the pieces of *Mirror*'s jigsaw start to lock together, because wind and air fans and feeds fire. Indeed, the five-year-old boy thinks immediately of his father when he hears the rustling bushes outside his bedroom. Editor Lyudmilla Feiginova comes back to this shot a few times: by day or night, sometimes in slow motion, sometimes in black-and-white, one sees the trees and bushes next to the house blowing in the breeze. This is an image of otherness – the primal otherness of the natural world. But it also evokes the father, and what he brings with him – the otherness of the outside world, in a realm of exile, marginalized. He exists in the outer spaces, like Cathy's ghosts in *Wuthering Heights*.

If the air is not full of drifting snow or driving rain in an Andrei Tarkovsky film, it might be full of seeds which float dreamily by (in *Andrei Roublyov*). These images of snow or seeds falling or hair blowing or reeds streaming out under water, give a sense of weightlessness, a lightness of touch rarely matched in cinema. Again, time flows by, life flows by, everything is in motion, everything is changing.

FLIGHT

Flying is transcendence, release, escape, transformation. In film it might be simulated by a helicopter, a crane, a dolly, a blue screen, visual effects or a Steadicam shot (as in Stanley Kubrick's *The Shining* [1980, U.S.A.] or *Birdy* [Alan Parker, 1984, U.S.A.] for example). Géza Róheim put it thus: the 'flying dream is an erection dream... the flying dream is the nucleus of shamanism' (154). The archaic shaman 'flies' to other worlds, s/he climbs up the World Tree, and so on. Film is a waking dream, in some ways, which rewrites reality. The image of flight, central to shamanism (and shamanism is the origin of all religion) seems well suited to religious cinema, and to cinema in general. The dream of flying is one of the oldest dreams, and cinema is well-equipped to portray it. Certainly since early cinema (Georges Méliès' *Le Voyage dans la lune* [1902, France] for example), flight has always been a prime cinematic image.

In Andrei Tarkovsky's poetic cinema, flight is largely sexual. People float above their beds, dreamily spinning in post-orgasmic trances. In *Solaris* there is a gratuitous weightlessness sequence. Equally gratuitous, though far more spectacular, is the opening of *Andrei Roublyov*, with the flying machine which looks like something out of Leonardo da Vinci's sketches of fabulous technology (Leonardo is supposed to have 'invented' the helicopter). Flight is part of Tarkovsky's belief in the miraculous. It is something that simply occurs. It is rather like the Grail: if one doesn't believe in it, one doesn't see it. The emphasis on flight, which is scientifically 'impossible' in the way Tarkovsky imagines it, recalls Tertullian the Christian theologian again: one believes *because it is absurd.*

Although Andrei Tarkovsky is known for using motifs like birds, and flight, and levitation, and the natural elements, like water and earth, the sky is contemplated far less than expected in his cinema. In Steven Spielberg's films, characters are often looking up at the sky, spaceships zoom out of the clouds, or the camera lingers on starscapes, or giant moons, but Andrei Tarkovsky concentrates on the earth, on pools or rivers, on churches and *dachas.* Tarkovsky's cinema rooted in the soil and water.

BIRDS

The bird is a shamanistic animal *par excellence,* associated with transcendence, soul and flight to other worlds. Birds flutter out of the Madonna's womb in *Nostalghia*; after this sequence, a feather flutters down beside Gorchakov. An angel walks in front of the *dacha.* Gorchakov has, like the Stalker, a feather-like streak of white in his hair. He is a 'marked man', one of the 'touched' – half-angelic. Later, before Gorchakov gives his long monologue, there's an angel under water. There is a bird in his Russian wife's bedroom.

The ancestors of the angel in Western religion is again the shaman, who danced like birds and donned costumes of feathers (the American Indian feathered headdress is a late example of the bird-shaman's regalia). Birds and women are again connected in *Mirror*: the mother kills the cockerel; a bird breaks the pane of glass in the *dacha*; a bird flaps beside the floating woman. Most oddly of all, a bird lands on Asafyev's head, a miraculous shot. A bird represents the soul very clearly in the narrator's grandiose setting free of the tiny bird (a sparrow) that he's been holding on his death bed. *Andrei Roublyov* contains geese, birds flying in front of the aerial camera in the Tartar raid, and when Boriska looks up at the tree when he's searching for the place to cast the bell.

HORSES AND DOGS

There are horses in most of Andrei Tarkovsky's movies. For him, as for most artists, they are noble and magnificent animals. Tarkovsky makes references to artists' depictions of horses: Michelangelo Buonarroti's equestrian statue in Rome (in *Nostalghia*); and Leonardo da Vinci's horses in the *Adoration of the Magi* and other works (in *The Sacrifice*). In *Andrei Roublyov*, the battle scenes recall Leonardo's wildly mobile orchestrations of people and horses. But horses are also pure strangeness, as in D.H. Lawrence's *St Mawr*, as well as being the prime totem animal of so many Hollywood Westerns and historical epics. A horse walks into the Cathedral after the battle in *Andrei Roublyov*, and the effect is bizarre: a horse inside a church. Yet Roublyov hardly turns his head to look (he's in shock after the raid). *Andrei Roublyov* closes with a vision of horses in the rain: it is an image of nature in harmony, with its fecund water, like the end of *Stalker*. A horse strays from the rain-soaked ending of *Andrei Roublyov* into the beginning of Tarkovsky's next film, *Solaris*. It walks about, strange and independent, like an alien presence, a premonition of the otherness Kelvin will experience later on in deep space. The same Russian horse appears in the credit sequence of *Nostalghia*. Like the *dacha* and the dog, the horse seems to be an icon of Russia for Tarkovsky. The DP films the horse as D.H. Lawrence wrote about it: as an animal of power and *mystique* which people cannot resist or analyze.

The Tarkovskyan dog appears in every Tarkovsky movie, apart from the 1962 feature (Tarkovsky had dogs as pets). Dogs are most prominent in *Nostalghia*: both Gorchakov and Domenico have dogs (it may be the same animal). Gorchakov's Russian dog, seen in his memories or dreams of Russia, appears in the Italian hotel, padding into the bedroom as if it's the most ordinary thing in the world. The dogs in *Nostalghia* appear at key moments: in Gorchakov's central dream in the hotel, in the final scene, and at Domenico's death in Rome. It is the dog, not the people watching, that cries out when Domenico burns himself to death. The dog is ironically the most 'human' voice present. Dogs appear in the home movies and dreams in *Solaris*. The barking of dogs is one of Tarkovsky's favourite off-screen sounds. Critics have also likened the dogs in Tarkovsky's films to Anubis, the ancient Egyptian god, and the dog in *Don Juan* by Carlos Casteneda. Cats also appear in Tarkovsky's cinema – notably in *Mirror*, before the burning house scene, when the two children play with a cat, pouring salt onto its head.

THE LOOKING GLASS

No object seems more suited to cinema than the mirror (as image, theme, motif, philosophy, etc). Andrei Tarkovsky is by no means the only filmmaker to be obsessed by mirrors: consider Jean Cocteau's *Orpheus* movies, where characters step backwards into mirrors on their way to the Underworld, or the moment in *2,001: A Space Odyssey,* where astronaut Bowman contemplates himself in horror after travelling through the Stargate. The mirror is the perfect object for embodying modernism, whether it is used in Egon Schiele's stylized self-portraits, André Gide's self-reflexive *mise-en-âbyme* fiction, or the films of Ingmar Bergman, Rainer Maria Fassbinder, Orson Welles, and the Marx Brothers. In *Mirror* the mirror functions as an interface between past and present – this is made clear when, after the raining room sequence, the mother looks at herself in the mirror, then she's seen as an old woman: she wipes the mirror. The movie subsequently travels, as the first poem says, 'beyond the mirror'.

Cameras can look into mirrors and one can't tell which is the reflection and which is the 'reality'. Cameras love mirrors, and make love with mirrors. Virtual, cyborg, real, dream, imaginary or contrived reality – all these blur in cinema. Only when the camera pulls back from a mirror can one see which side is which. Hundreds of movie-makers have exploited this kind of manipulation. The mirror is the perfect device for Jean-Luc Godard's postmodern explorations, where scenes are acted into mirrors (as in *Vivre Sa Vie*, 1962, France).

In *Nostalghia*, Gorchakov stares into a mirror on a wardrobe in the street and finds his *doppelgänger*, Domenico, staring back at him (it was a scene that came from the days of *Mirror*). This is a common motif of identification. At the end of the movie, as the camera slowly zooms out from the house and Gorchakov, the first indication the audience has that he is not back in Russia is from the reflection of the arches of the Cathedral in the pool in front of him. This sense of unease is exacerbated even further: the camera is set up so that where the reflection of the Russian house should be, in the pool, one sees the Cathedral: this reflection accentuates the unreality of Gorchakov's state of mind, and the ambiguity of his nostalgic achievement. Cinema is automatically nostalgic, Tarkovsky reckoned, due to its ability to replay the same scenes again and again (ST, 140).

In *Solaris*, the mirrors are of a different order: there are the circular windows that look out onto the vortex of the Ocean; and the video screens which reflect back a different kind of image. In *The Sacrifice*, Alex is filmed in mirrors, and the *Adoration of the Magi* reproduction in Little Man's room is shot under glass so it acts as a mirror. Meanwhile, the floor of the main room downstairs is so highly polished it acts as a mirror. Often in Andrei Tarkovsky's movies, characters stare at themselves in mirrors, in fascination, sometimes in vanity (adjusting their appearance), but also in fear, as if they're seeing something truly other. In *Hoffmanniana*, the mirror is the familiar seeing device of fairy tales: Hoffmann sees himself creeping down a corridor carrying a candle (CS, 348).

Stuart Hancock noted that:

> Mirrors abound in [Tarkovsky's] films, and often his characters speak to one another's mirror image rather than to each other. In carefully staged scenes, characters stare off in different directions, aiming their words into thin air, even though those words work into each other's hearts like daggers. (1996)

In movie after movie, Andrei Tarkovsky's camera dwells on reflections in water, and often water and glass together. There are glass jars and bottles scattered on the floor of Domenico's house; and a large jar or bottle features in the childhood sequences of *Mirror*. In *The Sacrifice* glasses tremble and the jar of milk smashes. In *Solaris* the chandelier rattles. At the end of *Stalker* the glasses which at the beginning trembled as the train trundled by, skid along a table. Fish swim in a glass bowl, itself afloat, in the Stalker's dream.

Glass objects – in the form of bottles, cups, mirrors, vases, or jugs – are part of Andrei Tarkovsky's large props bag of still-life artefacts, which he sets up on table tops, or chairs, or window sills: eggs, books, plants, candles, lamps, drapes, lace and bed sheets.

Glass is often associated with death (in European fairy tales and Celtic mythology), the double or twin, as well as Buddhist transparency, self-awareness, celestial power, purity, perfection, the light of God and the self-luminous. Water and glass possess magic for Andrei Tarkovsky. He makes glass appear like some strange element, some new addition to the Periodic Table of science. The glass containers in his films look like the precious phials, crucibles and vessels of some mediæval alchemist or magus – snatched from the laboratories of alchemists Paracelsus or Cornelius Agrippa, say. The mirrors and glasses are filters, veils, barriers, walls enclosing secret worlds beyond reach. One can't quite cross the threshold of the mirror in Tarkovsky's cinema, as one can in Jean Cocteau's *Orpheus* movies.

FIVE

The Worlds of Andrei Tarkovsky

TARKOVSKY'S WORLDS

Andrei Tarkovsky's worlds are unlike those of any other filmmaker. As soon as one starts watching an Andrei Tarkovsky movie one enters his worlds, and they are quite different from the worlds of, say, Shuji Terayama, Howard Hawks or Alexander Kluge. Stanley Kubrick might be associated with some bland five-star hotel foyer (out of *The Shining*) or the even blander space stations in *2001: A Space Odyssey*; Jean-Luc Godard's world is the cafés and boulevards of the Left Bank; Rainer Werner Fassbinder cruises Berlin's cosmopolitan streets; and Pier Paolo Pasolini inhabits a Southern Italian scrubland. And the world of Steven Spielberg would be the suburbs in middle America (as in *E.T.*, 1982, U.S.A. or *Close Encounters of the Third Kind*, 1978, U.S.A. or *Sugarland Express*, 1974, U.S.A.). Tarkovsky's worlds are trash-strewn landscapes quite at home as the background to a painting by Pieter Brueghel the Elder or Leonardo da Vinci. Tarkovsky's world is more like that of Luis Buñuel, or Pier Palo Pasolini in his Middle Ages trilogy, or Werner Herzog in his *The Enigma of Kasper Hauser* (1974, West Germany). Pasolini's and Herzog's scruffy, ramshackle, earthy mediæval worlds have parallels with Tarkovsky's timeless worlds. 'My heart is very close to the late Middle Ages', said Herzog.[1] Tarkovsky's heart is happy in the late Middle Ages and Early Renaissance. He is not, like Max Ophüls or Stanley Kubrick, a Baroque artist – nor is he a Neo-Classicist, like Alain Resnais or Peter Greenaway. Tarkovsky always includes a lot of grit and sweat in his filmic worlds: they always look believable, in the sense that people are seen to be standing in mud or snow or water (rather than on a smooth studio floor), they are often dirty, shabby, weary, right in the thick of things. Sam Goldwyn had famously responded to a reviewer who complained that the slums in his films looked too nice, without any real dirt: 'they should do, they cost us so much!'

MISE-EN-SCÈNE

For Andrei Tarkovsky, *mise-en-scène* must be realistic, concrete, plastic, actual. Rain must look like real rain, not the spray from a fire engine and rig that's been hired for the day's shoot. *Mise-en-scène* must be true to life, he says. 'By its very nature cinema must expose reality, not cloud it' (ST, 72). But the 'truth' is subjective, psychological, and comes from the actors and the essence of a scene (ST, 74). Part of Tarkovsky yearns for a *mise-en-scène* that is transcendent and universal, dealing in essences – rather like the sculptures of Constantin Brancusi. But the other part of him aims for a *mise-en-scène* that is lodged in the real, messy, unpredictable world, and is restrained, not didactic. One of the central tensions in Tarkovsky's poetic cinema is precisely this: between the symbolic, Neo-platonic, religious, iconographic yearning, and the realist, plastic, immanent necessity. For Tarkovsky, *mise-en-scène* should not simply illustrate some meaning in a scene, should not be schematic, clichéd (that would be too simplistic), but should 'startle us with the authenticity of the actions and the beauty and depths of the artistic images' (ST, 25).

Poetic cinema ought to be emotional, intuitive, intense, Andrei Tarkovsky asserted. In Tarkovsky's poetic cinema, two worlds are in conflict: the inner and the outer, the individual and the social, the spiritual and the materialistic, the past and the present, the dream and the 'reality', the human and the natural. The struggle continues up to the end (and beyond the finale) of the movies; in some, the personal and psychological aspect wins out (as in *Nostalghia*); in others, characters accept that they have to enter the social, material realm of the present again (*Andrei Roublyov*).

The production designers for the seven features directed by Andrei Tarkovsky included: Rashit Safiullin, Anna Asp, A. Merkulov, Mikhail Romadin, Nikolai Dvigubsky, Yevgeni Chernyayev, Ippolit Novoderyozhkin, Sergei Voronkov, Andrea Crisanti and Shavkat Abdusalamov.

THE HOUSE

The primary Tarkovskyan environment is the house of childhood, the Russian *dacha*, which appears in most of Tarkovsky's movies, but most fully realized in *Mirror*. This house is explored endlessly by the roving camera, which tracks around the rooms and picks out *that* particular table from memory and *this* magical window with its view over the buckwheat field and *those* bushes outside and the forest beyond.

In *Nostalghia* the *dacha* is longed for: it is the symbol for Gorchakov of Russia, of the homeland and the heartland. He yearns for it so much he transplants it into the Italian Cathedral where he ends up. *Nostalghia*, after all, takes as its plot the displacement of exiles and travellers from their heartlands. And in *Mirror*, significantly, the first newsreel images shown are of the Spanish civil war refugees, who are similarly displaced. Like the house in *Mirror*, it is shot in *Nostalghia* from the front, showing the porch and the people moving around outside it. Behind it are the trees of the Russian forest. In *Solaris* the house plays a similar role, the house of the father: Kelvin returns just as much to the house, with its lake and surrounding fields, as to the father and the family. The childhood home is a place of magic and ritual, where objects have a life of their own, where the Summers are resplendent, where children play endlessly (and often in slow motion) in the fields and trees.

In *The Sacrifice* the whole house is burnt to the ground: this is an act of œdipal violence, a Promethean rebellion against society, culture and the ghosts of patriarchy, to transcend the law of the father – as well as being a last, desperate attempt at transcendence (to kill the ego, to transcend the self, in the language of psychoanalysis). In *Nostalghia*, the wooden house is placed miraculously (but at great cost) inside the Cathedral (partially placating the personal and œdipal ghosts). But in *The Sacrifice,* the homeland is decimated in a calculated way (though using a magical agent, fire). Both movies indicate that the homeland (or the relation to the ancestors, earlier generations, the family forebears) is dead. And if it's not quite dead, then it should be burnt to cinders. Why? Because every past illusion and delusion and hope once clung onto must be shattered. In each movie Tarkovsky's protagonists realize that the idea of the homeland is an illusion, a false hope, a desire that can never be repaid (most of his protagonists are wanderers).

Houses that are returning to the nature are another recurring motif, dwellings that once contained families and childhoods which are now crumbling into ruin, overgrown. The opposite of the Russian house is the degenerate, dilapidated apartment or warehouse. Alexander and the Stalker live in places that look like disused warehouses. They are not workers' cottages or houses, but post-industrial wastelands. These settings are places which are not functioning as they used to any more, and the people who dwell in them cling on to existence by their fingernails. The inhabitants of the Tarkovskyan wastelands always seem to be on the edge, holding on for dear life.

THE BED

Strange to think of the bed as a major setting in Andrei Tarkovsky's cinema – he is not a maker of porn, for example. The bed is a major site of familial emotions in Tarkovsky's cinema: the relations of blood and incest are at their strongest here. Whole families sleep in beds (*Stalker*), young boys witness the primal scene in beds (*Mirror*), and couples float in sexual reveries (*The Sacrifice* and *Mirror*). The bed is also the platform for dreams, and thus for someone like Tarkovsky who loves dreams, who notes down dreams copiously (in the *Diaries*), and who films dreams, the bed is bound to assume great importance. Beds appear as part of the childhood wonderland in Federico Fellini's cinema (in *Amarcord*, 1974, Italy), and, satirically, in *City of Women* (1980, Italy; in this movie a row of men in a huge bed masturbate in front of giant images of screen goddesses).

Ingmar Bergman wrote that '[n]o other art medium – neither painting nor poetry – can communicate the specific quality of the dream as well as film can' (1986, 44). Generally, Andrei Tarkovsky sticks to straightforward dream or memory sequences: it is assumed that Gorchakov's dreams in *Nostalghia*, for instance, are what he is really dreaming about (the dreams are not simply Gorchakov's memories, though: the viewer isn't asked to assume that the *dacha*, the trees, the pool, the dog and the groups of women in Gorchakov's dreams are what his life in Russia is *really* like). Tarkovsky always investigates the past, how memories of happier times haunt the protagonist (like Ivan's dreams of his mother). He does not use flashforwards, for instance, of what the future might be like for the characters (in *Nostalghia*, though, Gorchakov has a vision of Eugenia and his wife, the embodiments (the spirits, the *anima*) of Italy and Russia, embracing). And Tarkovsky does not (usually) insert flash cuts to confuse the audience: his memory and dream sequences are usually clearly signposted as such (in *The Sacrifice* and *Nostalghia*, though, the segues between 'reality' and dreams are more ambiguous). In *Mirror*, it is more complex, because some of the dreams or memory sequences are not wholly from the narrator's (Alexei's) point-of-view. The flashback to Maria's ominous experience in the printing works, for instance, is not something the narrator had direct access to.

What Andrei Tarkovsky doesn't do is follow Hollywood's penchant for narrative strategies such as: 'oh, it was all only a dream', or the virtual and alternate realities of movies such as *The Matrix* (1999) or *Twelve Monkeys* (1995). Tarkovsky's movies don't withhold vital information until the end of the piece: like the revelation that Bruce Willis is a ghost in *The Sixth Sense*

(1999), or the ghosts-within-ghosts in *The Others* (2001), or that the 19th century community in *The Village* (2004) really exists in the present.

To suggest a move into a dream world, Andrei Tarkovsky & co. employ pretty much all of the classic cinematic devices: mysterious music, heightened sound effects, losing local sound, electronically treated sounds, black-and-white, altered film stock, unusual or subjective camera movements, discontinuities of space and time, doubling of characters within the same space, impossible or unrealistic combinations of props, sets or actors, and so on.

FOREST OF TREES, FOREST OF SYMBOLS

The forest in symbolism and mythology is the realm of testing and initiation, the feminine zone of the natural world, secrets, death and transformation. In Andrei Tarkovsky's magical cinema it is the realm of dreams, of childhood and fairy tales, of the Baudelairean 'forest of symbols'. The 'dark forest' is a key environment of fairy tales, as it is of horror and Gothic movies. It is the place of initiation and trial. It lies on the edge of the familiar, everyday world of the fairy tale. It is where the protagonist gets lost, meets strange creatures, undergoes transformations and spells. It is, typically, one of the first places the protagonist enters on the journey outwards from the home, in *Snow White, Little Red Riding Hood* or *Hansel and Gretel* for example, and, earlier, it is the opening scenario of Dante Alighieri's *Divine Comedy*:

> In the middle of life's path
> I found myself in a dark forest
> where the straight way was lost... (*Inferno*, I: 1-3)

In *Ivan's Childhood* there is the flooded forest; in *Andrei Roublyov* there is a birch grove which also featured in *Ivan's Childhood* (M. Turoskaya, 33). In *Mirror* and *Solaris* the camera lingers on trees, their forms and textures; in *The Sacrifice* the camera tracks around trees, and there is of course the 'Japanese' bo tree which is climbed by the camera on a crane, shaman-like, at the end of the movie. This latter tree is clearly a cosmic 'Moon-Tree' or 'World Tree' of mythology and shamanism, linking two worlds, heaven and earth, the sacred and profane realms. It is the *axis mundi,* standing at the world centre. The boy sits under the Tree of Enlightenment just like the Buddha. The camera climbs up the tree like the shaman who attains magical powers and flies to other worlds. In Qabbalism the top of the Tree of Life is *Kether*, the Crown, the One, the Tenth *Sephiroth*. In *kundalini* yoga serpent-power climbs up the *chakras* of the body to the top, the brain, the pineal gland, the third eye, the crown chakra. Tarkovsky's Tree of Life is also Christian (Russian Orthodox): it is both the Cross, and the Tree from which Adam and Eve picked the forbidden fruit: it is the symbol prime of the Fall and Redemption (the Cross is also linked in symbolism to the maternal realm – the man dies on the body of the mother). Salvation and redemption and the re-instatement of primal unity are Alexander's aims in *The Sacrifice*.

One origin of Andrei Tarkovsky's cinematic trees is probably those of his childhood home in the Ignatievo forest, the subject of his father's Arseny's poem:

> Embers of last leaves, a dense self-immolation,
> Ascend into the sky, and in your path
> The entire forest lives in just such irritation
> As you and I have lived for this year past.
>
> The road is mirrored in your tearful eyes
> Like bushes in a flooded field at dusk,
> You mustn't fuss and threaten, leave it be,
> Don't jar the stillness of the Volga woodland. (ST, 161)

CHURCHES

The abandoned church in *Ivan's Childhood*, the Cathedral in *Andrei Roublyov*, the ruined Cathedral in *Nostalghia*; these are settings which require no explication. The Cathedral in *Andrei Roublyov* is a major setting in that movie. It's seen with the white walls, before it's been painted; after the battle the icons and paintings are glimpsed behind the war-weary characters; the people take refuge in the Cathedral – the Tartars ride into it, the most powerful image of the secular realm invading the sacred in all of Andrei Tarkovsky's cinema. In *Nostalghia*, the ruined church is clearly a symbol of the dying (or dead) religion of Christianity (and the bankruptcy of all religions in the thoroughly secular world Gorchakov inhabits). But, as Gorchakov walks through it, a dialogue between God, no less, and St Catherine (or their earthly representatives), is overheard. This (incredible) dialogue, ironic though it is, shows that belief and faith is still valued in Tarkovsky's cinema. The churches, the external manifestations of

Christian faith, may be falling apart, but the inner spiritual search continues (think of the Stalker). Indeed, it is so powerful, it eats away at people, killing their bodies as well as their souls (as happens to Domenico in *Nostalghia*).

In 1978, Andrei Tarkovsky wrote that it was necessary 'to love. And to believe. Faith is knowledge with the help of love' (D, 168). If churches don't appear in *Stalker, The Sacrifice* and *Mirror*, images from churches – icons and paintings – do, emphasizing that for Tarkovsky the æsthetic dimensions of religion have a value beyond their poetic beauty. The emphasis on religion and spirituality throughout Tarkovsky's cinema suggests that though his cinema has a modernist, New Wave outer shell, inside it is very traditional and pre-modern. Tarkovsky argued for spirituality not materiality, for inner freedoms rather than external freedoms, addressing moral, not material problems.

COSTUMES

Nelli Fomina, Maya Abar-Baranovskaya, Lidiya Novi, Lina Nerli Taviani and Inger Pehrsson were the costume designers for the movies that Andrei Tarkovsky directed. An old overcoat is the basic requirement for the male Andrei Tarkovskyan anti-hero, preferably grey or black, knee-length, and very shabby. An old woolly sweater, again dark (blue or black), is also required. In this outfit the Tarkovskyan protagonist could wander around Franz Kafka's Prague, Bohemian Paris, *fin-de-siècle* Vienna or Stalinist or Dostoievskyan Moscow without bothering anybody, and without being bothered. The costume is classless, ageless, characterless. It is Existential Outsider gear, but not restricted to any particular time or place. The costume could've wandered out of any classic novel from the past 150 years; it's a familiar outfit from the fiction of Knut Hamsun, André Gide, Jean-Paul Sartre, Albert Camus, Fyodor Dostoievsky or Charles Dickens. It is not flamboyant, doesn't draw attention to itself, and wants to blend in with the background. It's the costume of Northern Europe and Russia, a cold climate, where it's always Autumn or Winter, where there's barely enough wood to light the stove.

For women, the costume designers Nelli Fomina, Maya Abar-Baranovskaya, Lidiya Novi, Lina Nerli Taviani and Inger Pehrsson favour white cotton dresses and dark shawls, for the Russian/ homeland sequences (as in *Mirror* and *Nostalghia*). This costume seems based on his mother, women of the olde worlde, relating to the mythologies of Mother

Russia. Again, it is timeless, a look that could be at home in the Middle Ages as well as the 20th century. The other sort of costume for women occurs in *Nostalghia* and *The Sacrifice*, the so-called 'modern woman', in long, floaty dresses, veils, shawls and scarves. The look ties in with the long, eroticized hair Tarkovsky favoured, and the Virgin Mary faces (women like Russian ikons). Eugenia, in particular, is very fashion-conscious – the effect is like Italian *Vogue* meets British *Home and Garden*. Again, dark, Autumnal colours prevail, and, as with the mother in *The Sacrifice*, the assertion is of independence. (*Nostalghia* was partly filmed in Milan, so the link to the fashion world is fitting. Costumes on *Nostalghia* were designed by Lina Nerli Taviani and Annamode 68).

The costume designers – Nelli Fomina, Maya Abar-Baranovskaya, Lidiya Novi, Lina Nerli Taviani and Inger Pehrsson – dress women as if they have wandered out of some imaginary Pre-Raphaelite painting entitled *'Redemption'*. Hair is worn long in most of Tarkovsky's female characters. Long hair is an object of fetishism, as in *Mirror* or *Andrei Roublyov* (the fool). When it is worn loose it is a display of sexuality: the witch in *The Sacrifice* has very long hair, which she lets down and twines about Alexander on her bed – a stereotypical representation of the woman as sexual spider or serpent, weaving webs of lust around the victim. She is like an Edvard Munch *Madonna* or one of Gustave Moreau's *femme fatales*. The daughter too, who slips about naked, has long hair, while Adelaide is austere, repressed, piling her hair up.

Costumes tend towards muted, dark colouration and soft fabrics. No pastels or primaries for Andrei Tarkovsky. Nothing like the bright reds, pinks, purples, greens, yellows and blues in Sergei Paradjanov's movies, for instance, or the saturated hues of contemporary Hollywood cinema.

Make-up and hair artists included: Vitali Lvov, Vera Rudina, Lyudmila Baskakova, Iole Cecchini, Giulio Mastrantonio, Kjell Gustavsson and Florence Fouquier D'Herouel (there were others – finding who worked in the hair and make-up depts of even recent productions can be difficult).

LANGUAGE

Pictures, visual images, are far better able to achieve that end [to pose questions and demonstrate problems that go to the very heart of our lives] than any words, particularly now, when the word has lost all mystery and magic and speech has become mere chatter, empty of meaning, as Alexander observes.

Andrei Tarkovsky, *Sculpting in Time* (228-9)

Language may not be a motif or a symbol, but it is certainly one of Andrei Tarkovsky's prime considerations. The Word is set against the Image. It can easily be seen from Tarkovsky's movies, which feature little dialogue but extraordinary imagery, the means of expression Tarkovsky prefers. The ability to speak is creative, one of the primary marks of being human – linking back to the Creative Word of God (and the artist). Tarkovsky uses verbal expression – the revelation of it – to begin *Mirror*. In many films there are mute people (in *Solaris, Andrei Roublyov, Stalker* and *The Sacrifice*); there are stutterers; there are the 'holy fools', who speak the unspeakable; there are the many extracts of poetry, spoken in voiceover or by the characters; in *Nostalghia* there is a discussion on translation (poetry is what is lost in translation, said Robert Frost). Here, Tarkovsky investigates how much cultural exchange there can be between two nations, and how deep it can be. Aleksandr Pushkin and Leo Tolstoy are set against Dante Alighieri and Francesco Petrarch (the poetic deities of Russia vs. those of Italy). If poetry or soul cannot be translated, then Gorchakov must have left his soul in Russia.

But surely much of religion (if not soul or spirit) is translatable? Otherwise, what about the *Bible*, which has been translated from Hebrew and Greek into Latin and English and countless other languages? After all, Christianity is not 'native' to Russia, yet Andrei Tarkovsky (apparently) believes in the Judæo-Christian God, a deity from 2,000, 3,000 or 4,000 years ago, created in another culture, another place, another time. The problem of language and translations is vast and very complex. Tarkovsky's way was to cut through it by making pictures, not words. The ambiguity is still there, but it's easier for Tarkovsky to deal with. 'Build your film on white, on silence and on stillness', wrote Robert Bresson (126).

In *The Sacrifice* language is in the foreground. 'Words, words, words' moans Alexander (quoting William Shakespeare and speaking in English in the movie). The lines are from *Hamlet*: Polonius asks '[w]hat do you read my lord?' and Hamlet answers '[w]ords, words, words' (II. ii. 195).

Alexander is surrounded by rustling grass, the sound is like the susurrus of words. His son, temporarily deprived of verbal agency, speaks of the Word at the end of the film. When the boy asks 'why?', the movie's answer is clear: the camera cranes up the tree, away from the boy, away from the human, chattering realm, into the dazzling whiteness of the sun, sea and tree. If one wants to discover the wonder, Andrei Tarkovsky says, simply contemplate this natural glory. (The irony consists in attempting to convey the transcendent or supra-lingual experience via cultural means. Like poets of all ages, Tarkovsky can only use language to point to something beyond language, that mystical realm Ludwig Wittgenstein evoked. Hélène Cixous remarked that 'everything is language'.[1])

The opening of *Mirror*, with its sequence of the birth (or rebirth) of language (or access to language), can be seen in the terms of Lacanian psychoanalysis. In their study of Jacques Lacan in *Film Theory*, Rob Lapsley and Michael Westlake wrote:

> The entry into language and the discovery of lack in the Other therefore precipitates the child into the constitutionally unsatisfiable state of desire. In a further sense, too, the entry into language is the birth of desire. (70)

In a sense, all of *Mirror*, and much of Andrei Tarkovsky's cinema and cinema in general, concerns Lacanian *manque à etre*, the lack, the desire. The narrator in *Mirror* goes back to the Lacanian 'mirror phase', in which his mother is the Other, as well as the mirror in which his self-idealization is reflected. So much of cinema replays the œdipal crisis of the entry into the symbolic order of Lacan, with its emotions of lack and desire. As Toril Moi crystallized Lacan's thought so concisely: '[t]o speak as a subject is therefore the same as to represent the existence of repressed desire'.[2]

SIX

Sound and Music

SOUND AND SPACE

It would be easy to make up an *Andrei Tarkovsky Sound Effects* CD, or an I-Tunes compilation of his favourite sounds. It would contain dogs barking, a buzz saw, birdsong, glass tinkling, drapes flapping, wind, thunder, a few rain showers, and twenty different 30 second bursts of water (dripping, running, gurgling, washing).

We're always talking about Andrei Tarkovsky here, as if the director did everything on a film. He didn't. There are plenty of people responsible for the sound in Tarkovsky's cinema. They include: Remo Ugolinelli, Danilo Moroni, Filippo Ottoni, Ivana Fidele, Massimo Anzellotti and Luciano Anzellotti (*Nostalghia*), Owe Svenson, Bosse Persson, Lars Ulander, Christin Lohman and Wikee Peterson-Berger (*The Sacrifice*), E. Zelentsova (*Ivan's Childhood*), V. Krashkovsky (*The Steamroller and the Violin*), E. Zelentsova (*Andrei Roublyov*), Semyon Litvinov (*Mirror* and *Solaris*), and V. Sharun (*Stalker*).

Generally, the sound mixers take one sound and mix it high, like Ingmar Bergman, against a background of silence. Andrei Tarkovsky praised Bergman's use of sound in *Through a Glass Darkly*, 'a sound on the brink of audibility' in the lighthouse scenes (ST, 159). Tarkovsky admired Bergman's selective sound, singling out a natural sound and enlarging it, making it expressive; Tarkovsky cites the scene in *Winter Light* where the body is found by the stream: '[t]hroughout the entire sequence, all in long and medium shots, nothing can be heard but the uninterrupted sound of the water' (ST, 162). Tarkovsky uses sounds out of context, and lots of off-screen sounds. His sense of the off-screen is highly developed. His movies are full of big spaces; they are spacious, for two reasons: (1) his use of off-screen sound, and particularly sounds which enlarge the sense of space, (2) the lack of chatter, of dialogue. Tarkovsky's movies have long chunks of silence, or a very few sounds, and these long passages are not kitted out with music, like so many other films. Tarkovsky is quite confident enough to allow many scenes to play in near-silence, whereas more inexperienced directors (or those with producers yelling for more action from the wings) might be inclined to cut to the next action beat or plot point. Tarkovsky uses Robert Bresson's aural ethics: '[w]hat is for the eye must not duplicate what is for the ear' (50).

Andrei Tarkovsky's handling of sound is sometimes deliberately ambiguous. 'His sounds destabilize; they make the coherent and comfortable seem suddenly strange and disorienting'.[1] In Tarkovsky's movies, sounds sometimes take a long time to become recognizable: the takes are long, and sometimes sounds fade up very gradually, as the camera tracks or zooms slowly. The key to Tarkovsky's ambiguous sound is the way he reveals sound sources, or deliberately obscures a sound's identity, or only selectively reveals a sound's source (ib., 237).

For example, in *Nostalghia* there are off-screen conversations which take some time to be identified. When Andrei and Eugenia visit the St Catherine Baths, the spectator hears a long conversation off-screen. Only after the languorous, slow tracking shot has moved to the far left of the Baths are the sources of the colloquy revealed (the bathers in the pool). In another off-screen conversation, over another tracking shot, as Andrei visits the ruined Cathedral, the interlocutors are not revealed at all – perhaps because they are St Catherine and God, or people standing in for them (Andrei Tarkovsky has filmed gods before, though: in *Andrei Roublyov* he shot Jesus in the Crucifixion scene).

In *Stalker*, sounds mysteriously appear then vanish: even a small waterfall makes a great din, but when the travellers reach the waterfall and river near the Zone, the sound of it is heard halfway through the tracking shot that reveals it. And when the pilgrims visit the same spot later on, no rushing water is heard at all.[2] Andrei Tarkovsky and the teams often used parallel sound to interweave reality, dream, memory and fantasy, as when Andrei in *Nostalghia* hears the dripping water or folk singing in the corridors of the hotel in Italy, or when the buzz saw from Domenico's memories invades his own memories. Tarkovsky's use of parallel sound is more subtle than cutting from black-and-white to colour, which indicates a movement from reality to memory, but can be also more insistent. While the eye is dazzled by the memory sepia sequences in slow motion in *Nostalghia* (such as Domenico chasing his son across the steps of the village square), the sound that accompanies the memory makes its presence felt upon the ear just as strongly. Parallel sound occurs in another place in *Nostalgia* when Andrei, thinking of his wife's voice, conjures up her sleeping form and says 'Maria'. She wakes and glances around, as if she had heard his voice in the room. She looks towards the camera, where she thinks the voice has come from.

Dripping water, one of the major Andrei Tarkovsky emblems, is a sound not normally audible in everyday life. Certainly during the day in urban or suburban areas, dripping water is not a common sound. The background sounds are too noisy. Only when one is out in the country, or at night, can such quiet sounds usually be heard. The sound of water suggests a 'transcendent, unlocated space', a place that has always been there, like the invisible, sacred, inner world. As such sounds are only heard in moments of quiet and calm, they are linked with states of meditation and repose: in short, religious states of being. A sound such as dripping water is at once relatively ordinary but it's unusual to hear it so often in so many locations, as it occurs in a Tarkovsky movie.

Some sounds in Andrei Tarkovsky's cinema play once only – such as the sound of the bottle dropping in *Mirror* in the *dacha*, or something (unseen) rolling on the floor in *The Sacrifice*, or the glass falling at the end of *Stalker*, a sound which merges with the rattling approach of the train. There's a kind of poetic genius in the way that Tarkovsky incorporates the sounds of unseen objects, like rolling coins on the floor. Often, these sounds have no onscreen (physical) motivation, but they expand the world of the films immensely. (The sound of coins in Tarkovsky's movies hint at bargains, wagers and sacrifices.)

In *Mirror*, in the first of the present-day scenes, at Aleksei's apartment, the camera tracks through empty rooms while Aleksei speaks to his mother on the phone. There is no indication that Aleksei is somewhere in the flat, or where his mother is. The telephone conversation may itself be a memory. There is no insert shot of a phone either, as in the typical Hollywood movie. In *Stalker*, as the characters go into the Zone on the railway car, Andrei Tarkovsky, Artemiev and Litvinov use a rhythmic sound of wheels clanking on the tracks; then they add electronic processing of the sounds. This technique – of rhythmic natural sounds or machine-made sounds later processed in a studio – is found in much of 1980s synthesizer pop music – in groups such as Kraftwerk, 'kraut rock', Orchestral Manœuvres in the Dark, Cabaret Voltaire and Depeche Mode. The sound of the railway in *Stalker* is very similar to OMD's *Sealand* (1981) and *The Avenue* (1984).

Andrei Tarkovsky's sense of sound is really remarkable, and a major factor in the power of his cinema. In *Stalker*, when the train runs by the Stalker's home, there is: (1) the sound of the train, (2) some metal rattling, (3) a brass band, (4) an aeroplane (this latter is added when the mother weeps on the floor).

SOUND IN *THE SACRIFICE*

In the long and often comical dialogue in *The Sacrifice* between Otto and Alexander, in Alexander's upstairs study, when Otto tells Alexander he must sleep with the witch Maria, the soundscape includes: (1) the creaking of Little Man's bedroom, (2) Swedish folk music, (3) singing from downstairs – a woman, perhaps Alex's wife, and (4) the sea, very quiet. These noises enlarge the screen space immensely, enriching the fictive world Tarkovsky & co. are creating. In the opening two scenes of *The Sacrifice* there are three bangs, like thunder claps or distant explosions, which accompany and underline particular moments: (1) when Otto mentions death, (2) when Alexander speaks of finding the house for the first time, and (3) when little Man jumps on his back. Each of these is a moment of emotional poignancy. The thunder cracks are unexplained – there is no storm, and no rain; they are used to create an atmosphere of unease, of tension before a storm (Alexander, though, does look off-screen as if he's heard one of the explosions. But because they also occur at emotional moments, as when Little Man leaps on Alexander, they also occur in Alexander's mindscreen).[1]

Thunder claps are heard over the image of Christ in *Andrei Roublyov*, where he appears as the Pantokrator. The effect here is of divine power and violence – Christ is portrayed as the stern deity who presides over the Last Judgment, over life and death. In the crowd scene in *The Sacrifice*, only footsteps are heard, not the cries of people nor other noises associated with a crowd (a Hollywood production, for instance, would incorporate all sorts of sound sweeteners for such a big scene). The location and time of the scene is not explained. During it, the sounds of Maria's house and Alexander's house are heard (emphasizing that it is a dream or fantasy).

Ambiguous use of sound occurs in *The Sacrifice*, when the bombers fly overhead. The sounds and images used to suggest the aeroplanes approaching – the maid with the glasses and the sound of vibrating glasses – seem to indicate that the sound comes from above (the maid appears to be glancing up at a chandelier). However, the rattling glasses and low rumble suggests an earth tremor; so when the source of the disturbance is revealed as jets flying overhead, the subversion of a conventional sound/ image association is unsettling (and the aircraft are never shown, similar to *Shame*. A number of jet sounds were mixed together to create the final effect).

Throughout *The Sacrifice* a female folk song is heard, often accompanying Alexander's dreams. By the end of the movie, as Maria cycles away from the burning house, the singing becomes a pastoral song, of a woman singing to a herd of cows, or a goosegirl singing to her flock (A. Truppin, 239). The goosegirl's song is linked to the image of the nude Martha chasing some geese in Alexander's house. As in *Nostalghia*, such rural folk songs relate to the memory of the homeland, the realm of the mother.

Occasionally Andrei Tarkovsky's cinema features complex mixes and sound-layering: during Alexander's dream, the soundtrack includes the voices of Maria, Alexander and his wife, a crowd's footsteps, the female folk song, Shakuhachi flute music, rattling glass, Alex sobbing (saying 'I can't'), and Maria comforting him like a mother nursing a sick child. The characteristics of these sounds alter as the dream develops. Each sound is mixed high, and the result is frenetic and disorientating. It only takes one or two noises to produce such dissonance, and the sound editors usually restrict themselves to one or two, instead of five or more.

SILENCE

Like Robert Bresson, Michelangelo Antonioni and Ingmar Bergman, Andrei Tarkovsky uses a lot of silence, or near-silence (sometimes called 'atmosphere' or room tone) in his art (much of the sound in art cinema consists of little more than 'atmospheres').

There is a further dimension to silence – the mystical aspect. In most historical world mysticisms (Catholicism, Taoism, Buddhism and Sufism, for example), there is a cult of silence. There are three different silences in Christian mysticism – of the mouth, the mind and the will. To hear the inner voice of God one must practise all kinds of silence.[1] Religious philosophies of silence included the Christian Quietist movement, which came to prominence in the 17th century, with mystics such as Madame Guyon, Miguel de Molinos and François de Sales. The emphasis was on passivity and reception.

SOUND EFFECTS

Glass tinkling (in many films); a dog barking; the creak of a bucket (in *Mirror*); coins rolling on the floor; wind rustling leaves and bushes; dripping water; running water; the seagulls and skirling birds in *The Sacrifice*; the creaking in Little Man's room; the wind in the grass; behind the Cathedral tracking shot in *Nostalghia*, focussed on Gorchakov walking, children and a woman conducting a religious ceremony are heard; the sound of the electrical saw in *Nostalghia* seems to be the perfect sound of a sunny, empty afternoon. Andrea Truppin suggests that the sound of the saw in *Nostalghia* is related to Christianity, to, specifically, Christ the carpenter (this may be stretching filmic analogies a little too far). The sawing sound is introduced when Andrei visits Domenico: Christian motifs abound here (in the Ludwig van Beethoven music, the bread and wine, the discussion of St Catherine, the objects in Domenico's house). Being an *electrical* saw rather than a hand saw (which is associated with Christ as carpenter) may relate to the movie's theme of having religious faith in the modern world. The long shot of Rome, for example, one of the great Christian centres of the world, is accompanied by a loud jet passing overhead. Such a shot encapsulates the tension between the old and the modern, the religious and the profane, the (old) world of the spirit and faith, and the (new) world of technology and the machine.

All these sounds add a dimension of mystery, narrative and meaning to the images. They are not narrative sounds in the conventional sense, and often they have nothing to do with extending the physical space. They are not psychological noises either, heard by just one protagonist. They are, rather, the sounds of spiritual states, the noises that accompany religious quests and states of being. Being silent magnifies local sounds so all one can hear is birdsong; or perhaps one hears dripping water. The ear can be as selective as the eye, and the movies explore the possibilities. Few sounds seem more suited to religious contemplation than running water, or rustling wind. These natural sounds are timeless. Not only have they occurred for millions of years (they must be some of the oldest natural sounds), they also induce a sense of timelessness. Running water or the wind blowing can have a hypnotic quality, suspending experience of time and space, letting the viewer dream while awake. Tarkovsky's cinema often gently nudges the spectator away from the world of words, numbers, rational thought, modern living. Sound is one of Tarkovsky's major tools in accomplishing those psychological and spiritual movements.

When the movie comes out of the title credits in *The Sacrifice* and the gorgeous, ancient sound of the sea and the seagulls is heard, a primæval world is evoked, a world that could be from ten million years ago. The soft but relentless beating of the waves induces a sense of tranquillity. Once established, Andrei Tarkovsky can go on to gently unveil his images. The sound crew also use many human-made noises, such as the jets in *Nostalghia* and *The Sacrifice*, or the trains that trundle by in *Stalker*. Tarkovsky's ultimate aim, he said, was to use only natural sounds: on the perfectly realized film (an unrealizable aim as any artist knows) there would be no place for music at all (ST, 162). He admits that he fails, and uses much music (ib., 159).

FOLK MUSIC

Andrei Tarkovsky generally chooses folk music by solo artists: the haunting flute in *The Sacrifice*, which plays through Alex's nightmare; or the woman singing at the end of *Nostalghia*. This latter movie in particular features a selection of women's singing: the praying of the witch-like devotees at the beginning, during the *Madonna del Parto* ritual; the Russian folk music; and, at the end, women talking fades into the single voice singing. The effect of this folk music is really haunting. The music is on its own very beautiful. Coupled with Tarkovsky's sensuous imagery, the effect is sublime.

SOUNDTRACK MUSIC

Incidental or specially produced soundtrack or theme music in the Hollywood movie manner is not so common in Andrei Tarkovsky's cinema – no *E.T.* themes or *Star Wars'* full orchestral extravaganzas for him. In Tarkovsky's cinema, there tends to be classical music and folk music in the later movies, and incidental music in the earlier films: Vyacheslav Ovchinnikov's conventional screen music for *Ivan's Childhood* and *Andrei Roublyov,* and Eduard Artemiev's eclectic soundtracks for the subsequent three movies (Artemiev suggested that Tarkovsky employed classical music to make cinema more 'serious' as an art form; Tarkovsky told Artemiev that cinema was a young artform, so he used classical music, like the references to the Old Masters in painting, to give his films a sense of history for the audience). Andrei Tarkovsky tries to use music as a poetic refrain, to parallel the visual image, and maybe open up 'the possibility of a new, transfigured impression of the same material' (ST, 158). Johann Sebastian Bach in *Solaris* is deployed in this way: at the beginning, middle and end of the movie, it acts as a refrain of the theme of the film. In *The Sacrifice* Bach is used in the same way.

Music could be a way of deepening and widening the audience's perception of a scene, Andrei Tarkovsky asserted. It didn't necessarily add anything that wasn't there already, but it did add a 'new colouring' (ST, 158). But music must always be in tune with the visual image, Tarkovsky claimed, enhancing it rather than going against it (ST, 158). And it shouldn't illustrate what was going on, shouldn't prop up the movie.

In his later movies, Andrei Tarkovsky moved away from employing a conventional score which would underpin the emotion or the action, towards heightened sound effects, and particular pieces of classical music. For Tarkovsky both music and cinema were artforms which dealt with reality, which had an immediate relation to the world, and which didn't require a mediating language (ST, 176). Plenty of cultural critics would violently disagree with that view. For many, both music and cinema are profoundly culture-specific, profoundly mediated, and affected by cultural contexts.

Andrei Tarkovsky's main composer, Eduard Artemiev, made some restrained but evocative music for *Solaris*, *Mirror* and *Stalker*. In *Mirror*, as the camera tracks in to the condensation stain on the table there is a tumultuous crescendo in the soundtrack that sounds like Giles Swain's *Cry*, or the György Ligeti music used in *2,001: A Space Odyssey*. Similar music, like an orchestra all playing sustained notes at once, occurs in *Solaris*. In *Stalker*, Artemiev's music is really beautiful (his best in a Tarkovsky movie): there is a theme tune for the Stalker character (a plangent folk melody played on flute); it begins and ends the film, and comes in at key points, such as the Stalker's dream. The music evokes Russia, combining folk melodies with electronic modernism.

Eduard Artemiev said that he composed and recorded a lot of music for *Stalker*, but the maestro concentrated on that one flute piece, using it again and again. There was also supposed to be a music cue for the tunnel (meat grinder) scene, but Andrei Tarkovsky didn't use the piece Artemiev had written (Artemiev remarked that every time he saw *Stalker*, there was a hole for him where the music should have been).

In *Sculpting In Time*, Andrei Tarkovsky said he was moving towards going without music in *Stalker* and *Nostalgia* (and Eduard Artemiev would agree with that), but he hadn't yet done without it completely (ST, 162).

During the opening of *Nostalghia* two pieces of music are mixed together – the Russian woman singing and Giuseppe Verdi's *Requiem*. The effect is startling, and states the theme in a grandiose fashion: the folky homeland of peasant Russian is being smothered by the heavier weight of baroque, operatic Italy. A similar juxtaposition of music occurs in *The Sacrifice*, where the Swedish folk song is contrasted with the Japanese flute music.

Eduard Artemiev remembered that Andrei Tarkovsky never went to music recording sessions, which was frustrating for Artemiev, because the movie director was for him the only one to have the overview of the film, the only one who could give useful suggestions. So Artemiev tended to compose and record lots of music without knowing how Tarkovsky would use it in the movie. Sometimes there were 5 or 6 or even 8 different versions of music that Artemiev wrote and recorded, and most wouldn't find their way into the final film. In *Stalker*, for instance, Artemiev recalled that there was lots more music created, but Tarkovsky only used the flute melody over and over.

CLASSICAL MUSIC

In some ways Andrei Tarkovsky's use of music is worse than that of Hollywood cinema. Hollywood patches up movies with awful sweeping strings and orchestras going at full speed (if everything else in a film has failed to move an audience, music is the last resort: music does so much of the emotional work in a Hollywood movie. And Hollywood movies, since the 1970s, have had music cues planted throughout, as if they don't trust the audience to react in its own way to a film, as if the audience has to be told at every stage what to think and how to feel). Tarkovsky goes even further; he selected key classical composers (Johann Sebastian Bach, Ludwig van Beethoven, Henry Purcell, Giovanni Battista Pergolesi, Claude Debussy and Richard Wagner), and chose very moving pieces of classical music: J.S. Bach's *St Matthew Passion* (in *The Sacrifice*); the opening of Bach's *St John Passion* (at the end of *Mirror*); Bach's slow, stately *Chorale Prelude in F Minor* (in *Solaris*); Beethoven's *Ode to Joy* (in *Nostalghia*); as well as the opening of Giuseppe Verdi's *Requiem*, with its melancholy double bass sliding ever deeper – a majestic piece of music. (Bernardo Bertolucci called Verdi mythic.)[1]

So it could be said that Andrei Tarkovsky bolsters up his movies with such powerful sounds, that he relies on music to do much of the work in his movies, as much as Hollywood cinema. The ending of *Mirror*, for example, wouldn't be nearly as moving without those restless violins and clarinets and voices which chase around in the air in Johann Sebastian Bach's *St John Passion.* Bach's music so phenomenally powerful, it would elevate even a mundane series of images.

Like movie directors such as Ken Russell, Martin Scorsese and Vincente Minnelli, Andrei Tarkovsky is a very musical filmmaker. Many sequences are shot with music in mind, and the classical (often choral) pieces fit so well with the visuals. One thinks of the extraordinary endings to Tarkovsky's movies.

JOHANN SEBASTIAN BACH

Johann Sebastian Bach (1685-1750) is the composer for Andrei Tarkovsky's cinema – not Wolfgang Amadeus Mozart, Ludwig van Beethoven, Johannes Brahms nor Maurice Ravel. Andrei Tarkovsky loves Bach for his highly devout Christian stance, and also because Bach is very emotional (Bach is also a 'musician's composer', like Tarkovsky is a 'filmmaker's filmmaker', a filmmaker beloved of other filmmakers. 'Bach's music can be matched to any situation. It's perfect', remarked Jean-Luc Godard, 'even when you play it backwards'). Bach, though, is Western European and Protestant Christian music, not quite with the same cultural roots as Tarkovsky's Russian Orthodox religion.

What does the use of Johann Sebastian Bach's music mean in, say, *The Sacrifice*? The music chosen is an *aria* from *St Matthew Passion.* It is musician's music: pure, precise, moving into the abstract. Holy, yes, and a little cold and brittle. The words are in German – not the languages of Swedish or English of the movie, nor the sacred language of the Church – Latin. The music is spacious, and very elegant – those emotional strings proceeding so gracefully – so airy and light. This music could be put with many kinds of visuals, it is so universal and abstract. Pier Paolo Pasolini used other parts of Bach's *St Matthew Passion* in his movie of Christ's life. Martin Scorsese's employed Bach over the opening credits of *Casino* (1995) and images of a car exploding (the juxtaposition of the sacred and the thoroughly secular (Las Vegas gangsters).)

In *The Sacrifice* the Johann Sebastian Bach *aria* is played twice – at the beginning and the end of the film, at the times when the Japanese *bo* tree is seen. The connection then is very religious, and very Christian: this pure, abstract classical music and perfect voice, singing of Christ's Passion, set beside the twisted, bare tree, so like Christ's Crown of Thorns, his Cross and the Tree of Paradise, the tree of so many mediæval and

Renaissance paintings. The ending becomes a poignant religious statement, backed up by the boy's words: the image deliberately alludes to the *Gospels*, to the Renaissance, to the *Old Testament* and to Christianity as a whole. But it is also very much an Oriental image – the first words Alexander says are that the tree looks Japanese.

Immediately, then, after the powerful *Western* religious imagery – of Johann Sebastian Bach's music and Leonardo da Vinci's paintings, Jesus, the Magi, the Tree of Paradise and the Cross – the 1986 movie shifts to *Eastern* philosophy, which seems so much better suited to Alexander and Otto and their philosophical debates. They are like a couple of old Zen Buddhist or Confucian monks. Surely there is added symbolism in their names: A̲lex and O̲tto, the Alpha and the Omega from the last book of the *Bible, Revelations*. Maybe this is going too far with this methodology of symbolism, but Tarkovsky had the *Revelations* in mind when he made this film – that's certain.

SEVEN

Production

FAST FILMS

Everybody makes films for themselves, really.

Andrei Tarkovsky (1993, 62)

The trouble that Andrei Tarkovsky had to go through to make some of his productions *seems* to have been tremendous. The *Diaries* are full of struggles, arguments, set-backs, continual reductions in budget and pay, all kinds of problems. But that's fairly typical of many films, and there are certainly many movies which had far, far more troubled routes to and through production (*Cleopatra, The Exorcist, The Twilight Zone, Apocalypse Now*, and so on). Deaths, violence, corruption, endless gestation periods, and schedules that run on for years are not unknown.

In fact, Andrei Tarkovsky enjoyed the protection and support of the Soviet film industry. He was favoured with high quality productions – look at *Andrei Roublyov* or *Solaris*. Those aren't low budget films by any definition of the term. Tarkovsky's epitaph is typical of him: 'The only condition of fighting for the right to create is faith in your own vocation, readiness to serve and refusal to compromise'.[1] And Larissa Tarkovskaya, his (second) wife, said of him in the documentary *Directed By Andre Tarkovsky*: 'he was the only Soviet director to do exactly as he wanted. He was absolutely uncompromising... he did as he wished'.

Andrei Tarkovsky was clearly one of those movie-makers who preferred to do as much as he could himself, and who only reluctantly delegated tasks. As Larissa Tarkovskaya said of Tarkovsky, 'whatever he could himself, he felt he ought to do'.

In the interview included in the documentary *Directed by Andrei Tarkovsky*, Andrei Tarkovsky said that filmmaking was not just a job for him, 'it's my life'; his movies and life were a continuum. A film, said Tarkovsky, is 'a fundamental act'. Here's the recurring Tarkovsky mantra of movie as art, as a statement, as self-expression, rather than movie as mass entertainment, or an industrial artefact, or a team effort. (This is a typical Tarkovsky pronouncement on entertainment: 'I am categorically against entertainment in cinema: it is as degrading for the author as it is for the audience' (D, 367). There must be millions of people who've been entertained by movies who wouldn't know what the hell Tarkovsky is talking about. That was typical of Tarkovsky's austere views of popular entertainment, but millions of punters wouldn't say they felt 'degraded' by watching a movie (well, maybe a Guy Ritchie or a James Cameron film, but not every other film).)

For Andrei Tarkovsky, commercial cinema and television degraded cinema, turned it into a factory assembly line (ST, 167). Commercial cinema for Tarkovsky debased the artform of cinema, because it cheapened people's tastes and expectations and sensibilities (ST, 179). Entertainment cinema 'extinguishes all traces of thought and feeling irrevocably', Tarkovsky claimed, so that movies were consumed like bottles of Coca-Cola. He's completely wrong, of course. Behind his attacks on what he called commercial cinema one can see the complaints of a filmmaker and artist who feels deprived of the big budgets, support systems, publicity, advertizing, and mass distribution networks that the major movie production centres enjoy. The 'tragedy' of cinema, for Tarkovsky, was that it was necessary for a filmmaker to have money, resources and a team of people in order to practise their art. 'One has to make money in order to make more films', Tarkovsky complained. 'It's completely different with other arts. One can write a book sitting at home – like Kafka who wrote but published nothing. But the book has been written'.

During Andrei Tarkovsky's movie career, the Soviet film industry was controlled by a centralized organization, Goskino. It ran all of the 40 Russian film studios, and all of distribution. Goskino ran the film archives (Gosfilmofond), the storage facility (the Central Film Base), the film school VGIK (All-Union State Institute of Cinematography), film processing laboratories, a script studio, the film actors' studio (Theatre of the Film Actor), a symphony orchestra, and the cinema journals *Iskusstvo kino* and *Sovetsky ekran*.

Goskino was led by the chairman (Alexei Romanov and Filip Yermash in Andrei Tarkovsky's time), and a governing body which included the heads of department (such as directors, scriptwriters, the board for feature production, the screenwriting board's head, and a KGB official). Mosfilm, the biggest studio in Russia, and the most important, was run by one of the deputy chairs of Goskino; during Tarkovsky's career, the executive directors of Mosfilm were V. Surin and N. Sizov.

In the Mosfilm hierarchy was a governing body of heads of department (such as scriptwriting, personnel, ideology and production), and an Artistic Council which included party officials, workers and filmmakers.[2] The movie production aspect of the Mosfilm studio was broken up into seven production teams, each run by a film director and a production manager. The teams also comprised editors and censors (mostly women), who oversaw the movies during production. Each production team had its own script boards, and its own artistic councils (made up of filmmakers), who approved scripts, music, costumes, casts, sets and so on.

In the Russian movie system there weren't producers in the Western use of the term; instead, the Goskino and Mosfilm executives acted in a similar manner to film producers in the West. Amongst the crew there were people who functioned something like production managers. On *Andrei Roublyov,* for instance, Tamara Ogorodnikova liaised between the filmmakers and Mosfilm, oversaw health and safety, and allocated the agreed budget (JP, 58). Obtaining additional money from Goskino and Mosfilm could be as difficult as with a Western movie studio.

Goskino controlled the release and distribution of films in the USSR. Once a movie was completed, it had to be presented to the Goskino authorities. At that stage, Goskino might ask for cuts and alterations. Films would sometimes go back and forth between the filmmakers, the studio and Goskino (similarly, in the Western film system, filmmakers sometimes negotiated cuts or changes with studios, backers and censors that go on for months). Sometimes Tarkovsky & co. would deliberately film scenes knowing they would be cut down (that's a regular practice among moviemakers – they give the censors something to cut so that other material can slip through).

Only when Goskino was satisfied would the film be approved (and only when a movie was accepted by Goskino would the cast and crew receive fees and bonuses). Like many filmmakers, Andrei Tarkovsky was very reluctant to agree to the demands for alterations. The bureaucratic movie machine (Goskino) had the power to withhold approval to the point where films could be shelved for long periods. This happened with *Andrei Roublyov.* Completed in 1966, it wasn't released in the Soviet Union until 1971.

The art film devotee (Andrei Tarkovsky's preferred audience) might rather have one Andrei Tarkovsky movie (or one Ingmar Bergman or Jean-Luc Godard or F.W. Murnau film) than ten thousand mainstream Hollywood films (which are caricatured by the arthouse crowd as tacky, trashy, shallow and violent movies, with enormous budgets, big stars and nothing to 'say' about anything). All films require business as well as art, but from Tarkovsky's point of view (or the art movie's point of view), Hollywood entertainment cinema seems to be all business and very little art. To say Hollywood cinema is a money-making industry is merely to state the obvious in a late capitalist, consumerist world.

Many post-New Wave filmmakers in Europe might be inclined to agree with Andrei Tarkovsky's reaction to the film *'Possession'* (Tarkovsky could be referring to *Amityville II: The Possession* [Damiano Damiani, 1982, U.S.A.], yet another of the many post-*Exorcist* cash-in horror movies, or it could be *Possession* [by Polish exile Andrzej Zulawski, 1981, France/ West Germany]):

> Saw an unspeakably revolting film called *Possession*. An American
> mixture of horror film, satanism, violence, thriller and anything else you
> like to name. Monstrous. Money, money, money... Nothing real, nothing
> true. No beauty, no truth, no sincerity, nothing. All that matters is to
> make a profit... It's impossible to watch... (D, 323-4)

While the Hollywood industry was churning out thoroughly formulaic, mainstream movies (which nevertheless generated tons of money), such as *On Golden Pond, Top Gun, E.T., Kramer vs Kramer, Ordinary People, The Dark Crystal, Footloose, Tootsie, Rambo* and countless sequels, in the mid-1980s, Tarkovsky made his last two movies, *Nostalghia* and *The Sacrifice*, which are full of space, silence, restraint and intensity. Tarkovsky's films are 'slow films' – in production and consumption as well as in subject and form.

Andrei Tarkovsky often lamented in the *Diaries* the lengthy gaps between his movies (it's a recurring gripe among all filmmakers). There were five years between the releases of *Mirror* and *Stalker*; and four years between *Stalker* and *Nostalghia*. Although this is longer than the usual two or three year turnaround of the Hollywood movie system, it's a better record than, say, fellow art film *auteurs* such as Robert Bresson or Carl-Theodor Dreyer or Sergei Paradjanov. In his diary for April 6, 1972, he wrote: '[h]ere I am forty. And what have I done in all this time? Three pathetic pictures. So little! So ridiculously little and insignificant' (D, 56).

Sometimes Andrei Tarkovsky regarded his own films as inadequate, emphasizing their faults above their merits (like many artists do). In his diaries, he wrote that he didn't like his own movies – 'there is so much in them that is fussy, ephemeral, false' (D, 174). At the same time, Tarkovsky also felt fairly confident about the value of his own work: 'other people's films are so much worse. Is that pride on my part? Perhaps it is. But it is also the truth' (ibid).

Andrei Tarkovsky's output was of a similar rate as Stanley Kubrick's or Lindsay Anderson's. But one of Tarkovsky's heroes, Japanese giant Kenji Mizoguchi, said don't rush: Mizoguchi wrote that '[i]t is essential that one should reflect for 5 or 6 years before beginning to film. Films produced very quickly are never very good'.[3] If Mizoguchi had practiced what he preached, he would have made seven movies in his thirty-four year career. In fact he made *ninety* feature films. This astonishing output (more than John Ford but not D.W. Griffith) might suggest that Mizoguchi's movies are poor in quality, but Mizoguchi is regarded as one of the greatest of all filmmakers.

Other art cinema directors who made a considerable number of movies but still maintained high quality over most of them include Ingmar Bergman, Luis Buñuel, Federico Fellini, Claude Chabrol, Yasujiro Ozu, Jean-Luc Godard, Nagisa Oshima, Eric Rohmer, François Truffaut, Andrei Wadja and Rainer Werner Fassbinder. Some of these directors were amazingly prolific: Fassbinder, Godard, Ozu, Bergman (as well as directing films, for instance, Bergman found time to direct theatre and opera and TV shows).

By comparison with many of the above filmmakers, Andrei Tarkovsky's output, including his opera, theatre and documentary work, is nowhere near as productive. But while one can lament that filmmakers such as Tarkovsky, Carl Theodor Dreyer, Sergei Paradjanov and Stanley Kubrick didn't make more movies, one also wishes that some directors had never started (James Cameron, Guy Ritchie, Paul S. Anderson [but not Paul Thomas Anderson], Simon West, etc).

It's worth repeating that Andrei Tarkovsky fared well in the Soviet movie system: he managed to shoot pretty much his scripts as he'd prepared them; he was allowed to film his own scripts (he didn't have to take on 'commercial' properties); he was allowed to take days off or rehearse actors in the middle of shooting; he was able to extensively rewrite his scripts (and even reshoot them from the beginning, as with *Stalker*); he wasn't a 'director for hire'; and his films were released very close to what he wanted (Tarkovsky acknowledged this in an interview published in *Cahiers du Cinéma* in 1987). None of Tarkovsky's films were butchered by Goskino, Mosfilm or censors, for instance.

SHOOTING

Andrei Tarkovsky made two movies in foreign languages (foreign to his native Russian, that is): Swedish and Italian (i.e, movies shot that were in those languages, rather than dubbed or foreign language versions of films. Pretty much any feature film director has to work these days in foreign languages, when (if) they oversee dubbed or foreign language versions. Some filmmakers, of course, hand over all of that to other companies).

Had he lived to make more movies after *The Sacrifice*, it seems inevitable that Tarkovsky would have eventually made a movie in English (especially if he had continued with European co-productions, where languages such as French, Italian, Spanish, English and German predominate). Many modern European directors have made English language movies: if they did not move directly into Hollywood, their English language films were acknowledgements of the international power of English. European art film directors such as Louis Malle, Volker Schlöndorff, Jean-Luc Godard, Wim Wenders, Roman Polanski and Alain Tanner all made movies in their native tongue then went on to make English language movies.

There are one or two moments in Andrei Tarkovsky's cinema where actors speak in English. Two moments occur in *The Sacrifice*: first where Alexander quotes from the William Shakespeare play that Tarkovsky directed, *Hamlet*: 'words, words, words' (this can be in English, because it's by the immortal Bard). The second time is where Susan Fleetwood speaks in English during her panic (Fleetwood's character is not an English speaker, but maybe Tarkovsky liked her delivery of the lines. It's not explained in the film why she speaks in English at that point).

Andrei Tarkovsky seemed to be moving further West (culturally as well as physically) from his native Russia: first to Italy, then to Sweden. France or Germany would maybe have been next, then perhaps Britain or America. The thought of an *American* Tarkovsky movie is intriguing: what would a Tarkovsky movie make of America? One thinks of other modern European filmmakers who have made movies in or about America, with an outsider's perspective: Wim Wenders with *Paris, Texas* (1984), an arthouse fave, or Werner Herzog with *Stroszek* (1977).

Unlike other European art film directors, such as Wim Wenders, Jean-Luc Godard and François Truffaut, Andrei Tarkovsky did not exalt American culture or American movies. While the *Cahiers du Cinéma* crowd and the French *nouvelle vague* enshrined Howard Hawks, John Ford, Frank Capra and dominant Hollywood cinema, Tarkovsky hardly mentions it in *Sculpting in Time* or his *Diaries*. If Tarkovsky does refer to directors, they are usually of the art cinema tradition: Luis Buñuel, Akira Kurosawa,

Federico Fellini and Ingmar Bergman. Not for him the affectionate *hommages* to American cinema of the French New Wave (to Humphrey Bogart and American detectives in Godard's *A Bout de Souffle* [1960], or to Orson Welles in Truffaut's *Les Quatre Cents Coups* [1959]). Tarkovsky was at times sceptical of American movies, and sometimes detested them (although people have described Tarkovsky discussing movies like *The Terminator* (1984) passionately; Tarkovsky could never have guessed then, however, that *Terminator* director Cameron would one day be producing a remake of his film *Solaris*).

If Andrei Tarkovsky had gone on to make a movie in or about America, it might not have been for some time after 1986: his projects in the planning stages included *The Temptation of St Anthony*, William Shakespeare, a Fyodor Mikhaylovich Dostoievsky film, and even a *New Testament* movie. However, if a big shot producer like Dino de Laurentiis or Scott Rudin had approached Tarkovsky around 1985-86 with a hands-off, final cut, free rein deal on an American picture, Tarkovsky might have been tempted. Say a version of Dostoievsky, but with an American star. That too, is not unknown: many arthouse directors cast American movie stars in their films: Jean-Luc Godard used Jack Palance in *Contempt* (1963), Wim Wenders cast Dennis Hopper in *The American Friend* (1977), Federico Fellini cast Donald Sutherland in his bizarre *Casanova*, and Bernardo Bertolucci and Luchino Visconti put Burt Lancaster in *1900* and *The Leopard* (but then, Wenders, Bertolucci and Godard are – or were – deeply fascinated by Americana). (Tarkovsky didn't use any American actors in his movies).

It's unlikely that we would have seen an Andrei Tarkovsky film starring Arnold Schwarzenegger, Vin Diesel or the Rock, with a trailer announcing: 'this season, 20th Century Fox presents Arnold Schwarzenegger in *The Brothers Karamazov...* from the director of *The Sacrifice* and *Nostalghia*'. But a picture with, say, Jack Nicholson or Johnny Depp, would have been a possibility.

Hollywood cinema is continually forging strange new alliances. Nobody could have guessed, for example, that Mel Gibson would make a film about Christ (*The Passion of the Christ*, 2004), that it would be shot (not dubbed) in Aramaic, and that it would be such a success with audiences (despite having no stars). (No doubt Andrei Tarkovsky would have had a few things to say about *The Passion of the Christ*, and he might not have completely hated it).

Among Andrei Tarkovsky's regular collaborators were fellow director and scriptwriter Andrei Mikhailkov-Konchalovsky, actors Anatoly Solonitsyn, Nikolai Grinko, Nikolai Burlyaev, Erland Josephson (a Bergman regular) and Oleg Yankovsky, composers Eduard Artemiev (*Solaris, Mirror, Stalker*) and Vyacheslav Ovchinniko (*Ivan's Childhood* and *Andrei Roublyov*), set designer A. Merkulov (*Mirror, Stalker*), cameraman Vadim Yusov (*The Steamroller and the Violin, Ivan's Childhood, Andrei Roublyov, Solaris, Mirror*), producer Tamara Ogorodnikov (*Andrei Robulyov;* she also acted in *Mirror* and *Solaris*), costume designer Nelly Fomina (*Solaris, Mirror, Stalker*), and editor Lyudmilla Feiginova (*Andrei Roublyov, Solaris, Mirror, Stalker*).

It seems Andrei Tarkovsky often had disputes with his camera people. He disagreed with the cinematographers on *Mirror* (ST, 136) and *Solaris* (D, 62). Most of *Stalker* was re-shot. Tarkovsky controls his camera meticulously, and although his movies are full of really stunning imagery, the camera person on a Tarkovsky movie needed to be slow, thoughtful and precise. No running around with a Steadicam for Tarkovsky, as seen in the films of Paul Verhoeven, Paul Thomas Anderson and John Carpenter and every Hollywood movie of recent times. Not as many big, sweeping, operatic camera movements, as with Bernardo Bertolucci and his director of photography Vittorio Storaro (though Tarkovsky employed some big crane shots: in the apples on the beach shot in *Ivan's Childhood*, for example, or the climb up the tree shot in *The Sacrifice*). No shaky handheld camera-work, either, as in early French New Wave cinema.

The most beautiful camerawork in Andrei Tarkovsky's cinema occurs in *Nostalghia* (shot by Guiseppe Lanci) and *The Sacrifice* (shot by Sven Nykvist), both made with Eastman Colour film stock. Nykvist is the celebrated cameraman of Ingmar Bergman's films, but Lanci's work on *Nostalghia* was equally gorgeously done. When he viewed the material for *Nostalghia*, Tarkovsky was amazed because it was 'completely homogeneous, both in its mood and the state of mind imprinted on it… the camera was obeying first and foremost my inner state during filming… I was at once astounded and delighted' (ST, 203).

Andrei Tarkovsky isn't known for fruitful and long-running collaborations with his director/s of photography like, say, Bernardo Bertolucci and Vittorio Storaro, Martin Scorsese and Michael Ballhaus, Ingmar Bergman and Sven Nykvist, or Oliver Stone and Robert Richardson. And the fact that Tarkovsky's last five movies (from *Solaris* onwards) all had different cinematographers says a lot. However, Tarkovsky's first three features were all shot by Vadim Yusov, so there is a continuity of style and a working relationship there.

According to contemporary accounts, Sven Nykvist found it tricky working with Andrei Tarkovsky on set of *The Sacrifice* at first, because of

Tarkovsky's habit of sitting beside the camera, and directing actors through the camera. As Nykvist liked to operate the camera himself, that could cause tensions. Some film directors never look through the camera, or steer clear of the camera crew. Some sit hunched behind the video monitors, but Tarkovsky was a supremely hands-on director. It was impossible for Tarkovsky to direct from a distance.

In Michal Leszcylowski's documentary on the making of *The Sacrifice* (*Directed By Andrei Tarkovsky*, 1989) a very intense filmmaker is depicted, often lost in thought, or wandering away by himself, or squinting through upraised hands, or discussing set designs, or raking water around on the grass, or moving stones around the model of the house, or carefully directing the actors, or clutching his head in exasperation. During the shoot in the city courtyard (for Alexander's nightmare), Tarkovsky was seen personally directing the dressing of the set, rather than leaving it up to the art director's team (and communicating through the interpreter, as ever on *The Sacrifice*), making sure there was plenty of newspapers and trash strewn about, plus black plastic, all sprayed down with hoses, and getting the car heaved into the correct position, on its side. Tarkovsky acknowledged the contribution of the team members in making a film, but he always insisted that the final word and conception comes from the director (ST, 33).

Andrei Tarkovsky is shown in *Directed By Andrei Tarkovsky* looking through the camera a good deal; sometimes he's on the camera dolly during shooting (but that may be due to the selection of the shot for the documentary – a film director sitting in a chair isn't quite as fun). He is depicted as a director who gets involved in every aspect of shooting. Indeed, Larissa Tarkovskaya quotes a line from his diary: '[d]on't bother other people with things you can do yourself.' Tarkovsky likes to do everything, to make sure everything is done properly. Collaborators said that Tarkovsky was involved with every aspect of filmmaking, down to the tiniest detail (the more the director reproduces the minutiæ of life in 'their concrete sensuous form', Tarkovsky said, 'the closer he will be to his aim' [ST, 154]). For Tarkovsky, the movie director was the final force or vision in a film. After all of the pages of script written, the locations chosen, the art director's sketches, and the actors cast, there was, finally, the director: 'only one person' stands alone, the director, 'the last filter in the creative process of filmmaking' (ST, 18).

In Michal Leszcylowski's documentary he is portrayed as an obsessive *auteur*, a genius energized by a religious vision – the artist as shaman and religious hero (like Vincent van Gogh, Arthur Rimbaud and Mark Rothko). Jeanne Moreau tells an interesting story of pre-shooting nerves: François

Truffaut used to pace up and down all night; Joseph Losey had an allergy attack; while Luis Buñuel, just before shooting, 'would touch everything, each object to reassure himself'.3

Art must take over the artist's life, Andrei Tarkovsky asserted, even to the point where it could endanger her/ his existence (ST, 188-9). American artist David Smith is one of many artists who have said the same thing (artists invited to teach in the academy often lecture their students like that, emphasizing the life-or-death necessity of making art). And many of the artists Tarkovsky admired – Vincent van Gogh, Fyodor Dostoievsky – do have that life-on-the-edge live-or-die extremism about them.

Andrei Tarkovsky made *The Sacrifice* with many Swedish actors and crew members. He had to speak through an interpreter. This perhaps helped his concentration – he wouldn't be distracted by what people were saying around him (in the same way, different groups of movie-makers communicating via internet, ISDN, broadband or other electronic links, such as a movie director in Hollywood and a visual fx team in London or Sydney, have said it was actually a better, more efficient way of working.) Yet despite problems in translating Russian ideas and commands into Swedish or English on the set, *The Sacrifice* is remarkably unified. The shooting seems have been a relaxed and coherent affair, with the crew working well together. It was not one of those sets where some obnoxious assistant director barks orders at the crew.

One can fully understand the utter relief the crew felt when the re-take of the very long and complex last shot of *The Sacrifice* was completed, because these things take so long to prepare for, to rehearse, and to shoot. After it, Andrei Tarkovsky says 'we all let go: we were nearly all weeping like children' (ST, 226). Tarkovsky's technique was to rehearse difficult shots again and again, so that he often only needed one or two takes. (That's another difference with the Hollywood practice of shooting thousands of feet of film and printing every take. It might be expected, for instance, for Tarkovsky to demand take after take, like Stanley Kubrick, famous for 50 or 60 takes just for simple shots, but that doesn't seem to have been the case.)

During shooting Andrei Tarkovsky's aim was to stick as closely as possible to the basic idea of the movie, which has been decided by the filmmaker (that means Tarkovsky himself, not a collective of writers, script doctors, co-producers, assistant producers and executive producers. Tarkovsky was co-writer on most of his films). He demanded total concentration from the other team members: they are there to make sure the vision is realized (ST, 125f). He was probably hell to work with at times (really, *really* hell).

For Andrei Arsenievich Tarkovsky, the screenplay was not literature (ST, 126), and he moved towards spontaneity, towards allowing things to happen during shooting (127, 131). The script and the shooting script were guides only. For Tarkovsky, the script wasn't a finished work of art, but was only successful in terms of how it could be transformed into a film (ST, 74). For Tarkovsky, 'a screen adaptation, always arises on the work's ruins so to speak. As a completely new phenomenon'.

Andrei Tarkovsky said that in the early days, he would plan shots and scenes exactly, but later tried to encourage an element of spontaneity about shooting. So that actors, locations, sets and the like could 'prompt one to new, startling and unexpected strategies' (ST, 127). Tarkovsky said he often thought of the psychology of the characters before shooting a scene, or the inner state of the scene, rather than specifics (ST, 132). Although he said he didn't alter the original conception of a movie too much during shooting and post-production (ST, 93), it wasn't until the last stages of post-production that a film's final form became crystallized (this was certainly true on *Mirror*). Sticking too closely to the script could be a grave or even fatal mistake (ibid.).

On *Mirror*, Andrei Tarkovsky said the crew used to visit the country house set at dawn just to experience the atmosphere of the place (ST, 106). Tarkovsky often improvized and changed his ideas for scenes as he went along (even a movie director known for rigorously sticking to the script and the storyboards, Alfred Hitchcock, in fact didn't, but incorporated new ideas and improvizations as he shot his pictures). New ideas were written for Margarita Terekhova in *Mirror*, for instance, 'to make use of her tremendous potential' (ST, 131). She became the present-day wife of the narrator, as well as his mother from the past (the character of Natalia wasn't in the original script). Via Terekhova came the idea for integrating the past and present scenes.

SCRIPT AND SCREENPLAY

Andrei Tarkovsky always wrote his movie scripts (Tarkovsky preferred to make films from scripts he'd been involved in writing), but most of his scripts were collaborations; he did *not* write them alone (unlike, say, Ingmar Bergman or Woody Allen, who tended to write on their own. A writer-director who works with other writers is much more common than a sole writer-director). Tarkovsky co-wrote *Andrei Roublyov* and *The Steamroller and the Violin* with Andrei Konchalovsky; *Mirror* was coauthored with Alexander Misharin; the Strugatsky brothers co-wrote *Stalker*; and Tonino Guerra co-wrote *Nostalghia*. *Ivan's Childhood*, meanwhile, was written by Mikhail Papava and Vladimir Bogomolov (who wrote the original book – the novella *Ivan*).

In the Soviet film system, a proposal was written first, then a longer 'literary script' (written as a story, rather like a treatment in Hollywood). The authorities would comment on each proposal and script draft. The 'director's script' was next (basically this was a shooting script, with notes on camera angles, locations, music, etc).

Andrei Tarkovsky was suspicious of talky scripts and movies: the dialogue, for Tarkovsky, only accounted for a small part of the overall impact of a scene or a film (ST, 75). The 'meaning' of a scene wasn't to be found solely in the words spoken by the actors; the characters' psychological state, the physical action, the setting, the images and so on were just as important for Tarkovsky (and usually given more significance than the dialogue). The best dialogue for Tarkovsky was that which fused with the *mise-en-scène*, the sounds, the textures, the psychology and the images of a movie.

Film critics continue to reduce films to dialogue and stories, as if the impact and experience of a movie can rest solely in the dialogue. But dialogue, as Andrei Tarkovsky rightly maintained, was only one component of many in a film. Dialogue was literary, and cinema transformed the literary into something else (ST, 134). And cinema wasn't literature: 'it bears no essential relation to literature whatsoever'. Tarkovsky made a distinction between a script written for the cinema, and a script which turned out to be literature. A movie script was written specifically so it could be turned into a film, Tarkovsky asserted. That was its only function. Too many screenplays were really literature for Tarkovsky.

'I don't believe in the literary theatrical dramatical construction,' Andrei Tarkovsky maintained, because it 'has nothing in common with the dramaturgy that is particular to cinema as art form'. Instead of describing and explaining actions, 'in film one does not need to explain, but rather to directly affect emotions'. His films were about inciting an emotional response, he claimed: 'the only thing I am after is for them to give birth to certain emotions'.

Ivan's Childhood, Solaris and *Stalker* are literary adaptions, but they are very much 'films by Andrei Tarkovsky', with the Tarkovsky stamp all over them (i.e., Tarkovsky's movies can boast a far greater degree of authorship than many Hollywood films possessing the personal credit for the director, which's more about economic status, ego, clout in the industry and agents' percentages than artistry). *Andrei Roublyov* was based on a real, historical figure (though it certainly wasn't the usual 'artist's biopic'). Early on in his career, Tarkovsky had been opposed to movie adaptions of classic literature or plays. They existed so perfectly within their own medium, they couldn't be adapted. Later, Tarkovsky altered his views, and contemplated adaptions of William Shakespeare, Fyodor Dostoievsky, Thomas Mann, Leo Tolstoy, and Venyamin Bulgakov.

Many of Andrei Tarkovsky's unmade films had literary sources. But whether the source book was by Thomas Mann, Hermann Hesse or Fyodor Dostoievsky, one knows the movie would have had Tarkovsky's signature everywhere. Tarkovsky was one of those filmmakers with an idiosyncratic style (one thinks of Orson Welles, Robert Bresson, Walerian Borowczyk or Jan Svankmajer), that turned whatever he made into a recognizable 'un film de Tarkovsky'. A Tarkovsky movie, like a Borowcyzk or Svankmajer film, could not be mistaken for anything else (which is an *extremely* rare phenomenon). *Auteur* or not, Tarkovsky was a filmmaker who was involved in every aspect of making cinema – from script to post-production and the press conference.

Andrei Tarkovsky was doubtful whether cinema had thus far had any filmmakers who could be counted alongside the great authors of world literature (ST, 173). It was perhaps because cinema was still developing its language and form. I'd say that any of the great *auteurs* Tarkovsky admired – Robert Bresson, Ingmar Bergman, Akira Kurosawa, Luis Buñuel – could stand beside the great authors (Dante Alighieri and Aleksandr Pushkin, say, or François Rabelais and Herman Melville).

In *Sculpting in Time* Andrei Tarkovsky describes how *Mirror* was transformed from being a series of somewhat unconnected memories and feelings of childhood to complexly interwoven webs of scenes, shots, episodes, gestures, newsreels, past and present experiences (*Mirror* was co-written with Alexander Misharin). He wrote:

> This account of the making of *Mirror* illustrates that for me scenario is a fragile, living, ever-changing structure, and that a film is only made at the moment when work on it is finally completed. (ST, 131)

Mirror only started to become a good movie during the editing (according to Andrei Tarkovsky), which Tarkovsky spent a lot of time on (however, one imagines that the beauty of the rushes must have been obvious to anyone who saw them). For Tarkovsky, cinema is not literature, as poetry is not prose. Cinema transforms literature into another medium. A film such as *Mirror* is intensely poetic, and lives in a different world from literature, from the printed word. There are incidents in it that are found in literature – the return of the father, for example, to his homeland and family. But this is filmed as one shot (the father in uniform holding his estranged children) in a complex montage which cuts between past and present and two images by Leonardo da Vinci accompanied by the strains of an opera singing of the veil of the temple being rent. Time and space are squashed through the eye of the needle of Tarkovsky's cinematic virtuosity, and changed utterly. The script might be born in prose and literature, but after cinematic transformation it ends up as something else entirely – a series of images and sounds. The poetry of cinema takes over.

Similarly, with *Nostalghia*, Andrei Tarkovsky spent ages working on the screenplay with Tonino Guerra, who co-wrote many of Michelangelo Antonioni's movies (including *Red Desert*, *L'Avventura* and the excellent *Identification of a Woman*, 1982, Italy). Scenes were shortened, re-written or dropped to make the script attractive to the financers. Every so often, because of the delays and set-backs, Tarkovsky tried to remind himself of the film he was trying to make:

1. *Madonna del Parto*
2. Foyer of the Hotel du Palma. Reminiscences and 'translation'.
3. The windowless room. Eugenia. The well. Conversations. The dream.
(D, 289-290)

But the script bears little resemblance to the finished movie. As in many novels, all the work of research is buried under the surface. It's there, but one has to dig. In the later films, the written screenplay, outline, treatment or shooting script is completely transcended by the cinematic image. Take Gorchakov's death scene in *Nostalghia*, for example: a man carries a candle across some drained Baths. A simple enough operation. Could be done in a couple of shots, lasting three seconds each. Or even ten or twenty seconds each:

Shot 1: L.S. Man walking across Baths. 15s.
Shot 2: M.C.U. Man placing candle on ledge. 9s.

Instead, there is a nine-minute continuous take, without dialogue, with few sounds, without music, without big acting, without voiceover. The image becomes primary. This is not prose, dance, painting, music or sculpture. The only concrete relation is to a person walking in a drained Italian pool, the actor on the screen (but it is also plainly an act that's operating on other levels). It is the spiritual relation that counts here – the relation to mythic, tragic ritual, to fire symbolism, to the Christianity of the *Gospels*, to mediæval mysticism, to religious faith and self-transcendence.

BUDGET

Andrei Tarkovsky's movies seem to have been made under quite different conditions to the Hollywood system. There was a political, ideological and social pressure upon Soviet filmmakers unmatched in Western Europe or America. Tarkovsky felt he was victimized. He hated the Mosfilm system, calling the people who ran the Soviet movie industry 'idiots' (D, 14). Yet the repressive institution enabled him to make as his second feature a large-scale historical drama, with many locations, a large cast and hundreds of extras. Produced by Hollywood at the time, such a film might have cost ten or more million dollars (the average Hollywood feature budget for 1965 was $1.5 million), or $80-140 million today (consider comparable epics of the early Sixties such as *King of Kings* [Nicholas Ray, 1961, U.S.A.] or *El Cid* [Anthony Mann, 1961, U.S.A.]). *Ben Hur* (William Wyler, 1959, U.S.A.) cost 15 million dollars, and *Spartacus* (Stanley Kubrick, 1960, U.S.A.) cost $12 million. (In talking about budgets and money, one must always keep in mind inflation, comparisons with the average budget of the time, and not least the socio-economic system of a film's production. United Artists' *The Greatest Story Ever Told*, Fox's *The Sound of Music* and MGM's *Dr Zhivago*, for instance, made at the same time as *Andrei Roublyov* in the mid-1960s, were produced in a very different political environment as well as a different movie production system.)

Like *Andrei Roublyov, Solaris* has high production values; it is certainly no low budget sci-fi flick like *Dark Star* (1974) or *Plan 9 From Outer Space* (1958), with wobbly sets, scrounged costumes and low power performances. For *Mirror*, which was shot under schedule, the production team went to considerable lengths in the design of the film (you had to on a Andrei Tarkovsky film): they rebuilt Tarkovsky's childhood home, as well as re-planting the nearby field with buckwheat so that it would accord with Tarkovsky's memory of the place (ST, 132). 'The average Soviet feature costs about 600,000 dollars to produce, with budgets scarcely ever rising above 1 million dollars' wrote David Cook in 1990, adding '[a]s in other Eastern European countries, both filmmakers and performers are modestly paid by Western standards' (775). The low pay of cast and crew enabled a Russian film like *Andrei Roublyov* to be produced for far less than it would have done if it had been made in the West. In the Russian system, the crew was paid a standard wage during production, having to wait (sometimes for a long time) for the bonuses.

Andrei Tarkovsky estimated that *Nostalghia* would cost about $750,000. £500,000.[1] Tarkovsky was paid around $100,000; he also tried to dispense with an assistant director and claim the salary for himself, according to

Toscan du Plantier (JP, 306). By 1982 prices, this is cheap (the average Hollywood feature budget in 1982 was $10,000,000).

Information on the exact amounts spent on Andrei Tarkovsky's movies is difficult to find, partly because it's always tricky find out out *exactly* how much a film costs to make, in any system.

Filmed in dilapidated warehouses and industrial zones, *Stalker* looks at times like some student post-Holocaust thriller (like *The Last Battle* [Luc Besson, 1983, France] or *Mad Max* [George Miller, 1979, Australia] to pick two low budget examples of the same era). Except that *Stalker* wasn't low budget (by Soviet standards). Andrei Tarkovsky was able to re-shoot much of the movie, which is a luxury granted to few movie-makers (usually only the prestigious ones, like Woody Allen or Stanley Kubrick, can secure extensive re-shoots. Film studios only very reluctantly allow filmmakers to substantially re-shoot movies. Often, if the executives think a film can't be salvaged, they prefer to scrap it and write off the loss).

Andrei Tarkovsky complained in his diary that it wasn't possible to make movies without the permission of the State (D, 10). Tarkovsky felt that the Soviet film system had held him back from making more movies. He complained to Filip Yermash, Goskino's chairman, that up until 1983 he had directed only five films in 22 years in the USSR. That's true, but it's not the whole picture, because when Tarkovsky wasn't directing, he was writing scripts (including for other directors), developing movies, and directing theatre. He wasn't sitting about waiting for the Soviet authorities to give him the green light.

If Andrei Tarkovsky had been working in the Western movie industry (in Western Europe, say), he might have directed even fewer films, as Vida Johnson and Graham Petrie rightly point out (1994, 6), because his movies were not commercial, box office-friendly products. They tended to be complex art movies, the kind of movies which have often found it difficult to find an audience, or even a theatrical release at all (the number of movies *not* released outside their country of origin in Europe is depressingly *huge*).

Andrei Tarkovsky's films were not historical epics favoured by French-Italian-German co-productions, for example, or cool, hip thrillers with sexy stars aimed at the youth markets in, say, Spain or the Netherlands. Maya Turovskaya reckoned that Tarkovsky might not have made many more films, had he lived longer, because he tended to work very slowly anyway.

Andrei Tarkovsky had to fight for much of the budget of *Nostalghia*, because he was outside the Russian movie industry (for the first time on a feature, though he had made the documentary *A Time To Travel* in 1981). Tarkovsky realized how difficult other Western filmmakers found movie finance. But it could be simply that he moans about the budget of *Nostalghia* so much in his *Diaries*. The film is indeed his most sparse – a few actors, and a few choice locations – Rome, Monterchi, the Milan hotel courtyard, the St Catherine Baths. But Tarkovsky makes the $750,000/ £500,000 the show received from Italian television (RAI TV) go a very long way, because *Nostalghia* looks like it cost twenty or even a hundred times its budget. One of the reasons is the use of existing locations: filming in the centre of Rome, for instance, gives a movie an instant enormous setting too expensive to build. Another reason is the luxurious feeling for textures and layers (smoke, rain, snow, backlight), which give the impression of a slick, costly, perfectionist sheen to his films. A shot may only consist of one actor and smoke drifting over a field, but Tarkovsky can make it look like a *lot* more.

The money and resources for *The Sacrifice* came from Argos Film, Paris, Swedish Film Institute, Film Four International, London, Josephson and Nykvist, Sverige Television/ SVT 2, and Sandrew Film & Teater – a European co-production, with finance mainly from television companies (the French Ministry of Culture was also involved). This was a typical financing pattern for 1980s art movies (and continues to be today). With a complex financial package like that, the producer of a film needs to be a canny negotiator, in order to liaise between so many backers, which will all have their own priorities and stipulations. (In the case of *The Sacrifice*, the producers were Anna-Lena Wibom of the Swedish Film Institute, and Katinka Farago of Farago Film) – two female producers, unusual, and a first for Tarkovsky.

One of the producers of *The Sacrifice* was Anatole Dauman, one of the key figures in European art cinema scene of the 1960s and 1970s. Dauman's *resumé* on the art cinema circuit (via his company Argos Films) was impeccable: Alain Resnais (*Hiroshima Mon Amour, Last Year At Marienbad, Muriel*), Jean-Luc Godard (*Masculin-Féminin, Two or Three Things I Know About Her*), Robert Bresson (*Au Hasard Balthazar, Mouchette*), Nagisa Oshima (*In the Realm of the Senses, Empire of Passion*), Volker Schlöndorff (*Circle of Deceit, The Tin Drum*), Walerian Borowczyk (*Immoral Tales* and *The Beast*), and Chris Marker (*Sunless*).

All of Andrei Tarkovsky's movies look as if the director achieved everything he had planned in pre-production. He gets the sets and locations he wants; the right actors and crew members; and final cut (though not always). And he also got to make films which he had originated or scripted himself – a *very* important point. That is, Tarkovsky wasn't a movie director for hire, he wasn't assigned to projects he hadn't initated (except for *Ivan's Childhood*, which Tarkovsky was invited to direct, taking over from the director Eduard Abalov). Rather, Tarkovsky originated and developed his projects and scripts himself, and presented them to the studio. That's the paradigm of the classic *auteur*, the film director as artist, rather than the other view, of the film director as hired hand, a jobbing worker. It's important because Tarkovsky could have a sense of ownership of a project, of being the prime mover. He could get excited about making the project, feel motivated to do it, because he initiated it.

By the time of *Nostalghia* and *The Sacrifice*, Andrei Tarkovsky had refined his filmic technique to the point of maximum clarity and beauty. These two movies in particular look really stunning, especially considering their modest budgets. But there are many cases of films looking striking on a tiny budget: *Breathless* (1959), *Eraserhead* (1976), *Chimes At Midnight* (1965), *Effi Briest* (1974), *The Seventh Seal* (1957), *Scorpio Rising* (163), *Rashomon* (1950), *The Blood of a Poet* (1930) and *Un Chien Andalou* (1928).

ANDREI TARKOVSKY'S UNMADE FILMS

One can never make the movie of one's dreams, Jean-Luc Godard remarked; it always eludes the filmmaker. 'The film of your dreams never happens. Not for Fellini, not for anyone'.[1] The film that Andrei Tarkovsky most wanted to make but never did was probably the one by or about Fyodor Mikhaylovich Dostoievsky (1821-81). For a long time he nurtured the idea of filming Dostoievsky. Most of the lists of projects in the *Diaries* feature Dostoievsky. Tarkovsky produced a detailed treatment of *The Idiot*, in which he discussed the problems of adapting Dostoievsky (his 'realism' and 'anti-naturalism', and 'his own affinity to cinema' [D, 375]). Akira Kurosawa said that making his vision of *The Idiot* (*Hakuchi*, 1951, Japan) 'was very hard work. It was extraordinarily difficult to make... Dostoievsky is very heavy'.[2]

A list of possible movies for Andrei Tarkovsky of 1970 (D, 14) included *Joan of Arc, The Plague* (Albert Camus), *Kagol* (about Borman's trial), *A Raw Youth* (Fyodor Dostoievsky), *Joseph and His Brothers* (Thomas Mann), *Matryona's House* (Anatoly Solhenitsyn), and intriguing titles such as *Two Saw the Fox, The House With a Tower, Echo Calls* and *Deserters*. Tarkovsky loved Thomas Mann, and likely would have based a film on something by Mann had he lived longer (he calls Mann a genius in his diary [D, 7]). He cherished Mann's *Tonio Kruger* and *Doctor Faustus*. He had discussions, in 1970, of shooting *Joseph and His Brothers* in Italy.

Many of Andrei Tarkovsky's ideas for movies are literary adaptions: Albert Camus' *The Plague*, Thomas Mann's *Joseph and His Brothers* and *Doctor Faustus,* Anatoly Solhenitsyn's *Martyrona's House* (D, 143), *Hamlet*, Fyodor Dostoievsky's *Crime and Punishment*, *Hoffmaniana* (D, 153), *A Light Wind* (adapted by Tarkovsky and Friedrich Gorenstein from Alexander Belyaev's *Ariel*), *The Double*, Venyamin Bulgakov's *The Master and Marg-anita*, Leo Tolstoy's *The Death of Ivan Ilyich*, and so on (D, 211).

If Andrei Tarkovsky had filmed them, some of these movies would have been remakes (*Crime and Punishment* and *Hamlet*, for instance). But they wouldn't have been 'faithful' adaptions of the books (it's impossible). Tarkovsky's idea for *Hamlet*, for instance, was to do it with almost no dialogue (pretty radical for one of the wordiest plays in history. William Shakespeare's characters, if nothing else, talk incessantly, using ten lines where one would do. Taking away their dialogue is already a major departure from the plays). Tarkovsky was still contemplating making *Hamlet* in 1984 (he had also been offered to direct it by the Royal Shakespeare Company in Britain). Tarkovsky's adaption of Fyodor Dostievsky's *The Idiot* would run through the narrative twice over, from the point-of-view of two characters (Mishkin and Rogozhin), splitting the narrative into two movies.

Another idea for a film was *Life of Archpriest Avvakum*, which Andrei Tarkovsky was considering after making *Andrei Roublyov* (Archpriest Avvakum Petrovich, 1620-1682, was a prominent churchman and leader of the Old Ritualists or Old Believers). In 1959, Tarkovsky co-wrote a script with Andrei Konchalovsky: *Antartica, Distant Land* concerned a Russian expedition of scientists in Antartica, but although it was submitted to two Soviet directors (Grigory Kozintsev and Edmond Keosayan), it was never made.

E.T.A. Hoffman (1776-1822) was a favourite author with other filmmakers – Michael Powell and Emeric Pressburger had created their own version of the *Tales of Hoffman* (1951), a bold, operatic endeavour, which was (like many of Powell's and Pressburger's best movies) also about the magic of cinema. In amongst Hoffman's fantasia, Powell had been fascinated by the concept of automata – puppets and dolls that come to life. That would doubtless have featured in Tarkovsky's take on Hoffman. According to Michal Leszcylowski, *Hoffmanniana* was going to be Tarkovsky's next movie after *The Sacrifice*, to be started in Autumn, 1986. Tarkovsky had scouted locations (in Berlin, at Charlottenburg Palace), and would have been helped by the Bavarian movie programme. (It was going to be a German co-production when it was developed in the 1970s).

Much of Andrei Tarkovsky's cinema has literary origins. Conversely, if writers such as André Gide, Novalis or Fyodor Dostoievsky had made films, they could have been like those of Robert Bresson or Tarkovsky – austere productions with everything stripped away leaving spiritual faith and the search for truth. In the realm of literary adaption, Tarkovsky's interests chime with those of Luchino Visconti, who directed movies of Dostoievsky's *White Nights* (*La notti bianche*, 1957, Italy), Albert Camus' *The Outsider* (*Lo straniero*, 1967, Italy) and Thomas Mann's *Death in Venice* (*Morte a Venezia*, 1971, Italy). These three writers (Camus, Mann and Dostoievsky) recur in Tarkovsky's list of potential projects.

Andrei Tarkovsky changed *Stalker* considerably (from the book by the Strugatskys) and one is sure that his adaptions of Fyodor Dostoievsky, Thomas Mann, William Shakespeare and others would have been similarly pared down and idiosyncratic. Among the more intriguing but never-to-be Tarkovsky films is *Joan of Arc* – 'a latterday *Joan of Arc*' he called it (D, 153). One wonders how it would compare to the powerful *Joan of Arcs* of Carl Theodor Dreyer (1928, France) and Robert Bresson (1961, France). (It probably wouldn't have been like the Hollywood *Joan of Arc* (1948) with Ingrid Bergman, or the ridiculously over-the-top French-U.S.A. *Messenger: The Life of Joan of Arc* (Luc Besson, 1999)). Perhaps Tarkovsky's interpretation of Dostoievsky would have recalled Robert Bresson's beautiful adaption of *White Nights*, shot so hypnotically in Paris, under the title *Four Nights of a Dreamer* (1971, France).

In 1970 Andrei Tarkovsky was toying with the idea of shooting Thomas Mann's *Joseph and His Brothers* (a favourite book) in Italy; Tarkovsky had met Dino De Laurentiis's Italian production manager (Robert Coma) on the Russian-Itallian co-production of *Waterloo* (D, 21). Tarkovsky, though, reckoned the powers that be wouldn't greenlight it (D, 25).

Other intriguing plans of Andrei Tarkovsky's included a 'film based principally on [Carlos] Casteneda' (D, 166). This could have been something wonderful, a journey into shamanic, magical territory. At one point Tarkovsky toyed with the idea of doing a sequel to *Stalker* (D, 169), with the same actors, in which the Stalker turns into a 'votary', a 'fascist', '[b]ullying them into happiness'.

A movie of Hermann Hesse's fiction – *The Glass Bead Game* or *Steppenwolf* – could also have been tremendous (D, 79). One would imagine Andrei Tarkovsky's version of Hesse's Existential, mythic fiction (or Albert Camus, Franz Kafka, Jean-Paul Sartre or Knut Hamsun) to be something like *Stalker*, the most Hesse-like of his films. Tarkovsky raved about *The Glass Bead Game* in his journals: 'brilliant', 'a spiritual symbol of life. A novel of genius' (D, 23). Tarkovsky quoted Hesse in *The Glass Bead Game*: 'truth has to be lived, not taught. Prepare for battle!' (ST, 89)

Sardor was written for Uzbek filmmaker Ali Khamraev by Andrei Tarkovsky and Alexander Misharin in the early 1970s; the proposal didn't go anywhere, and the full script was written later, at the end of 1978, for another Uzbek director, Shukhrat Abbasov, then head of Uzbekfilm (CS, 420).

Flying was at the heart of *Light Wind* (a.k.a. *Ariel*), co-written with Fridrikh Gorenshtein. The people who can fly are used to spread religious beliefs. Although there are sequences where characters fly, Andrei Tarkovsky rewrote the script to turn it into an exploration of philosophical and spiritual issues. There are references to Jacob Boehme.

Towards the end of the decade (in 1978), Andrei Tarkovsky listed potential movie projects as *The Country* (a 16mm documentary of reflections); *Italian Journey*; *The Master and Margarita* (from Venyamin Bulgakov's novel); *The Horde*; and a film based on Carlos Casteneda (D, 160). *The Country* was a low budget 'amateur' film that Tarkovsky contemplated making while waiting for other movie projects to bear fruit. It would have been shot in Spring, in April and May, and would have featured actor Alexander Kaidanovsky as Tarkovsky himself (D, 168). A year or so later, another list of movie projects included *The Idiot* (Fyodor Dostoievsky), split into 2 two-hour films; another Dostoievsky project, *The Double* (but this time a biopic); a movie about the last years of Leo Tolstoy's life called *The Escape*; *The Death of Ivan Ilych* (from Tolstoy); *The Master and Margarita* again; and *Nostalghia* (D, 211).

At one time (1980), Ingmar Bergman expressed interest in collaborating with Andrei Tarkovsky on a film, according to Tarkovsky in his *Diaries* (248). What they might have done together, however, is mouth-watering but indistinct. For instance, both were perfectionist directors who also originated and wrote their own material. Would one have written and the other directed, or would it have been an anthology piece? Although Tarkovsky did write scripts or ideas for other directors (such as *Sardor*, for Ali Khamraev), he didn't do that much, preferring to spend his energy on his own projects. (But then, Bergman and Tarkovsky avoided each other when the maestro was in Sweden in filming *The Sacrifice*!).

But perhaps the most fascinating of Andrei Tarkovsky's many unmade films is of Samuel Beckett's (1906-88) novel *Molloy*, the first of *The Unnameable* trilogy. What a meeting of talent that could have been: Beckett and Tarkovsky. In the *Diaries* Tarkovsky jots down a few ideas on *Molloy*:

> A diagram of the life of someone who is seeking (actively) to understand the meaning of life... 1. Two actors. 2. Unity of place. 3. Unity of action. 4. It would be possible to be aware of nature in the background now and

again (as it grows dark or light. (D, 101)

However, although Samuel Beckett's art is regularly produced in the theatre around the world, and has been adapted for TV and radio, there are hardly any feature movie versions. Albert Camus and Franz Kafka have been filmed a few times – equally 'difficult' Existential fictions – but not Beckett. You'd think there'd be a well-known movie of *Waiting For Godot* produced by now, and used by literature students who are advised to watch the versions of *Romeo and Juliet* (1968 and 1996) or *Henry V* (1945 and 1989).

Although Andrei Tarkovsky didn't film Samuel Beckett's fiction, there are elements of Beckett's disaffected, shambling derelicts in Gorchakov in *Nostalghia* (he always appears in a grey overcoat, a very Beckettian costume), and the characters in *Stalker*. The Stalker's home is out of Beckett's fictional world – the run-down building, the family squashed together in the old iron bed, the trains clanging by outside. This could be out of Beckett's *The Expelled*, or *Molloy*. What Tarkovsky's characters lack is the vehemence and utter despair of Beckett's down-and-outs. Tarkovsky has a spiritual hope which Beckett does not (could not, would not) entertain. The pragmatic negativity in Beckett's art would have to be tempered by Tarkovsky, who would not have been able to embrace the darker, miserable aspects of Beckett's œuvre. Even during the most downbeat moments of crisis in Tarkovsky's cinema, there is faith and belief.

EIGHT

Andrei Tarkovsky and Painting

PAINTING AND FILM

One essential difference is time: the painting can be contemplated for hours at a stretch, while film always takes up the same time each viewing. The painting is physically still, while the film image flickers. Painting and cinema offer different (but related) depictions of death, time, change, being and otherness. Andrei Tarkovsky's poetic cinema moves towards the condition of painting, in his nine minute takes, lighting out of Jan Vermeer or Georges de la Tour, vistas out of Pieter Brueghel, and his (often) static presentation (scenes staged as enigmatic, mnemonic *tableaux* served up in Renaissance space for the viewer). Further, painting has a physical presence that can be seen as far more complex than that of film: in painting the spectator considers: the size and the scale of the painting, the nature and colour of the frame, the canvas, the various media, the texture, the relation to other paintings, the relation to the viewing space, the lighting and viewing height, and so on. Cinemas differ as spaces, but once the lights go down, the movie is pretty much the same. Theatrical release prints can be tatty or new, sound can be clear, Dolby, surround sound 7.1, loud or muffled, and the screen can be large or small, but the film is essentially the same.

PAINTING IN ANDREI TARKOVSKY'S CINEMA

Using paintings as a basis for *mise-en-scène* was derided by Andrei Tarkovsky in his writings (ST, 78), although he did just that a number of times in his movies. Tarkovsky used painting many times, often incorporating discussions of painters in his dialogues or visuals. There is Leonardo da Vinci in *Mirror* and *The Sacrifice*; Piero della Francesca in

Nostalghia and *The Sacrifice*; the snowscapes referencing Pieter Brueghel in *Solaris* and *Mirror*; part of Jan van Eyck's *Ghent Altarpiece* in *Stalker*; Albrecht Dürer's *Apocalypse* in *Ivan's Childhood*; Vincent van Gogh is alluded to in the face and hands of Gorchakov; Byzantine icons appear in *Mirror*, *Andrei Roublyov* and *The Sacrifice*; and *Andrei Roublyov* has the painter's icons crowning it at the end.

Andrei Tarkovsky's penchant is for uncluttered artists: he dislikes the Baroque, the mannered, the ornate, the over-rich. Hence his love of Albrecht Dürer, Vincent van Gogh, Leonardo da Vinci, Piero della Francesca and Pieter Brueghel. One can see in Tarkovsky's cinema affinities with Fra Angelico's simple, lyrical Quattrocento depictions of religious faith – Angelico's art is the culmination of mediæval Christian fervour. One can find the intense mystical feeling of Early Netherlandish painters in Tarkovsky's sacred cinema. Painters such as Jan van Eyck, Rogier van der Weyden, Quentin Massys and Petrus Christus depicted events from the *Bible* in dark but luminous paintings, filled with a miraculous, exquisite, detailed light (the translucence in Early Flemish art is infinitely more enriching than the light in the Impressionists, who're usually celebrated as painters of light but turn out to be opaque and limited).

But though the Goddess and the Church is broken or decayed, Christ (Christ-like fervour) still burns in Andrei Tarkovsky's progatonists: one can see connections between Tarkovsky's Christianity and that portrayed in, for example, Rogier van der Weyden's stupendous *Descent From the Cross* (1439-43, Prado, Madrid), and the *Crucifixions* by Petrus Christus, Dieric Bouts, Gerard David and Hieronymous Bosch. This Northern European painting tradition is, like Russian mediæval icon painting, Tarkovsky's visual ancestry and inheritance.

Although Andrei Tarkovsky does use landmark artists of the Italian Renaissance in his movies (principally Piero della Francesca and Leonardo da Vinci), his art is geared to Northern Europe and Russia. The art of the intenser Italian Renaissance artists – Masaccio, Giotto, Andrea Mantegna – chimes with Tarkovsky's visions of the world (but not the blander, airy art of Raphael Sanzio, Francesco Parmigianino, Garfalo (Benvenuto Tisi) or Lorenzo Lotto, nor the later Mannerist, Roccoco and Baroque painters: Annibale Caracci, Guido Reni, Domenichino, Guercino (Francesco Barbieri) and Padre Pozzo).

Andrei Tarkovsky is part of this tradition of painting – where spiritual issues are portrayed in an anguished, subjective, expressive fashion. One can see how Tarkovsky developed the Christian depictions of modern Western art (such as Emil Nolde, Max Beckmann, Egon Schiele and Eric Gill) – each of whom portrayed some event in the Christian story in a modern, Expressionist manner. The tradition of mystical darkness, as found in mystics such as Dionysius the Areopagite (fl. 500), St John of the Cross (1542-91), Meister Eckhart (c. 1260-1328) and *The Cloud of Unknowing* (14th century), is another ancestor of this approach to spiritual issues.

The typical way in which painting is introduced into Andrei Tarkovsky's movies is by an actor leafing through a book (in *Ivan's Childhood*, *Mirror* and *The Sacrifice*). This may have been the way in which Tarkovsky first encountered painting – not at school or in museums, but at home, via a book, in privacy. (In a way, it's a modest, perhaps even too obvious method of weaving in a subplot about painting into the films. But perhaps Tarkovsky's characters are the sort of highly educated people who might look through a book of paintings). Of all the arts, Tarkovsky folds painting and music into his cinema more than any other. He does not, for instance, make references to the history of cinema, or dance, or ballet, or musicals, or sculpture, or opera (Ingmar Bergman's movies often reference theatre, for instance, while jazz (and the Marx Brothers) are never far from Woody Allen's movies). Both painting and music are significantly non-verbal artforms with a tendency towards lyricism and expressionism (and they're abstract enough to fit into Tarkovsky's cinematic scheme).

ANDREI TARKOVSKY AND LEONARDO DA VINCI

The skillful painter must paint two main things, man and what is going on in his mind.

Leonardo da Vinci[1]

Leonardo da Vinci (1452-1519) is the unsurpassed master of darkness, ambivalence and strange beauty. He is the highpoint of figurative art in the West. There are many aspects of Leonardo that single him out as Andrei Tarkovsky's favourite artist: his vast curiosity, his restlessness, his perfectionism, his ambiguity, his solitary outsider lifestyle, his *sfumato* painterly style and the timelessness of his art. (Tarkovsky spoke of Leonardo's ability to observe the world from outside, detached, but accurate.) Leonardo is also one of the supreme examples of the artist-as-hero, something that Tarkovsky identifies with. Tarkovsky portrays Andrei Roublyov as a quiet wanderer possessed by genius. There is a lot of Leonardo's personality in the character of Roublyov (Roublyov as misunderstood genius, as a perpetual exile, as in advance of his era, and so on). (Leonardo's art enjoyed a new surge of interest in the 2000s, following author Dan Brown, *The Da Vinci Code* book and movie, and countless cash-ins).

Like Andrei Tarkovsky, Leonardo da Vinci produced only a few 'finished' works (and every artist can identify with that, the eternal dissatisfaction with one's work, the mind flitting to other projects, the ease of being distracted). But the ones Leonardo did make are the apotheosis of the Renaissance, and the whole Western art tradition, unparalleled in their sense of depth, darkness and mystery. Leonardo is an occult exponent of the invisible – he makes the invisible visible, in the German painter Max Beckmann's sense. Beckmann's aim, like Tarkovsky's, was 'always to get hold of the magic of reality', as he put it.[2] In Leonardo's art one finds a sense of the invisible and the beyond more compellingly rendered than in just about any other painter. Leonardo's occultism is his ability to make manifest the inner spiritual dimensions of things. He investigates his subjects on so many levels – the social, spiritual, physiological, personal, hermetic and scientific.

Leonardo da Vinci's people – the women, angels, saints, outcasts, children and madmen – inhabit a twilit world of shadows. Leonardo's subjects are half-angels, half-devils, supremely ambiguous, tantalizing, mocking and mysterious. None of Andrei Tarkovsky's people are as fully imagined as Leonardo's softly smiling angels and goddesses (as great as Tarkovsky is, I don't think he would put himself on the same level as Leonardo). It's practically impossible to portray a Leonardo face in cinema. The famous Leonardo Gioconda Smile, as enigmatic as Buddha's grin, is also unfilmable. At one point in *Mirror*, Tarkovsky tries to do it: he cuts from the *Portrait of a Woman* (Ginerva Benci?, c. 1474-76, National Gallery of Art, Washington), a.k.a. *The Young Woman With the Juniper,* to Natalia, the wife of the narrator. The mythicization stems from the montage, which is bold (ST, 108).

The sitter in *The Young Woman With the Juniper* (used in *Mirror*), Andrei Tarkovsky called at once 'attractive and repellent. There is something inexpressibly beautiful about her and at the same time repulsive, fiendish' (ST, 108). Leonardo da Vinci's portrait was effective, Tarkovsky reckoned, because the viewer couldn't single out any particular aspect of the painting from the whole, it couldn't be grounded in one particular interpretation. Instead, the artwork offered up the 'interaction with infinity', an opening out into infinity (ST, 109). Easy to see how Tarkovsky might like a similar response to his own art: that the viewer wouldn't be persuaded to dissect his movies, to take them apart detail by detail, but to apprehend them as a whole. It was the *whole film*, Tarkovsky asserted, that was the work of art, not any particular element. Dividing up a movie into components was to miss the point (114, 177). Only a film as a whole can carry the meanings and values that audiences ascribe to them, Tarkovsky said, not the dissection of individual shots or scenes.

Themes common to both Andrei Tarkovsky and Leonardo da Vinci include: the twins, seen in Leonardo's two mysterious *Virgins of the Rocks* (*c*. 1483-86, Louvre, Paris, and *c*. 1503, National Gallery, London and other works). The twins appear in *Mirror*, and the double in *Nostalghia*. The myth of the Two Mothers – in Leonardo's beautiful *The Virgin and Child with St Anne* (*c*. 1510, Louvre) and the London *Cartoon* (*c*. 1498, National Gallery) – are found in *Nostalghia* (the Russian women in Gorchakov's dream); and in *Mirror* (the aunt and the mother). At the end of *Mirror* the matriarchal trinity is seen: the grandmother, mother and (in this case two) children, a familial configuration like that of Leonardo's *St Anne* images, where the grandmother is depicted as a Dark Mother, a Black Goddess figure.

The double or *doppelgänger* is one of the long-standing motifs of cinema, found in *Doctor Jekyll, Kagemusha, The Prisoner of Zenda, Persona, Vertigo* and many other movies). One of Andrei Tarkovsky's favourite devices, employed on all of his films from *Solaris* onwards, was to put several versions of the same character on screen at the same time, without resorting to cutting or visual effects. This was achieved simply and in-camera by using stand-ins of the lead actors, with the same costumes, hair and make-up, positioned carefully on set. Examples include the multiple versions of Hari in *Solaris*, or Gorchakov's dreams of Russia and his home in *Nostalghia*. Sometimes Tarkovsky cuts back and forth between the same space in different states: the *dacha* in *Mirror*, for instance, is depicted empty and desolate one moment, then as it was in the past in another. Sound effects or music smooth over these transitions.

In Andrei Tarkovsky's and Leonardo da Vinci's art women are exalted – as well as feared and stereotyped. Like Leonardo, Tarkovsky's cinema enshrines the strange power of women (the familiar depiction in masculinist art of women as unknowable, unreachable Other). The scene where the mother Maria flails her arms in the raining room in *Mirror* is like the modern filmic equivalent of a scene from a long lost Leonardo painting (one can imagine Leonardo – or post-Leonardoan artists like Gustav Klimt or Gustave Moreau, artists with similarly ambiguous views of women – applauding Tarkovsky for that scene. To an artist like Michelangelo Buonarroti or Gianlorenzo Bernini it would appear bemusing).

Women in Andrei Tarkovsky's cinema recall those in Leonardo a Vinci's art – there is the same emphasis on ambiguous sexuality, fetishes (long hair), arcane gestures, prominent eyes, swan-like features, serenity, restlessness and strangeness. (Leonardo's women are the precursors of the *femme fatales* in Symbolist and *fin-de-siècle* painting or 1940s *film noir*). It was the memory of his mother, Sigmund Freud wrote of Leonardo, 'that drove him at once to create a glorification of motherhood'.[3] The same could be said of Tarkovsky, in *Mirror*. Both artists glorify the mother: she is a gigantic figure, never fully understood by the child. She is at once dangerous and deeply desired.

LEONARDO DA VINCI'S *ADORATION OF THE MAGI*

There is something terrifying about Leonardo da Vinci's *The Adoration of the Magi* when one sees it in the flesh, as well as something beautiful and mysterious. The square painting (1481-82, Uffizi, Florence) depicts a moment of maximum religious revelation. Fervent spirituality spirals out from the calm centre of the Madonna and Child. Leonardo pushes back the frontiers of pictorialism. Oswald Spengler in *The Decline of the West* called it 'the most daring painting of the Renaissance'.[1] The half-angelic/ half-dæmonic beings slipping through the painting have surely the most beautiful faces in Western art. The event they celebrate is an epiphany, when the Godly nature of Jesus is publicly revealed. Leonardo depicts the manifestation of the divine, the experience of the numinous, the *mysterium tremendum*. Here the deification is enacted, with a host of witnesses, the witnesses being a cross-section of humanity, from the lowly sub-proletariat in the background, around the horses, to the royal figures in the foreground.

Andrei Tarkovsky aims for such an epiphany in his movies, where God-in-nature is mysteriously revealed. This is (partly) what Tarkovsky seems to be going for when he films the rain at the end of *Stalker*, for instance.

Andrei Tarkovsky and his team chose to focus on the Magi in *Adoration of the Magi*, in the first shot of *The Sacrifice* (over the opening credits). The abasement of Balthazar, Caspar (or Jasper) and Melchior is total: one of the kings kneels down so low his head nearly touches the ground. The Child soaks up this adoration, while the Virgin deflects it with her expression of humility. She is absolutely the heart of the painting, visually, although the Child is the centre, spiritually, in the orthodox view. Early Leonardo sketches for an *Adoration* work show the Virgin doing all the adoring; she kneels with her arms outspread before the Child, as in the *Adorations* of Early Netherlandish art (it's a moment of adoration before the Magi appear, and is known as *The Adoration of the Virgin*, based on an account by St Bridget of Sweden following a visit to Bethlehem in 1370). In the *Adorations* or *Nativities* of Fra Filippo Lippi, Piero della Francesca, and the Early Netherlandish painters, the Madonna holds her hands together in humble prayer before the majesty of the Child. In Leonardo's drawings, her arms are outspread: her awe at the Child below her is also a self-glorification.

Andrei Tarkovsky acknowledged that he was one of those artists who created their own inner world, rather than recreating reality (ST, 118). The innerness or interiority that Leonardo depicts has been the province of poets for centuries. It is the unknown, dark, nighttime, inner space of poetry, symbolized by the night, by stars, blackness (death), and infinite spaces.

Andrei Tarkovsky used *The Adoration of the Magi* to frame the narration in *The Sacrifice*. Sven Nykvist holds his camera on the central portion of the painting for many minutes at the opening of the movie. Sometimes in the rest of the film the painting is shot so that the glass over it acts as a mirror. Sometimes it shifts within a shot from being a painting to a mirror. There is a flicker of humour when Alex tells Otto that the painting is a print, not an original. Alex's joke is another reference to the authenticity of religion, religious images and religious faith in a modern, Godless world. The painting presides over Alex's dream. The central gift in the painting, from a King to Christ, echoes the gift of life Alex gives to his mute son at the end of the film – the gift of life as the ultimate sacrifice. The upward tilt shot, at the opening credits, visually connects the gift of the sacrifice with the tree above. The tree lies vertically above the gift of the King in the painting, connecting father and son together spiritually.

Andrei Tarkovsky saw Leonardo's *Adoration of the Magi* in Florence in August, 1979 (D, 200). Two days later he saw Leonardo's *St Jerome* (*c.* 1480, Vatican, Rome), and noted: '[a]bove all – the Leonardos' (ib.). The tortured image of St Jerome is fixed to the wall in Alex's upstairs study in *The Sacrifice*, like the *Adoration of the Magi*. Alex is clearly identified with St Jerome in the saint's guise as dishevelled penitent – the Jerome who had a vision in the desert of angels announcing the Last Judgement (which is the plot of *The Sacrifice*, except the angelic messenger service is television, and the Last Judgement comes in the form of nuclear war, a common motif in movies of the Cold War period). St Jerome is sometimes shown in Renaissance paintings listening to the angels' trumpets blowing over his head. In *The Sacrifice*, the Apocalypse is announced by the missiles or jets screaming overhead – latterday technological angels.

The severe *Self-Portrait* by Leonardo da Vinci (*c.* 1512, Royal Library,

Turin) appears in *Mirror* as the father returns to the homeland. Andrei Tarkovsky's father was a poet, an artist, and the appearance of the Leonardo sketch at this point underlines the significance of the father as a creative person, and that the film is an æsthetic construction and inquisition – in part the Story of the Birth of an Artist. The self-reflexivity of Leonardo's art is part of his mystery, and probably one of the reasons that Tarkovsky was attracted to him.

ANDREI TARKOVSKY AND PIERO DELLA FRANCESCA

Piero della Francesca's (1415-92) art makes geometry mystical. It is bright and timeless, like Classic Greek fresco and relief. Piero's paintings fetishize architectonic precision. Piero extends space beyond Euclid and Isaac Newton towards an Einsteinian four dimensional worldview. His spatial mysticism looks towards Cubism and modern abstraction, to quantum mechanics and the New Physics. Piero della Francesca is regarded as the first Cubist,[1] a realist,[2] and the 'greatest geometrician of his age'.[3] Piero's large blocks of colour and light are musical, like choral sounds. His art is unified, supremely, by his vision. As in Ludwig Wittgenstein's philosophy, Piero makes mathematics transcendent. Like Leonardo da Vinci he is a scientific artist, but this is not the reason Tarkovsky puts his work into his movies.

Piero della Francesca created two monumental *Madonna* paintings – the *Madonna della Misericordia* (*c*. 1460, Town Hall, Sansepulcro, Italy) and the *Madonna del Parto* (*c*. 1450-55, Cemetery Chapel, Monterchi, Arezzo). It is the latter painting that presides over the opening of Andrei Tarkovsky's Italian film, *Nostalghia*. Piero's parthenogenic Goddess exudes a noble magnificence, with her belly pushed forward, her cool, sky-blue dress, her quickened womb and attendant angels. But it is the face, the extraordinary Pieroan face, that turns this *Birthing Madonna* into a Black Goddess, a deity who 'presides especially over marriage and sex, pregnancy and childbirth' (as Marina Warner wrote in *Alone of All Her Sex* [274]). In 1979 Tarkovsky noted in his *Diary*:

9 August, Bagno-Vignoni
    Early this morning there was a thunderstorm, very beautiful. Rain. This morning we looked at the hot water baths – St Katherine. It's a fantastic place for a film.
    Tivoli showed me the stream, and the room with no windows for the 'Companion' and for the film. *Madonna del Parto.*

> We filmed Piero della Francesca's *Madonna of Childbirth* in Monterchi. No reproduction can give any idea of how beautiful it is.
> A cemetery on the borders of Tuscany and Umbria.
> When they wanted to transfer the *Madonna* to a museum, the local women protested and insisted on her staying. (D, 196-7)

Piero della Francesca's *Pregnant Madonna* is a thaumaturgic image, thought by locals to have magical properties (Piero, 98). The Madonna is a powerful matriarch, an archaic image of Mediterranean motherhood. In *Nostalghia* she is part of a women's ritual, as the local women gather and kneel and pray before the image of the pregnant Goddess: birds are symbolically released from the statue's womb. Eugenia is identified with the Goddess as Tarkovsky cuts from one to the other in a piquant piece of montage (why bother with subtlety, or complex staging, when the point can be made with simple cross-cutting?). The scene plays out with a slow tracking shot moving into the face of Piero della Francesca's austere Earth Mother painting. On May 3, 1980 Tarkovsky explained the scene:

> The first episode, in the mist. Madonna del Parto. The pregnant women come crowding here like witches, to ask the madonna to ensure them a safe delivery, and so on. The mist lies in layers around the church. (D, 245)

(That aspect of the women's ritual – that they were pregnant – wasn't quite made clear in the movie.)

NINE

Philosophy and Religion in Andrei Tarkovsky's Cinema

PHILOSOPHY AND RELIGION

Few film artists have been so obsessed by religious matters as Andrei Tarkovsky. One thinks of Ingmar Bergman, Yasujiro Ozu, Luis Buñuel, Carl Theodor Dreyer and Pier Paolo Pasolini, among others. Tarkovsky is regarded as a religious filmmaker (and Tarkovsky was a believer, unlike Bergman, Buñuel and Pasolini. Indeed, among European and Russian filmmakers of the 1960s to 1980s, Tarkovsky is unusual in believing in God and the redeeming power of spiritual faith. Jean-Luc Godard, Bernardo Bertolucci, Donald Cammell, Paul Verhoeven, Peter Greenaway, Krzysztof Kieslowski, Andrei Konchalovsky – the last thing those cosmopolitan, sophisticated movie directors would do is admit to religious beliefs, in their public personas at least. The odd thing, of course, is that filmmakers like Ingmar Bergman, Werner Herzog or Woody Allen spent a lot of time in their films exploring religious and spiritual issues).

But Andrei Tarkovsky made no secret of his religious beliefs, and religious issues lie at the heart of his work. Tarkovsky was fascinated by questions of faith, purity, integrity, good and evil, doubt, suffering and sacrifice. In part Tarkovsky's notions of faith and hope derive directly from Christianity. *Stalker* was about a man having crises of faith, only to find himself renewed by each bout of despair, Tarkovsky said (ST, 193). For Tarkovsky, the Stalker was 'an extremely honest man, clean, and, so to speak, intellectually innocent. His wife characterizes him as 'blessed'... the last idealist'. The three travellers at the end of *Stalker* become aware for Tarkovsky of the most important thing in life: faith (ST, 199).

At the end of *Stalker*, Andrei Tarkovsky aimed to make a genuine affirmation of love (for some, his way of going about it might have seemed eccentric). He has something of the determination and obstinacy of the early Christian fathers in this continual affirmation of notions such as love and faith. Tarkovsky is no fire and thunder *Old Testament* prophet – or he doesn't seem to be, because of his quiet, serious, scholarly surface (i.e., in his media profile as intense Russian poet-filmmaker). But it's no surprise that some critics have likened Tarkovsky to a saint or martyr, or employed the language of religion to describe his cinema. 'The one thing capable of resisting the universal destruction is love... and beauty. I believe that only love can save the world', Tarkovsky confessed (D, 26).

Remembering the significance of religion in Andrei Tarkovsky's cinema (people pray, characters debate theological issues like Buddhist monks, God is overheard talking to a saint, Crucifixions are staged, and so on), it's worth recalling some of the tenets of Christianity, and in particular the fervent sort of belief that Tarkovsky's cinema indulges in (as well as questions).

VISION QUEST

Only one journey is possible: the journey within. We don't learn a whole lot from dashing about on the surface of the Earth... And of course we cannot escape from ourselves; what we are we carry with us. We carry with us the dwelling place of our soul, like the turtle carries its shell. A journey through all the countries of the world would be a mere symbolic journey. Whatever place one arrives at, it is still one's own soul that one is searching for.

Andrei Tarkovsky (1982)

The Andrei Tarkovsky character is on a 'vision quest', and each Tarkovsky picture is structured on the vision quest of the archaic shaman.[1] The quest is to find the sacred amongst the secular, the timeless amongst the temporal or transitory, the valuable amongst the banal. Sometimes the quest is for being, truth, wholeness, meaning, childhood – the terms change, but the quest remains essentially the same. Pier Paolo Pasolini, in rejecting the conventional fiction film, went instead for the truth. 'My ambition in making films', he wrote, 'is to make them political in the sense of being profoundly "real" in intent'.[2]

In some movies directed by Andrei Tarkovsky, the quest has an external dimension – *Andrei Roublyov, Solaris, Nostalghia* and *Stalker* contain outward journeys in the world which mirror the protagonist's inner quest (the outer dimension is essential for a dramatic medium). *The Sacrifice* is a seemingly static film; but it is modelled on the Dark Night of the Soul of mysticism (made famous in the writings of Spanish mystic St John of the Cross), on the Night Journey of Muhammad and the ancient shaman's travelling to other worlds (which is the model for all religious journeys or quests or pilgrimages). And within the film there are journeys which reflect Alex's state of mind: to the Japanese tree; to the city in the dream; to the witch's house; to the trees outside the house where he talks with Maria.

The journey in *Mirror* is the complex flight between past and present, between memory, dream and fantasy, between wife and mother, between youth and age, between the family then and the family now. In *Solaris* the journey is ambiguously away from and towards the secular world of the Earth, with its technological cities, cars and televisions, to the sacred, inner world of dreams and the past (embodied by Hari, Kelvin's dead wife). *Solaris* is all about atoning with the past, about guilt, redemption and forgiveness. *Solaris* may represent Tarkovsky's most radical inward turn, an interiorization continued in *Mirror*.

Nostalghia's outer journey is from Russia to the Italian countryside then to Rome. Gorchakov wanders about not so much like a mediæval pilgrim on a quest, as the modern, dispossessed exile. Gorchakov has to be given his quest by Domenico (to carry the candle over the water). In a way, Gorchakov is adrift because he has no quest, no goals, no *desire* left. In a typical narrative movie, the aims are often shifting over the course of the story. But in *Nostalghia*, Gorchakov is searching for something, but he doesn't know what it is, or even if he would want it if he found it. (It's not erotic desire or women – Gorchakov spurns Eugenia when she offers herself to him; she mocks him when he declines to take her). When he wanders into the ruined Cathedral, God is heard talking about Gorchakov and his uncertain spiritual state, but the man cannot hear him. One imagines that even if God sent an unmistakable sign (a burning bush, say), Gorchakov would still ignore it.

Stalker is modelled on the pilgrimage of the faithful to some shrine, temple or Cathedral, a Rome or Mecca or Lourdes. The 1979 film consciously evokes religious pilgrimages, and suggests many other films as well as real pilgrimages undertaken throughout history. Each of the three pilgrims takes a problem or question to the shrine, as in mediæval romances and fairy tales. This recalls the questions in mediæval Arthurian romance, such as 'whom does the Grail serve?' The answer offered in the movie is that the Zone or the Room serves life, or the sacred manifested in life. The narrative line of *Stalker* for critic Peter Green plots 'a path that skirts hazardously close to hocus pocus or schoolboy adventure' but manages to rise above them, and the sci-fi component, to attain a metaphysical plane.[3]

Each Andrei Tarkovsky film has a mythic structure. *The Sacrifice* has something of *King Lear* and *The Tempest* about it, consciously elegiac, a movie about consciously revaluating one's life and maybe turning one's back on everything that one once was and accomplished (Prospero's breaking of his staff and drowning his books). *Mirror* relates to *Hamlet* and *Oedipus Rex*, with œdipal material particularly prominent. Like *Solaris*, *Mirror*'s about being haunted by the past, about being unable escape the past, or transcend one's origins. *Stalker* has elements of the *Odyssey* and Greek myths in it, as well as many Biblical overtones (for instance, ancient Greek mythological quests such as Jason and the Golden Fleece, or Orpheus in the Underworld, or Odysseus travelling back to Ithaca).

FAITH

Each Andrei Tarkovsky protagonist is driven by faith. The faith of the Tarkovsky protagonist is called into question in each movie: what does s/he *really* believe in? How important is faith for the individual? Can s/he live without it? By the end of each film personal faith has been challenged. Sometimes the quest is to find it again (while acknowledging the impossibility of such a task). Sometimes it is to encourage its significance for others as well as oneself.

The Stalker frantically re-asserts his faith at the end of the Mosfilm movie. In *Nostalghia* the protagonist sinks back into a glamourized past, into a dream-vision of a yearned-for Russia – comprising the *dacha*, the snow, the pool, the dog, the ululating women on the track. In *The Sacrifice*, Alex's faith is tested to the limit, and the resultant shift in his mental state (from neurosis to psychosis) encourages him to burn down his world in a ritual conflagration accompanied by the Japanese flute music, which represents the otherness and religious unity of Eastern mysticism he has always yearned for and now can no longer achieve. The deep breathing in Zen Buddhist meditation and breathing of the flute was linked; the breath, wind, sound, and spirit were connected. The Japanese flute music is a spiritual music, which emphasized emptiness, the gaps between the sounds and breaths. The mantle of shamanic power is passed on to his son as Alex drives right past him in the ambulance. The first act of the narrator in *Mirror* is to interrogate the past on the telephone to his mother. His last act, while (apparently) on his death bed, is to release the bird, a symbol since time immemorial of freedom and the soul (hinting at metempsychosis, as well as the soul flying to heaven. Whether Tarkovsky gets away with someone releasing a bird on their deathbed is another question. In an MTV pop promo it would be cheesy and silly enough to be accepted in an ironic, playful fashion, and kids in Seattle or Seoul might find it cool when their pop idol goes all arty on them, pretending to die and release a bird. But in a serious art film it's something else: it's meant very seriously).

Faith is blown apart or re-affirmed, or replaced by something else in Andrei Tarkovsky's sacred cinema. Few modern artists, and even fewer filmmakers, talk about religious faith. Yet it is a central concept in Tarkovsky's philosophy. There is the æsthetic dimension: one needs faith to make art; and the ontological aspect: without faith life is severely impoverished; 'only faith interlocks the system of images', he wrote (ST, 43). The Tarkovskyan protagonist is marked by her/ his faith – 'people whose strength lies in their spiritual conviction' (ib., 207). In this sense, in his devotion to faith, Tarkovsky is like some mediæval mystic, nurturing his religiosity.

TRUTH

Andrei Tarkovsky's philosophic thinking pivots around big metaphysical terms such as Faith, Truth, Time and Experience. The search for 'truth' is, like spiritual conviction or faith, central to his philosophy. For him, art is a noble undertaking, a search 'for the spiritual, for the ideal' (ST, 38). Art is a revelation of the world, an awareness of the infinite, 'the eternal within the finite, the spiritual within matter, the limitless given form' (ST, 37). (It could be Johann Wolfgang von Goethe or Henry Thoreau or Aleksandr Pushkin talking). The aim of cinema, said Tarkovsky, must be for truth. This 'truth' is concrete, achieved by getting as close as possible to 'the images of life itself' (D, 355). The artist can only approach the absolute through faith and creativity (ST, 39). Art was not simply self-expression for Tarkovsky; there was always a higher calling – to do with spiritual communication, forging a spiritual bond, and sacrifice (ST, 40). Tarkovsky wrote and directed like someone with complete conviction, someone believing utterly in what he does. In the *Diaries* he noted on March 24, 1982:

> The most important thing and the hardest thing to have is faith. Because if you have faith, then everything comes true. Only it's impossibly hard to believe sincerely. There is nothing more difficult to achieve than a

> passionate, sincere, quiet faith. (D, 308)

This reaching out for absolute faith and belief in truth is the basis for the narratives of *Nostalghia* and *The Sacrifice* in particular, but it is a theme in all Andrei Tarkovsky's movies. The films and the protagonists become increasingly desperate and tragic, because it is increasingly difficult to maintain or even search for religious faith in a very secular world, a world in which God has been dead, officially, for a hundred or so years, since Karl Marx, Sigmund Freud, Charles Darwin and Friedrich Nietzsche helped to kill him. Films of what Will Rockett called 'upward transcendence' are rare (23). There are many movies of sideways (social) transcendence, and of downwards transcendence (the descent into horror and the supernatural).

As with the Christian father and theologian, Quintus Septimus Florens Tertullian of Carthage (*c.* 160-220 AD), the Tarkovsky character believes because it is absurd ('I believe because it is absurd [*credo quia impossible*]', said Tertullian of Christ's life). There is no total nihilism, and even the character who burns himself to death (Domenico), in what seems to be a very desperate gesture, is a passionate believer. 'True poetry goes with a sense of religion. An unbeliever cannot be a poet', says Tarkovsky (D, 321). This might be true for Tarkovsky, but plainly it is not true for many unbelievers who were also brilliant poets: William Shakespeare, Arthur Rimbaud, and Thomas Hardy (or perhaps their belief was in different things – but certainly not God in the traditional sense of the term). Thomas Hardy, for example, said he had been looking for God for fifty years and hadn't found him. On the other hand, poets such as Francesco Petrarch, Dante Alighieri, Emily Brontë and John Donne might agree with Tarkovsky.

REBIRTH

> *We should long ago have become angels had we been capable of paying attention to the experience of art, and allowing ourselves to be changed in accordance with the ideals it expresses.*
>
> Andrei Tarkovsky (*Sculpting In Time*, 50)

As with Ingmar Bergman, Robert Bresson and Michelangelo Antonioni, many viewers might say Andrei Tarkovsky's cinema is bleak and pessimistic. In fact, Tarkovsky is very optimistic. 'Artistic creation is by definition a denial of death. Therefore it is optimistic, even if in an ultimate sense the artist is tragic', commented the director (D, 91). Tarkovsky takes his cue from Christianity and Buddhism, which are religions of negation (known as the *via negativa* in mysticism). The greater the denial, the greater the reward. Hence there is in Tarkovsky's sacred cinema an emphasis on the denial of self, ego, personal desire. William James wrote of this self-sacrifice in *The Varieties of Religious Experience*:

> They [Buddhism and Christianity] are essentially religions of deliverance: the man must die to an unreal life before he can be born into the real life. (131)

This is the way of the teachings of Jesus: the 'dying-to-self' before the rebirth. As Jesus said in the *Gospel of St John*: '[v]erily, verily, I say unto you, Except that a grain of wheat fall into the earth and die, it abideth by itself alone; but if it die, it beareth much fruit' (*John*, 12: 24). What Tarkovsky's religious cinema tries to do is to film the agony of this dying-to-self, this making oneself into a seed, ready to be reborn ('[a]n image is a grain, a self-evolving retroactive organism', Tarkovsky wrote in 1974 [D, 91]). On a Marxist/ materialist level, it means identifying with the very basic forces of life – killing and eating. As Joseph Campbell put it: '[l]ife lives by killing and eating itself, casting off death and being reborn, like the moon' (1988, 45). At a deeper level, it means cultivating the sense of self – nurturing it in order to lose it. D.H. Lawrence wrote: '[h]ow one must cherish the frail, precious buds of the unknown life in one's soul' (1934, 375). The whole process is difficult, painful and time-consuming. Tarkovsky's films are long and slow partly because of (depicting) this ontological and spiritual difficulty.

(A few critics have interpreted Andrei Tarkovsky's movies in terms of the 'hero's journey', as Joseph Campbell called it, a myth criticism approach which's very popular in Hollywood screenwriting, and American movie criticism. The heroic or single myth has very familiar elements: the call to adventure, the quest or goal, the journey, the obstacles, the acts of sacrifice and catharsis. Each stage in the hero's journey is easy to apply to Tarkovsky's films – and vague enough to be applied to any part of any of the movies. Tarkovsky's movies, however, differ greatly from contemporary Hollywood cinema's because the journeys are so intensely interiorized. His movies don't have Luke Skywalker battling the Dark Father, or Mad Max or Tom Cruise saving a community from villains).

RELIGIOUS EXPERIENCE

Part of the problem of the religious movie, or the movie that uses religious subject matter, is that religion deals with the unseen, the unknown, with absolutes that don't lend themselves readily to being filmed. The problem in cinema is always how to visualize things, no matter how 'real' or abstract. And it's especially tricky when trying to dramatize an inner life. The traditional feature movie demands drama and conflict. The Hollywood formulaic treatment means, in short, extreme dramatization.[1] Tarkovsky shies away from excessive, expressive approaches, over-determined dramatization and exposition. He relies heavily on the abilities of his actors to communicate his sense of the religious. He also uses many cinematic techniques, ranging from slow motion to special print processing in order to change the texture and colour of the image.

Andrei Tarkovsky's poetic cinema *suggests* the religious – in its performances by actors, its narrative structures, in the juxtaposing of images and sounds. Where Hollywood cinema might resort to dialogue, exposition or voiceover to explain a state of mind, Tarkovsky uses very long takes, or one of his regular motifs (rain, water), or sound. Tarkovsky's sense of the noetic, the divine, is not that of Hollywood cinema, yet he is a psychological director, trading in states of mind (just like any Hollywood movie in fact). 'The Truth is not to be spoken but lived', said Hui-Neng, the 8th century Zen Buddhist master (J. Ferguson, 200). As far as cinema is concerned, Truth, Essence, Spirit (or whatever one calls it), must be lived, portrayed, filmed. It must pass through the many gates and filters of the cinematic process. (If it's amazing that any movie gets made at all, with so many obstacles to overcome, it's even more extraordinary that a *religious* film can survive the process).

Each of Andrei Tarkovsky's protagonists experiences fully their moments of doubt and pain when their faith is called into question. The agony is wholly internal – the diametric opposite of the conventional narrative movie, which always seeks to dramatize experience with external action. Tarkovsky is something of an Existentialist – his religious self-questioning philosophy (some would say self-torture) has similarities with the thought of 20th century theologians such as Nikolai Berdyaev, Paul Tillich, Bernard Lonergan, William Johnston, Karl Barth and others – and also modern philosophers such as William James, Martin Heidegger, Jean-Paul Sartre, Maurice Merleau-Ponty, Edmund Husserl, Claude Lévi-Strauss, Gaston Bachelard and Søren Kierkegaard, and not forgetting Friedrich Nietzsche. (Tarkovsky might not personally feel so many affinities with the postmodern cultural theory philosophers and gurus, such as

Jacques Derrida, Fredric Jameson, Teresa de Lauretis, Homi Bhabha, Jacques Lacan, Michel Foucault, Jean Baudrillard, Hélène Cixous, Paul de Mann and Umberto Eco. Although some of them – Luce Irigaray and Julia Kristeva, for example – have written lucidly of spiritual issues. In fact, although contemporary cultural philosophers appear at first to be ultra cynical, seen-it-all-before, world-weary thinkers, they write a lot about spiritual and religious matters, and regularly employ the language of religion in their gnomic tomes).

For Andrei Tarkovsky, religion begins with the individual, and is founded upon the individual. His movies are (partly) about religious upheavals in individuals. Tarkovsky does discuss wider, societal issues (the world going down the drain in *The Sacrifice,* or the alienation of cities in *Solaris*, or the historical battles and events that formed Russia in *Andrei Roublyov*). But he concentrates on the individual, isolating him/ her from other people and from society. In the late films this is all the spectator sees: the individual alone, stripped of the societies that enculturated them, going through painful Existential transformations. The emphasis in Tarkovsky's philosophy is on personal experience, and the importance of the personal response. The personal is not so much political in Tarkovsky's cinema, but tragic, mystical, desperate. 'In cinema, works of art seek to form a kind of concentration of experience, materialised by the artist in his film' Tarkovsky wrote in *Sculpting In Time* (85).

THE HUMAN AND THE DIVINE

One can't film the divine, so one has to film people who stand at the interface of God and his creation, the natural world. This is where psychoanalysis and anthropology sites its studies – in the human animal. One of the supreme embodiments of the meeting-point of the human and the divine in the West is Christ. Although he filmed Jesus in close-up only once (there was a Calvary scene in *Andrei Roublyov*), Tarkovsky makes many references to him (Hari 'resurrects'; Andrei Roublyov is nearly crucified; and the Writer in *Stalker* dons some twisted twigs as a Crown of Thorns, echoing the *Ecce Homo* image of Christian iconography). Certainly, Tarkovsky was a believer – he invokes God in the *Diaries*, in times of stress. But clearly his faith had been shaken many times – particularly in the early 1980s, when the Americans were talking about a 'limited nuclear war' and global catastrophe seemed very close (explored in *The Sacrifice*).

GOD AND THE BOMB, OR RELIGION AND NUCLEAR WAR

God has retreated from the worlds of Andrei Tarkovsky's movies, or at least it looks that way: so many barren or wintry landscapes, full of broken machines, smashed-up buildings, broken hearts, broken egos, shattered psyches and battered souls. It is global desacralization that Tarkovsky's sacred cinema explores, coming down on the side of mystery and interiorization. And in *The Sacrifice* Tarkovsky used the reality of nuclear war as an equivalent or embodiment of desacralization on a global scale.

Stalker takes place in a post-holocaust (post-nuclear) landscape; *The Sacrifice* occurs just before an air-strike; the Tokyo freeway sequence in *Solaris* is a hell of noise and light. In Tarkovsky's cinema, God is elsewhere, but yearned for (*how could he abandon us?* is the cry of the religionist facing the horrors of the 20th century). In vain Alex kneels and clutches his hands together and recites the Lord's Prayer as the camera bears down upon him (in *The Sacrifice*). (Orson Welles remarked somewhere that there are two things impossible to film: one was prayer, someone praying. The other was sex.) But after the dream has revealed the pain to be internalized, a figment of Alex's tortured psyche, there is no cut to a balming, life-affirming shot of the clouds. (This occurs at the end, with the final shot, of the tree and ocean). God lies under the surface (a ghost, a memory, a trace): in the icons in the book Alex leafs through, or in Leonardo da Vinci's *Adoration of the Magi*, or in the arms of the 'witch' Maria. God doesn't appear in *The Sacrifice*, and the final, longed-for revelation of God doesn't occur. Instead, Tarkovsky's protagonists learn about their frailties, and capabilities. They learn about altruism and responsibilities; and they learn that nothing is certain; that everything is fragile and in flux; and that religious absolutes do not come from God but are elements of human adaption.

THE SUPERNATURAL IN ANDREI TARKOVSKY'S CINEMA

What does appear many times in Andrei Tarkovsky's *œuvre* (instead of – or despite – God) is the supernatural. 'Supernatural' is probably the wrong kind of word, being associated now with the kind of movies Andrei Tarkovsky despised. But the præternatural, the miraculous or mysterious is central to Tarkovsky's sacred cinema. Doors creak open by themselves (*The Sacrifice*); objects roll around and fall to the floor (*Mirror*); or they rattle (*Stalker*); birds flap in alcoves, or burst from statues (*Nostalghia*); a bird lands on a boy's head like a blessing (*Mirror*); a bird breaks a pane of glass (*Mirror*); a lamp keeps going out and relighting itself (*Mirror*); a candle stays miraculously alight (*Nostalghia*).

Andrei Tarkovsky's movies are full of objects behaving in strange ways (as if a poltergeist were at work on the sets, but a poltergeist with a star-fixation, who only moves objects when the camera's rolling). The known, empirical world is not everything: behind it lies a vast unknown: the invisible is everywhere; the known world, it turns out, is not known at all, but is full of mystery. Tarkovsky imbues objects taken for granted with mystery. The world of the inanimate has a life of its own, is as dynamic as the human world. Long after the people are dead in those Russian houses, doors will still be creaking open, and glass bottles will still be mysteriously falling to the floor, though with no one, and no camera, to see them, to give their actions value, to mythicize them.

Andrei Tarkovsky has an elemental view of the world — like John Cowper Powys or Walt Whitman. Fire, rain, wind, rivers — these are the cosmic, powerful elements in Tarkovsky's filmic world. In this sense, Tarkovsky is something of a magician, and his præternatural sympathies recall the mages and alchemists of old, such as John Dee, Elizabeth I's court wizard who communicated with angels, or alchemists Paracelsus, or Cornelius Agrippa, or visionaries such as William Blake or Emmanuel Swedenborg. Like John Dee and Blake, Gorchakov is associated with angels and angelism; and, like Joan of Arc, Gorchakov hears voices, hears God talking to St Catherine.

Andrei Tarkovsky's religious cinema doesn't depict Christ or God, but does reveal a world in which the unknown is not in the next country or the next town but right here, in this building, in this room. The filmic world of Tarkovsky is not so much Christian as pagan and animistic, not full of God and holiness but the paranormal, the unusual, the unexplained and the strange. Tarkovsky loves, like the writer Bruce Chatwin, the miraculous (Chatwin said his life had been one long search for the miraculous). Tarkovsky's unmade movie of St Anthony would have been full of bizarre occurrences. In Tarkovsky's poetic films, a glass of water becomes a strange object, with a magic of its own. Like the motifs of fire and rain, these magical objects are the hallmarks of Tarkovsky's cinematic style. They are devices which enable him to separate his filmic worlds from those of any other movie-maker. The Tarkovskyan magic world exists in its own time and space, far away from Hollywood, but also far away from Beijing, Rome, London, Berlin, Bombay, or any other film capital or industry.

THE MYSTICAL DIMENSION

Intense Christian spirituality haunts Andrei Tarkovsky's movies – in particular *Andrei Roublyov*, *Nostalghia*, *Stalker* and *The Sacrifice*. The imagery of the Russian Orthodox Church recurs in Tarkovsky's films – the candles, icons, fire, crosses, angels and rituals. Elements of the Orthodox Church religion appear in Tarkovsky's sacred cinema: the veneration of icons (with images having divine auras); the lived spiritual life; the Seven Sacraments (Baptism, Conformation, Mass, Confession, Holy Orders, Matrimony and Extreme Unction); celibacy and the monastic way of life; and the belief in the Virgin Mary. There are examples of the Catholic rites of penance, Eucharist, baptism, pilgrimage, sacrifice, resurrection, Crucifixion, purification and apotheosis in Tarkovsky's religious films. These rituals are not always performed in a manner that's obvious or immediately recognizable (such as the snowbound Crucifixion in *Andrei Roublyov*). Domenico hands Gorchakov some bread and wine in *Nostalghia*, a clear reference to the Last Supper and Eucharist. This very obvious piece of symbolism is integrated quite naturally into the movie – the actors carry on discussing things as if no gigantic symbol has just been flashed at the audience (and no doubt it went unremarked by many viewers). Domenico's crucifixion is a much more strident ritual, more essential to the plot of *Nostalghia* than the bread and wine which Gorchakov receives, yet it is also self-conscious and contrived (an audience may be more inclined to interpret Domenico's self-immolation in religious terms because just prior to doing it he has been haranguing onlookers about moral, religious matters).

In *Andrei Roublyov* Andrei Tarkovsky clearly enjoyed recreating those moments in history when important Christian images (Andrei Roublyov's icons) were being made. Here the Christian imagery, of churches, holy men, icons – is required by the subject and the era. In the later films, the Christian images had to be suggested rather than shown directly, in order for Tarkovsky to maintain his realism, his sense of the concrete. *Nostalghia* is full of religious references, yet it remains 'realistic' (although it is a very stylized of realism). The movie begins with a religious ritual: there is a Last Supper, a Crucifixion, a ruined Cathedral, a sermon and a baptism. Yet, as in *The Sacrifice*, the religious allusions are integrated with the realistic aspects of the narrative.

Yet Andrei Tarkovsky also used fantasy and the fantastical throughout his films – as when Alex and Maria levitate while they make love (On depicting love as flying, Tarkovsky told Layla Garrett, that 'love is a miracle – it transcends the gravity of the material world. People in love must levitate' [1997, 23]). But Tarkovsky's fantastical reinterpretations of

Christian ritual didn't go as far as Luis Buñuel – in *Viridiana* (1961, Spain), for instance, Buñuel savagely parodied the Last Supper.

THE LEFT-HAND PATH

Other religious influences in Andrei Tarkovsky's cinema include: Georg Gurdjieff (D, 277), Rudolf Steiner and anthroposophy (D, 344), Zen Buddhism and Taoism (he mentions Lao Tzu and the *Tao Te Ching*, for instance, and *haiku* poets like Matsuo Basho), the humanism of William Shakespeare, Leo Tolstoy, Arthur Schopenhauer and Fyodor Dostoievsky, as well as the idealism of Johann Wolfgang von Goethe and Hermann Hesse. Despite his belief in suffering, Tarkovsky is not a Buddhist: he is an idealist and Romantic, and Taoism connects with this Western stance.

Andrei Tarkovsky was personally interested in Rudolf Steiner, telekinesis, ESP, astrology, and Oriental philosophy (Taoism and Buddhism). Tarkovsky also tried meditation (including Transcendental Meditation). Tarkovsky would refer to numerology – the magic of numbers (his birth date, he said – April 4, 1932 – added up to the number five in numerology). 'That is the key to my soul, the key to my character. It stands for temptation, contradictions and extremes. I'm like Leonardo's Man – crucified in a circle of life', Tarkovsky said.[1] (I don't think Leonardo meant his *Vitruvius Man* to be crucified – but it's typical of Tarkovsky to interpret things like that!).

The magical side of Andrei Tarkovsky, the side that believes in the miraculous, has much in common with Neoplatonic thought (Philo, Prophyhry, Plotinus), with hermeticism and the occult 'theory of correspondences' (the 'theory of correspondences' was taken up by poets such as Charles Baudelaire and Arthur Rimbaud, and European Symbolist artists like Gustave Moreau. It's related to the notion of synæsthesia, where colours have equivalents with sounds, or touches with smells, and so on).

Andrei Tarkovsky thinks in poetic, intuitive ways, and he continually makes poetic connections. His visual motifs – milk, rain, fire, water – work in this way. The connections are of what hermeticism calls the lunar, left-hand, feminine, unconscious kind (the stuff of nighttime, of dreaming, of the unconscious). In no sense could Tarkovsky be termed a mathematical, scientific and mechanical filmmaker. Films are not for him machines (as they are sometimes described by Steven Spielberg, James Cameron or Brian de Palma. However, Tarkovsky had to be very technically proficient in order to control every aspect of production, cinema being an intensely technological medium).

Films for Andrei Tarkovsky are anguished, personal spiritual statements that are torn from the depths of one's being. Art itself can create a spiritual experience in the viewer, equivalent to a religious experience, Tarkovsky maintained; 'Art acts above all on the soul, shaping its spiritual structure' (ST, 41). Tarkovsky's movies are conceived first on the experiential level – as moments and images and feelings. Werner Herzog said: 'I believe the real power of films lies in the fact that they operate with the reality of dreams' (J. Franklin, 113). Like Herzog's, Tarkovsky's cinema is deliberately anti-intellectual and anti-rational. Their logic is of poetry not science ('art does not think logically', like science, Tarkovsky said [ST, 41]). Tarkovsky mistrusts science: for him, the transcendent lies in the mystical sphere of life. Tarkovsky could not see that science can be mystical, but in the New Physics, cosmology or quantum mechanics, with its talk of black holes, event horizons, superstrings, quarks and babyverses, it can be. (Many writers and scientists have discussed the links between religion and science, God and cosmology, among them: Stephen Hawking, Fritjof Capra, Russell Stannard, Carl Sagan and Arthur C. Clarke).

SAINT TARKOVSKY

In the Tarkovskyan film persona there are elements of a range of religious types: the alchemist, the magician, the shaman, the philosopher, the mystic, the martyr and the pilgrim. The Writer in *Stalker*, for instance, laments the passing of magic from the world: the world is all triangles and numbers now, he claims (his speech is an instance of Tarkovsky being rather clumsy and too-obvious in his denigration of science and logic). Yet the Writer too is a pilgrim, filled despite his world-weariness with yearning (he's searching as much as any Tarkovsky protagonist, perhaps for a miracle which will restore his faith – because only a miracle could do that). In the Tarkovskyan character, in the persona of the *auteur* who made the movies, there is something of an alchemist, an arcane searcher for the Philosopher's Stone. In Tarkovsky's magic cinema, the Grail, the goal, the transmutation of base matter into gold or the 'Great Work' of alchemy, is spiritual fulfilment, embodied in a single, beautiful shot. Each film ends in an ecstatic vision or moment which has been striven for throughout the picture (and is sometimes achieved despite the death of the character). Here the Tarkovskyan character is like a mediæval saint or martyr at the end of some pilgrimage across wastelands or through a Dark Night of the

Soul. The Stalker is something of a chivalrous knight, a guardian of the holy of holies, which's the wish-fulfilling Room (a Grail image, a cauldron of plenty).

THE GOSPEL ACCORDING TO SAINT TARKOVSKY: TARKOVSKY AS PROPHET

What some observers are unsure about is Andrei Tarkovsky the Prophet. His movies seem to be teaching something. They interrogate spiritual issues. But what, precisely, is he saying? What is *The Gospel According to Tarkovsky*? He is saying that spiritual feelings should be nurtured • that faith is essential • that the modern secular world destroys spirituality • that humility is important • that the individual must test these things for her/ himself • that there are no leaders to tell people what to do • that spiritual feelings can be experienced anywhere, by anybody • that getting in touch with one's spirituality is the most serious business there is • that the process is long and painful, with no promise of completion.

Andrei Tarkovsky's movies take spiritual doubt and turn it into torment (that's what art does, what drama is). Sometimes the religious journey ends in death (*Nostalghia, Mirror*) or in near death (*Stalker, The Sacrifice, Solaris, Andrei Roublyov*). But Tarkovsky, as a prophet, retains a sense of mystery and ambiguity. He is a poet who wishes to remain a little abstract and ambivalent, rather than a prose-writer who has to be much more literal. What Tarkovsky likes about film is its ability to remain ambiguous and mysterious, while also being immensely didactic, concrete and authoritative. Film communicates powerfully, but in Tarkovsky's sacred cinema it communicates mystery. No explanations, no answers, and often only half-formed questions. (However, Tarkovsky did contribute a book of his thoughts, views, ideas and discoveries: the 'gospel' of Tarkovsky was published as *Sculpting In Time: Reflections On the Cinema* in 1986. The book is Tarkovsky's principle æsthetic statement, outside of his movies (the collected screenplays and the diaries count as secondary sources).)

TEN

Structure and Narration

DIRECTIONS

Andrei Tarkovsky uses many devices of the art cinema tradition, as noted in the introduction: open forms, abstract and formalist approaches to narration and ambiguity. Structurally, Tarkovsky's movies are in some ways classic narratives; they begin, they develop, they end (with more closure of narrative strands than one might expect, though usually with ambiguity intact). His films work within the realm of conventional dramaturgical techniques: from exposition through rising action to climax and closure. There are conflicts, questions, journeys, decisions and problems in Tarkovsky's cinema, as well as simile, metonymy, metaphor, synedoche and much figurative discourse.

BEYOND TRAGEDY

The typical structure of an Andrei Tarkovsky film is to start with dissatisfaction and end with a partial resolution of tension. There is no classic closure in Tarkovsky's movies, because the questions are unanswerable, the problems unsolvable, the attitudes indissoluble. In Tarkovsky's cinema there is no easy way out, and the hard way is nearly impossible to achieve. The gateway is very narrow, and it's closing in. The intensity increases over the course of a movie, but it often loses its sense of direction. There are no happy endings to Tarkovsky's fairy tales, because the problems raised in his films are gigantic. There is no hero, no Grail, no Grail knight, no cowboy, no private detective or police chief great enough to rejuvenate the wasteland, to solve the mystery, to reunite estranged people, or find lost souls. There is no woman to be saved and wed. There is no reward. There is no climatic chase or violence or confrontation. There is no villain. There are few (if any) comic moments. No smiles. No laughter. No consolations.

ENDING IN ECSTASY

And yet the endings of Andrei Tarkovsky's movies are moments of ecstasy – some of the most rapturous finales in all cinema. It's not just the music that makes these endings so powerful, nor the fact that the bored viewer is joyful because the film is nearly over. No, these are genuine ecstasies, that grow out of the material. They are false in some ways: the music helps to boost the rapture. Yet there is something life-affirming about Tarkovsky's movie endings. Tragedies his films are not. The situations of the protagonists are tragic – in their bleak worlds of restlessness and spiritual bankruptcy. Yet the view of the films is life-affirming. The catharsis comes from seeing someone being so close to the edge. The endings are thus transcendent. Not utterly transcendent – there are always ambiguities to grapple with, elements in life that cannot be overcome. Gorchakov's ecstatic placement of Russia in the midst of Italy, for instance, is achieved at a massive cost to his soul (indeed, the ambiguity of the ending of *Nostalghia* has Gorchakov die in the Baths, after carrying the candle, so that his vision of the Russian *dacha* in the Italian Cathedral is achieved only in death, in spirit. Perhaps it's the embodiment of his dying moments?).

With his penchant for desperate figures out of Fyodor Dostoievsky's fiction, and his love of Shakespearean tragedy (he directed *Hamlet* for the theatre), Andrei Tarkovsky might be expected to make pessimistic films, like those of Joseph Losey, Erich von Stroheim, or Luchino Visconti. Stanley Kubrick's cinema could be seen as either nihilistic or realistic (but seldom idealistic). At the end of Kubrick's assault on the Vietnam experience, *Full Metal Jacket* (1987, U.S.A.), Private Joker says 'I'm in a world of shit, but I'm alive and I'm not afraid'.[1] This is the bottom line in Kubrick's cinema: to be alive not dead. Just survival. Similarly, Rainer Werner Fassbinder's bleaker movies (such as *Fox and His Friends* [1974]) or Werner Herzog's dark comedy *Stroszek* (1977), could be seen not as pessimistic but realistic. Tarkovsky is infinitely more positive than modern cinema's pessimists and realists (Fassbinder, Martin Scorsese or Kubrick). Some filmmakers appear to enjoy rubbing the viewers' faces in the dirt.

Words such as 'hope', 'faith' and 'truth' are used without irony by Andrei Tarkovsky. In an Alain Resnais or Rainer Werner Fassbinder movie, these words are used with lashings of irony. Tarkovsky seems to lack the same sense of irony. Tarkovsky, after all, is the artist who wrote in *Sculpting in Time* (his prose testament which enlarges the last will and testament of the films): '[i]n *Stalker* I make some sort of complete statement: namely that human love alone is – miraculously – proof against the assertion that there is no hope for the world' (ST, 199). One could not imagine a similar statement coming from Fassbinder, Roman Polanski, Jean-Luc Godard, Luchino Visconti, Terence Malick or Luis Buñuel. Andrei Tarkovsky is rare among filmmakers in his adherence to such notions as 'love', 'faith', 'truth' and 'hope' (for pessimists and realists, these are at best self-delusions).

CULTURAL STRATEGIES: POLITICS, IDEOLOGY AND CULTURE

Andrei Tarkovsky's movies work in a cultural space veering between abstraction and naturalism, between subjective psychology and objective realism, between spiritual asceticism and utterly indulgent Romanticism, between religion and demystification, between formal simplicity and cinematic complexity, between Communist Russia and the capitalist West, between the cinema of the (Soviet) State and the art cinema of Europe. In Tarkovsky's major cinematic device (the long take) there is a tension between stasis and movement, between dramaturgy and duration, between realism and artificiality. Tarkovsky's sequence shots, like those of any filmmaker, draw attention to themselves as pieces of virtuoso cinema, even as they strive for naturalism and verisimilitude. One kind of cinematic sequence shot is a good example of artifice, technofetishism and acute self-consciousness: the long Steadicam shot. Although Tarkovsky didn't use the Steadicam, it was inevitable that he would have done had he made more films, camera movement being absolutely vital to his cinema (and from his first movie, *Ivan's Childhood*, Tarkovsky had showed that he loved to use all of the technical tools of cinema available, such as extreme wide angle lenses, or big cranes, or very lengthy tracks).

Andrei Tarkovsky's sequences are so long they move beyond the self-conscious stage in which the mechanics of cinema are all too obvious, and shift into another realm, where the point of the shot is made clear. Tarkovsky transforms the temporal element alchemically into something spiritual. All the best religious cinema must use a *gestalt* method, a theory of dialectical montage, in which the religious aspect, x, is more than the sum of its parts. In relativity physics, mass is a form of energy; similarly, in the religious film, transformations from secular film material to sacred thought are possible. A film may *be* a religious experience in itself, as well as *depicting* a religious experience (it's not just sci-fi geeks who consider watching *Star Wars* or *Star Trek* a spiritual experience: many filmmakers speak reverently of the first time they saw *Citizen Kane*, or *Fantasia*, or *Persona*, or *The Seven Samurai*, or a Ray Harryhausen movie).

Andrei Tarkovsky regards his films in this way: he is an alchemist, changing the nature of his subject, just as Hari, who is made up of neutrinos, slips in and out of the quantum realm, and changes herself in *Solaris*. Hari is formed of ripples on the quantum sea; but for Tarkovsky the quantum realm is full of spirituality, not atomic and sub-atomic particles.

Culturally, Andrei Tarkovsky is a Romantic, an inheritor of the Romanticism of Aleksandr Pushkin, Friedrich Hölderlin and Johann Wolfgang von Goethe (and, later, the poetic, dream-haunted *avant garde* Surrealism of André Breton, Jean Cocteau, Joseph Cornell and Luis Buñuel rather than the de Sadean, Freudian aggression of Antonin Artaud, Hans Bellmer and Georges Bataille). Giorgio de Chirico rather than Pablo Picasso; Fyodor Dostoievsky rather than Leo Tolstoy; E.T.A. Hoffmann and the Brothers Grimm rather than Charles Perrault and Hans Christian Andersen. And Russian poets such as Alexander Blok, Mayakovsky, Osip Mandelstam and Anna Akhmatova. (Tarkovsky was dubious about the idea of the *avant garde*, about progress, and about experimentation. There couldn't be any real experimentation in art, Tarkovsky maintained; and the idea that art was 'progressing', getting better all the time, was false (ST, 97). As Tarkovsky put it, 'how can Thomas Mann be said to be better than Shakespeare?' (ibid.).)

Andrei Tarkovsky is a conservative stylist who sometimes resorted to radical formal innovations. He is as anti-rational as an anti-scientific artist can get. He is an artist of the right hemisphere of the brain in the terms of split-brain psychology. Intuition, not rationality; imagination, not reality; sacred, not secular. In Lacanian terms, Tarkovsky goes for the Imaginary realm, not the Symbolic realm, with its psychic unity found in the mirror phase. A cinema of the Kristevan semiotic *chora* by way of the dream realm of the Freudian unconscious. Cinema as dreamwork (post-Freudian psychotherapy). A cinema that eschews the œdipal authority of the Symbolic realm (the Law of the Father), but can never outface it, of course. The suture in Tarkovsky's religious cinema is to reconcile the private, inner dream world and the outer, social world. The movies operate at this interface. Tarkovsky holds a mirror up to himself, but the mirror reflects back a personality not pure but severely modified by the demands of enculturation, identity, ambition and œdipal tensions.

Politically, Andrei Tarkovsky's cinema is as bourgeois as they come, as seen from a Marxist, materialist ideological perspective. Tarkovsky's films are full of religion (opium), moneyed aristocratic down-and-outs who live in dilapidated splendour (a house next to the sea or a romanticized *dacha* in the woods), stylized poverty and sumptuously filmed settings (it looks like poverty, but it isn't, really. A socialist realist documentary on poor folk living in slums a Tarkovsky film ain't).

The rationale of Andrei Tarkovsky's cinema is 'fiction = mystification = bourgeois ideology' (P. Wollen, 89). On one level, Tarkovsky's cinema is all mystification and mythicization. Through Tarkovsky's powerful poetic abilities, everything in his movies is romanticized and spiritualized. Nothing is radical; Tarkovsky's politics are conservative and reactionary. Societal change will only occur in Tarkovsky's cinematic world if there is a *spiritual* transformation in the individual. This is a stance Marxists and Maoists find laughable. Tarkovsky's films were criticized by Goskino and Soviet film establishment as being too personal, too religious, and not nationalistic, communist or Russian enough. There was no looking East for Tarkovsky, no looking towards China, Maoism and Communism, as there was with many of Western Europe's intellectual movie-makers in the late 1960s and early 1970s (for example, Jean-Luc Godard, Michelangelo Antonioni and Bernardo Bertolucci). This move to China and the Red East also occurred with the Parisian intellectuals, such as those in the *Tel Quel* group (Julia Kristeva, Roland Barthes, Philippe Sollers, François Wahl, Marcelin Pleynet and others). Meanwhile, at the same time, the West (America) went to war with the Orient.

NARRATIVE DEVICES IN ANDREI TARKOVSKY'S CINEMA

Andrei Tarkovsky employed different kinds of narrative forms within in his movies. The dream sequences are the most obvious instances, but there are also home movies (in *Mirror*, for example), flashbacks, memories *and* imagined memories (in *Nostalghia*), TV reports (*Solaris*), TV broadcasts (*The Sacrifice*), newsreels, pseudo-documentaries (the hypnotism scene in *Mirror*) and documentary footage.

Consider some of the formal elements in Andrei Tarkovsky's cinema: of the many *looks* found in cinema there are few looks of relationship in Tarkovsky's art, of characters looking at each other. Instead, they look down, wearily, or look away from each other (consider the way Tarkovsky blocks a typical two-hander dialogue scene: the actors are standing at right angles, or with their backs to each other. The central dialogue scene between Domenico and Gorchakov in *Nostalghia*, for instance, has the religious proselytizer wandering around the room discoursing while Gorchakov listens). Further, the *network of looks* in conventional editing (shot/ reverse shot) is negated by the sequence shot technique (for instance, the editors Ludmila Feganova, G. Natanson, Olga Shevkunenko, Tatyana Yegorychyova, Erminia Marani, Nina Marcus, Amedeo Salfa, and Michal Leszcylowski seldom choose to cut reaction shots into his sequence shots). *Cause-and-effect linearity* is also negated, or used infrequently. The trajectory of the Tarkovsky movie is one long digression bound only loosely by œdipal, æsthetic, spiritual, emotional, nostalgic and artistic constraints. *Spatial and temporal verisimilitude* is generally affirmed, but there are times when Tarkovsky deliberately subverts this. For instance, he uses Brechtian *distancing devices* occasionally – a character will look into the camera (like Maria when she kills the cockerel in *Mirror*). In cinema this is regarded as a modernist technique, breaking the fourth wall, though it is ancient in the theatre. Many times in a Tarkovsky film *dramaturgy* is subverted in favour of poetic realism: *continuity* and *sequentiality* are often discarded in favour of a dramaturgy of dream that moves into spontaneity and intuition.

Andrei Tarkovsky does employ *foreshadowing* (for example, in *Nostalghia*, Domenico gives a candle to Gorchakov and he uses it at the end of the movie). *Visual rhymes* and *puns* are another favourite device.

Classical or *continuity editing* is generally deployed, but again editors Ludmila Feganova, G. Natanson, Erminia Marani, Nina Marcus, Amedeo Salfa and Michal Leszcylowski often subvert it in favour of poetic logic. As noted above, *poetic* or *symbolic montage* is Tarkovsky's main method of cutting. He rarely uses *rapid cutting* (only at moments of crisis, and then rarely). *Cross-cutting* is rare too, as is *parallel action*. A Hollywood editor would have definitely cut the two fire rituals climaxing *Nostalghia* together, in an attempt at maximum drama. Tarkovsky merely places one scene after the other (notice how he delays the reaction shots of Gorchakov's candle-carrying right to the end of the shot: nothing must disturb the intensity and suspense of that nine-minute take. During Domenico's fire sermon, however, Tarkovsky makes good use of the many extras hired for the day, with elaborate tracking/ reaction shots).

Andrei Tarkovsky's *découpage* pivots around poetry. Yet Tarkovsky is conservative with his editing techniques, compared to some *avant garde* filmmakers: he does not use *Hollywood montage*, which is ideal, really, for his kind of poetic cinema (he might have been tempted to if he had lived into the age of digital editing on computers, where optical effects and speed ramping are easy to achieve, and don't require optical printers or expensive laboratory processing). Tarkovsky rarely employs *fades* (to white or black). *Jump cuts* are used, but not nearly as much as one might expect from a dream-bound *ciné*-poet (and not as much as in Tarkovsky's New Wave contemporaries, such as Jean-Luc Godard, François Truffaut and Wim Wenders). Tarkovsky does employ extensive *montage sequences*, though, most obviously in his dreams, memories and flashbacks. Here his editing style is distinctly modernist and New Wave.

But Andrei Tarkovsky & co. do use many *dream devices*: *flashbacks, connecting motifs, refrains, memories, flashforwards* (the end of *Nostalghia* is a kind of flashforward, of an imagined future), and hundreds of *hypersituated objects* (highly foregrounded objects, such as the bottles of milk, books, candles and the fires). *Visual rhymes* are a form of *refrain*. Tarkovsky happily quotes from his own films, just like Jean-Luc Godard or Steven Spielberg. He uses *intermediate spaces,* actionless spaces between scenes. He loves elaborate *tracking shots* (some are *extremely* complex). He always prefers to have the camera on a track or dolly and seldom employs *handheld camera*. He's very fond of extravagant crane and boom shots, like Sergei Paradjanov or Vincente Minnelli (it's very fitting that the final shot of his final movie should be an elegant crane upwards, echoing the opening shots of his first film, *Ivan's Childhood*). Sometimes Tarkovsky uses radical camera movements, such as *360° pans* (early on in *Andrei Roublyov*, for example, there are two very slow three-sixty pans around the interior of the hut where the monks listen to the jester).

Andrei Tarkovsky never wastes an opportunity to move the camera: if there's time (and money) to rehearse and shoot a complex camera move, he'll do it. One of the great pleasures of Tarkovsky's cinema is the way he moves the camera (it's the same with Orson Welles, Theo Angelopoulos or Bernardo Bertolucci). But while even great movie directors sometimes seem to be moving the camera for the sake of it (Martin Scorsese, Peter Greenaway, Terry Gilliam), there's never that sense in Tarkovsky's films. Favourite Tarkovsky camera moves include: craning down with an actor as they bend down to the ground; craning up trees; and very long tracking shots – the longer the better (through woods, over fields, over water). Sven Nykvist remarked that Tarkovsky seemed to be one of those movie directors who had been trained at film school to move the camera where possible (Nykvist had also worked with Roman Polanski and Stanislav Barabas, who also liked to move the camera good deal).

Andrei Tarkovsky's *camera angles* can be as clever, self-conscious and showy as a film student going out with a camera for the first time (or a bored, jaded pop promo director trying to spice up another dreary pop act). Tarkovsky never lost his liking for unusual camera angles: they're everywhere in his movies as well as his early films. Tarkovsky often favours a camera angle slightly above an actor's head, and very often his camera is tilted down at an actor lying on the ground (in *Stalker,* for instance).

Dreams are sometimes indicated by treated *colouration,* or black-and-white or sepia-and-white, but just as often by no obvious signs. Andrei Tarkovsky enjoys manipulating a variety of filmic codes in order to achieve his results. *Exposition* is dropped in Tarkovsky's cinema in favour of long and slow visual effects which sometimes relate only tenuously to a character's situation or psychology. The horse at the beginning of *Solaris,* for example, does not fit in with the exposition. Unless perhaps it shows that other-worldliness and beauty can be found right here on Earth as well as in space. One doesn't have to travel thousands of miles to distant planets to find authentic strangeness and beauty (beauty and the beautiful was very important for Tarkovsky). The horse perhaps embodies Earth's natural wonder (and it's also, of course, Tarkovsky quoting himself: the slo-mo horse at the end of *Andrei Roublyov*).

Sometimes, Andrei Tarkovsky's exposition is *very* clumsy: Alex in the first scene of *The Sacrifice* rattles off pages and pages of exposition during that lengthy tracking shot over the grass, and quite a bit of it is unnecessary, and could've been woven into the movie in a more imaginative manner. Many movie producers might've been tempted to advise her/ his director to consider cutting it, but perhaps one doesn't do that with Tarkovsky. (Tarkovsky's clearly not that interested in it anyway, and seems to be trying to get it out of the way).

Point-of-view in an Andrei Tarkovsky flick is generally very *subjective*, bound up with notions of individual psychology, with a religious search, with spiritual matters. Total *objectivity* (social or ideological) is not found in Tarkovsky's cinema. Nor does he use, like, say, Michelangelo Antonioni, a cool, dispassionate point-of-view; No; like Federico Fellini and Werner Herzog, Tarkovsky is bound up completely in his creation, and the point-of-view in his movies reflects that degree of involvement (Freudians would call it 'emotional investment').

Andrei Tarkovsky's *narrative style* owes something to the stream-of-consciousness method (of the literature of James Joyce, Virginia Woolf, D.H. Lawrence and John Cowper Powys, among British novelists). *Mirror,* especially, is a sequence of thoughts, dreams, memories, newsreel and symbols. The movie was so open in form Tarkovsky admitted it was edited in twenty different ways (and no doubt, if Tarkovsky had lived on into the age of DVDs and director's cuts, he might have returned to editing the film: *Mirror* isn't 'finished', as no work of art is really 'finished'. Films, especially, can be reworked on so many levels in so many ways – months and months can go by. Some filmmakers, like Orson Welles, Stanley Kubrick or Francis Coppola, were famous for editing their films up to – and beyond – the release date). What, ultimately, fused these disparate forms of *Mirror* together was probably Tarkovsky's personal vision, his emotional commitment (and the skill and patience of editor Lyudmilla Feiginova and her assistants). The deeply psychological and poetic nature of Tarkovsky's movies nevertheless means that they are very anti-psychoanalytical, non-deterministic, anti-reductionist and anti-secular in their worldview. Instead, a post-Orthodox Christian pantheism is advocated, an affirmation of the God Within, and an inkling of the emergence of a Goddess Within.

ELEVEN

Childhood, Family and Character

AFFIRMATION OF THE FAMILY

Each of Andrei Tarkovsky's last five movies ends on a note of affirmation of the family, of child-parent relations, of childhood, of the maternal realm, and of familial, emotional bonds. The past in Tarkovsky's cinema is feminized, presided over by powerful matriarchal figures: the mother, grandmother, wife and Spanish lady in *Mirror*; the spouse and changeling daughter in *Stalker*; the wife and mother in *Solaris*; the wife, daughter, maid and witch in *The Sacrifice*; and the powerful Madonnas and matriarchs who surround Gorchakov and his dreams of the Russian motherland in *Nostalghia*. In *Mirror* the familial affirmation is of the classic (archaic) matriarchal trinity: daughter, mother and grandmother (made even more personal by the director's mother, Larissa Tarkovskaya, playing the grandmother, and the same actress, Margarita Terekhova, playing the wife and mother in the different time periods); the endings of *Solaris* and *The Sacrifice* offer an image of patriarchy spanning the generations, as father and son embrace. At the end of *Stalker*, as in *Offret*, the child turns magical and performs a psychic/ spiritual act or ritual. At the end of *Nostalghia* the protagonist is all alone with the family dog, but the homeland is miraculously re-affirmed, with Russia in Italy, the snow and, above all, the female ululations on the soundtracks. (Significantly, none of the Russian women are standing in this 'Russian' landscape, as they have every time this dream, memory or fantasy has been shown throughout the movie).

THE MYSTERY OF CHILDHOOD

In movies such as *Ivan's Childhood, Solaris* and *Mirror*, Andrei Tarkovsky explored the world of childhood and remembered childhood, always filtered through memory, desire and regret, and never presented without mnemonic filmic devices. Tarkovsky used his films, like many artists, to investigate his own childhood and emergent psychology, to exorcize ghosts and re-experience pains: '[i]f you are serious about your work, then a film is not merely the next item in your career, it is an action which will affect your whole life' (ST, 133). Art was a serious business for Tarkovsky. Like the painters Mark Rothko or Max Beckmann, Tarkovsky took his work very seriously.

Andrei Tarkovsky measured his experience of childhood against that of other artists, and against commonly-held beliefs. In *Mirror* he goes back to feel again the ambiguity and pain the absent father caused (Ingmar Bergman and Steven Spielberg revisited their troubled childhoods in films like *E.T.* and *Fanny and Alexander*). Tarkovsky's films act like fairy tales – mechanisms in which the unconscious is uncensored, and anguish can be powerfully expressed (a 'what if?' scenario which's allowed to run unfettered). *Mirror* works as exorcism; but it is also about the birth of the artist, and the experiences that shape the artist's life.

Andrei Tarkovsky shows childhood to be something essentially mysterious. The kids in *Mirror* are simply there, out in the garden, or pouring salt onto the cat's head, or running, or watching a fire. There is doing, but being takes precedence. In the Tarkovskyan childhood, everything is strange, but not necessarily threatening. There is none of that occasionally sinister and unsettling treatment of children found in American movies, where children are often either sentimentalized in a cloying, gooey manner, or they are soon to be witnesses of meaningless violence.

In Andrei Tarkovsky's cinema, children are closer to the magical, præternatural world than adults: the boy Aleksei in *Mirror* has premonitions; the bell-caster Boriska in *Andrei Roublyov* has magic gifts; in *Nostalghia* the boy asks terrifying questions in all seriousness ('is it the end of the world, papa?'); in *The Sacrifice* the boy Little Man sleeps in a mysterious twilit bedroom, builds houses with witches, lies like Buddha under a bo tree, and utters the divine words of Creation ('in the beginning was the Word'). Significantly, all the important children, from Ivan to Little Man, are boys (except for the daughter in *Stalker*.)

Andrei Tarkovsky's cinematic depiction of childhood has affinities with that of Federico Fellini: the bed, the furniture, the house and its environs are seen as magical spaces, where the individual was first formed, where her/ his first encounters with a larger world took place. In movies by both Federico Fellini and Tarkovsky sheets and drapes billow mysteriously in the wind; the house is presided over by a Madonna; words are not spoken, nor remembered – childhood is experienced primarily, sensually, physically, viscerally, and before language.

Children in Andrei Tarkovsky's *œuvre* are solemn beings, lonely creatures, often estranged from their parents (think of Little Man, or Ivan, for instance). Like many people, Tarkovsky said he had problematic relations with his parents (he described his relations as 'tortured, complicated, unspoken'). 'It's patently clear that I have a complex about my parents' (D, 19).

RELATIONSHIPS

> [*Solaris*] ends with what is most precious for a person, and at the same time the simplest thing of all, and the most available to everybody: ordinary human relationships, which are the starting-point of man's endless journey.
>
> Andrei Tarkovsky (*Diaries*, 364)

The relationships valorized in Andrei Tarkovsky's poetic cinema include those of children and parents, initiate and guru, follower and leader, husband and wife. The endings of many of the movies shows the strength of the child-parent relation: fathers and children (*Stalker, The Sacrifice, Solaris*) or mothers and children (*Mirror, Nostalghia*). The children themselves are strange: they are not regular kids: the fiercely independent orphan in *Ivan's Childhood*, a wartime spy in his tweens, mature beyond his years; the blonde boy in *Nostalghia*, unsettlingly angelic; the mute, injured Little Man in *Offret*; the silent changeling girl in *Stalker*.

The husband-wife or lover relation is rarely seen in the same depth as the child-parent relation (and there are no significant homosexual or gay relationship in Andrei Tarkovsky's cinema). The couples in *Mirror* and *Stalker* argue bitterly. In *Andrei Roublyov* there is the unconscious sexuality in the relation between the chaste monk-like painter and the mute woman. Between Alex and his wife Adelaide in *The Sacrifice* there is hardly any loving contact. In *Solaris*, a man succumbs to loving an artificial woman composed of neutrinos millions of miles from Earth.

Sexual relations between men and women are fraught with difficulties, as in the fiction of Thomas Hardy or Leo Tolstoy. Ambiguity, paranoia, self-doubt and fear reign; ambivalence is the hallmark of the Tarkovskyan human sexual relationship. There is no explicit sexuality, nothing more liberal than a kiss; Tarkovsky's movies have the restraint (some call it prudishness) of Japanese cinema (Kenji Mizoguchi, Hayao Miyazaki and Yasujiro Ozu, but not *animé* like *The Legend of the Overfiend*).

So, no nudity (except in the pagan festival in *Andrei Roublyov*, and one or two other moments).[1] Unwilling or unable to depict explicit sexual encounters, for critics like G. Petrie and V. Johnson, Andrei Tarkovsky transferred sexuality to the sensual depictions of the natural world (the swaying weeds in the streams in *Nostalghia* and *Solaris*, for instance, or the Stalker lying back in the grass in the Zone [JP, 249]).

The kiss in *Andrei Roublyov* is a unique instance of a profound erotic gesture: after it the painter and the woman are bound up together. Tarkovsky employs the kiss in the manner of Production Code era Hollywood cinema, as a synecdoche to stand in for sex. He doesn't need to show Roublyov and the woman having sex, because it's clearly signposted in a number of other places too (such as the shot of Roublyov running away to join the revellers, or Roublyov appearing shamefaced to his assistants the following morning, or the way he pointedly averts his eyes as the naked woman swims past his boat).

CHARACTER TYPES, ARCHETYPES, STEREOTYPES

The central Tarkovskyan character is the white, middle-aged, Western male: cynical but also innocent; world-weary but also hopelessly idealistic; highly educated but not very wise; sceptical but also religious; an exile from his culture who nevertheless cannot escape his culture (and an exile who can never go 'home'); a drifter; painfully sensitive; a man at a crisis point (not always a mid-life crisis, but with many of the same symptoms); a fallen angel, someone who was once successful but is now in decline.

He is, of course, the classic outsider, the stranger, the loner: solitary, melancholy, a wanderer and nomad. It's a figure found in much of modern literature. In, for example, J.-K. Huymans' Des Esseintes, D.H. Lawrence's Paul Morel, Albert Camus, Jean-Paul Sartre, Franz Kafka, Knut Hamsun, André Gide's Edouard and Lawrence Durrell's Darley. A masculinist, modernist creation fashioned to express the Existential alienation and emasculation experienced by modern men. Often frail, with tragic personalities, Andrei Tarkovsky's men have drifted out of Fyodor Dostievsky's underground novels. Tarkovsky's men would be at home in the fictional worlds of Franz Kafka's Prague, Andrei Gide's Paris or Fyodor Dostoievsky's Moscow.

Andrei Tarkovsky's main characters (apart from all being male, except for Maria/ Natalia in *Mirror*), are not action men or heroes in the conventional sense. They are artists (Roublyov), scientists (Kelvin, the Scientist, Domenico), actors and critics (Alexander), and writers (Gorchakov, the Writer). They're usually highly intellectual, and cite William Shakespeare, Aleksandr Pushkin or Fyodor Dostoievsky at the drop of a hat. Tarkovsky said his characters were weak, not tough heroes, but out of their weakness came strength; it was the conflict that was strong, not the characters: 'the central characters are almost always weak persons whose strength is born out of their weakness, out of the fact that they just do not fit in, and are at odds with their surroundings'.

The women in Andrei Tarkovsky's cinema, meanwhile, take on stereotypical dimensions. There are virgins (Martha in *The Sacrifice*, the red-haired girlfriend in *Mirror*), whores (the witch in *The Sacrifice*, the pagan woman Marfa in *Andrei Roublyov*), crones (the grandmother in *Mirror*), maids and helpers (the aunt in *Mirror*, the maid in *The Sacrifice*), and 'modern', liberal women (Eugenia, Hari, Natalia and others).

Generally, women in the cinema of Andrei Tarkovsky are assigned patriarchically-defined roles – mothers, wives, lovers and grandmothers. They are often seen in a bad light: as seducers, who can easily tease men into submission. The pagan woman, Eugenia, Hari, Natalia, Maria and Martha each play this role. They are often hysterical, or insane, or difficult: there are a high number of hysterical scenes in Tarkovsky's cinema.[1] There are women as mothers, reassuring and bathing their fretful, fearful male charges. And, with their long, Pre-Raphaelite hair, veils, shawls and long dresses, there are the archetypal 'evil woman', the *femme fatale*, the Medusa or Black Venus type,[2] as found in much of Western culture, from Petronius through Dante Alighieri and William Shakespeare to Charles Baudelaire and Gabriel d'Annunzio, to Raymond Chandler, *film noir* and neo-noir films.

(An actress having her hair up or down is a simple but recurring indicator of her personality or intent in Andrei Tarkovsky's cinema. In *Mirror*, for instance, Maria as the mother has her hair up; but when her husband visits her, in the raining room scene, her hair is down. And her modern-day counterpart, Natalia, plays with her hair a lot, as does Eugenia in *Nostalghia*. The Italian translator has the most obviously eroticized hairstyle in Tarkovsky's movies, in contrast to Gorchakov's Russian wife, whose hair is tied in a demure bun. But Eugenia lets her long, curly hair down at every opportunity. Tarkovsky's fetishism for long hair – preferably wet as well – is immediately apparent).[3]

Often, Andrei Tarkovsky's women have magical powers – the mute woman in *Roublyov*, Maria the witch, *Solaris*'s Hari, the grandmother in *Mirror* and the Stalker's daughter all have special abilities. The mythology, politics and ontology of women dominates European art cinema (certainly Jean-Luc Godard, François Truffaut, Carl Theodor Dreyer, Ingmar Bergman and Akira Kurosawa all evoked women reverently, as well as negatively).

In Andrei Tarkovsky's cinema, women are exalted, exaggerated, denigrated and pigeon-holed. He limits their personalities, their potential, their sphere of action. The men always have a larger world of agency and thought, as in most other arts. The mother in *Mirror* is magnified as an Earth Goddess, a Mother-of-All. She is a working, single parent. Beyond this, her sphere of influence is limited. Although she works, and is seen at work, her chief characteristic is to 'be'. *Mirror*'s modern day wife Natalia is a powerful and independent woman, who keeps the child, despite the narrator's complaints (the narrator in *Mirror*, Aleksei, may be Tarkovsky's most self-critical and honest portrait of a modern, 'feminized' man; but he may also be Tarkovsky's unapologetic criticism of men who were brought up – like himself – mainly by women). Like Eugenia, Natalia can move beyond the man. The narrator, meanwhile, is never seen (except part of his body), but he controls the narration, the action, the whole plot of the movie. The movie pivots around the mother/ wife's personality, but it is the narrator's drive that sets the movie in motion, and shapes its course (the movie is his dream, his memory, his life).

ACTORS

Like many theatre directors and some film directors, Andrei Tarkovsky had a group of performers that he used again and again. Anatoly Solonitsyn was his favourite: Solonitsyn's function is similar to Jean-Pierre Leaud's in François Truffaut's films (why are Truffaut and Léaud always trotted out as a classic example of a director and star collaboration? For my money, Jean-Luc Godard and Léaud were far more interesting – consider the marvellous *Masculin-Féminin* for instance).

Andrei Tarkovsky liked actors who looked tortured and haunted. His favourite face seems to be something that looks like Vincent van Gogh – thin, pinched, bony, haggard, but also noble, aristocratic, cultured. (He calls attention to Oleg Yankovsky's resemblance to van Gogh in

Nostalghia). Aleksandr Kaidanovsky (the lead in *Stalker*) has a bony face made even more distinctive because of the shaven head. Erland Josephson brings a maturity to the tragic, tortured Tarkovskyan face – and adds the Ingmar Bergman dimension.

Andrei Tarkovsky has a knack of choosing intriguing faces: Nikolai Burlyaev (Ivan), Gudrun Gísladóttir (the witch), and Yuri Nikulin (the Cathedral Treasurer in *Andrei Roublyov*). *Andrei Roublyov* is a panoply of interesting faces (faces out of Hieronymous Bosch or Hans Memling) and different acting styles. (But the undoubted champion of art film *auteurs* who had an uncanny eye for extras and actors is Pier Paolo Pasolini. His movies probably have the most extraordinary faces in world cinema of the 1960s and 1970s or any era of cinema).

Andrei Tarkovsky hated vulgar gestures, actors who pander to audiences, and cerebral, analytical actors who have to dissect their roles (ST, 145). He had problems with Donatas Banionis who played Kelvin, because Banionis kept trying to analyze his character (ib., 145). And it shows: *Solaris* is a weaker movie because of Banionis's mannered performance (or because of the disagreements between the director and the actor). Tarkovsky prefers psychological truth (ib., 155). Authenticity is essential – an intuitive, emotional realism: '[i]n front of the camera the actor has to exist authentically and immediately, in the state defined by the dramatic circumstances' (ib., 139).

Andrei Tarkovsky is not as good with actors as, say, Orson Welles or Jean Renoir (i.e., he hasn't got the reputation of being an 'actor's director'), but he does get some good performances from his cast. Best of all is Margarita Terekhova, who is exceptional in *Mirror* (though Erland Josephson in *The Sacrifice*, Aleksandr Kaidanovsky in *Stalker,* and Nikolai Burlyaev in *Ivan's Childhood* and *Andrei Roublyov* are also marvellous). Tarkovsky wasn't known for holding extensive rehearsal periods prior to shooting like, say, Francis Coppola (Coppola's technique of read-throughs with the whole cast, then video taping rehearsals and editing them as an animatic or 'electronic storyboard' was not Tarkovsky's method. A lot more of the rehearsal time on a Tarkovsky picture was for technical stuff). Tarkovsky tended to give actors only a little direction, like Woody Allen or George Lucas, preferring to cast the right people and hope that they would deliver the goods (although, if an actor was having difficulties, Tarkovsky would patiently advise them).

The directorial approach Andrei Tarkovsky took with actors wasn't the theatrical tradition of discussing every fine point of a character's personality, motivation or actions (which some actors found frustrating). Actors found that Tarkovsky was reluctant to explain in detail about their character. He tended to think in images, Donatas Banionis remarked (Banionis complained that at times Tarkovsky was only interested in how an actor looked physically). Tarkovsky told actor Alexander Kaidanovsky on the set of *Stalker* that he didn't need 'your psychology, your expressiveness... The actor is part of the composition, like the tree, like water' (JP, 45). Tarkovsky didn't like his actors to act knowing everything about their characters, or about the whole narrative. Sometimes he would deliberately withhold information about the plot (ST, 140). In a 1966 interview, Tarkovsky said he preferred not to tell actors about motivations or functions within a scene, but what s/he has to respond to, what her psychological or emotional state should be (D, 358).

Instead of giving actors specific and helpful suggestions on how to play a scene, Andrei Tarkovsky often preferred to muse on the philosophical aspects of the film. Actors have recalled that Tarkovsky was difficult on set, and something of a tyrant. Working for him could be physically and mentally exhausting. Tarkovsky didn't employ stand-ins for actors, so each actor had to perform the actions for real each time. Tarkovsky would goof around sometimes, but generally the atmosphere on set was fairly serious, about getting the work done.

Actors often do well in an Andrei Tarkovsky movie for the simple reason that the films are so good (a good movie makes everyone look good). Although he may not be one of the celebrated directors of actors like Elia Kazan or Robert Altman, Tarkovsky does have the knack of creating a space where great acting can occur, if the performer is up to the challenge. For instance, Tarkovsky employs plenty of long takes, which (most) actors love: it gives them room to explore a character. Also, Tarkovsky's lead roles are truly leading roles: the characters are in most every scene, and have ample opportunities for serious acting.

Andrei Tarkovsky asked his actors to suggest inner turmoil but without resorting to over-the-top performances. The most difficult task for a Tarkovsky actor was to portray spiritual crises with minimal means. Tarkovsky asked his actors to carry much of the weight of the spiritual exploration in his movies. The camera, the music, the sound fx, the lighting, the costumes, the dialogue and all the rest of it were doing their bit, but the actor was the focus of the viewer's attention.

TWELVE

Love, Gender and Sexuality

In the end everything can be reduced to the one simple element which is all a person can count upon in his existence: the capacity to love. That element can grow within the soul to become the supreme factor which determines the meaning of a person's life. My function is to make whoever sees my films aware of his need to love and to give his love, and aware that beauty is summoning him.

Andrei Tarkovsky (ST, 200)

Judging by what Andrei Tarkovsky says, love seems to be at the heart of his philosophy. He wrote that 'human love alone is – miraculously – proof against the blunt assertion that there is no hope for the world' (ST, 199). Here Tarkovsky echoes the mythos of the Western world from early Christianity to 1960s counter-culture: the belief that love is a transformative power in society, political as well as sexual or familial, that 'all you need is love'. Tarkovsky is a romantic idealist, and his sentiments chime with those of artists such as Novalis, Johann Wolfgang von Goethe and Emily Brontë. Yet there are few images of romantic love or expressions of grown-up sexuality in his movies. (And Tarkovsky doesn't go anywhere near the wilder sides of sexuality, such as the pornography, S/M, transsexuality and eroticism in the fiction of Georges Bataille, William Burroughs, Marquis de Sade, Jean de Berg or Pauline Réage, or their equivalents in modern cinema: Walerian Borowczyk, Ken Russell and Pier Paolo Pasolini). No lesbian, gay or homosexual relationships, either, in Tarkovsky's films.

The most erotic moment in Andrei Tarkovsky's work is probably when the naked Marfa (the pagan woman) kisses Andrei Roublyov on the mouth (there's a biographical aspect to this scene: the nude woman is Tarkovsky's wife, and she's embracing his lead actor, and an actor who was an alter ego on screen for Tarkovsky). Roublyov is tied to a post – his situation deliberately echoes Christ on the Cross (and just so's the viewer doesn't forget, it's mentioned in the dialogue by his captors – narrative signposting as obvious as a Hollywood popcorn movie). The scene has many religious precedents. In the *Song of Songs* in the *Bible* (one of the most erotic religious texts in the Western tradition), there is the line 'let him kiss me with the kisses of his mouth'. Another precedent is Mary Magdalene tending the wounded Christ after he's been taken down from the cross. Tarkovsky echoes this in *The Sacrifice*, when Maria washes Alex's hands; and that scene is itself a re-run of the one in *Solaris*, when Kelvin's mother bathes him. In Renaissance painting, Sandro Botticelli produced two tender *Pietà* paintings, with the Magdalene clasping the dead Christ's feet. And in 20th century art, Eric Gill produced a woodcut, *Nuptials of God* (1922, University of Texas), which exactly prefigures Tarkovsky's image: a naked, long-haired Mary Magdalene kissing the crucified Christ. The set-up – men teased and tempted by naked women – also recalls many Christian saints and martyrs, in particular St Anthony (about whom Tarkovsky planned a movie, with assistance from the Pope, no less [D, 345]). The long-haired, sexually predatory woman – this is one of the archetypal Tarkovskyan women – whether it's Maria in *Offret*, Natalia in *Zerkalo*, Hari in *Solaris* or Eugenia in *Nostalghia*.

The sexual act in Andrei Tarkovsky's cinema is portrayed by flying or floating. When Alex sleeps with the witch Maria in *Offret*, she strips her clothes off and caresses him like a mother tending a child. They rise off the bed, spinning slowly. The lights dim gradually and the room becomes a womb. It's more like a regression to early childhood than sex between adults, more like a mother comforting a son (look at – or listen to – the way Alex behaves in this scene). The sex act is elevated from the realm of realism to the mythic, transcendent realm. (The links between flying and erection, intercourse and orgasm were pointed out by Sigmund Freud, among others. What's great about Tarkovsky's cinema is that he can take something as obvious as flying = sex and make it work. It could so easily backfire, and come across as a crude joke).

The floating scene in *Mirror* is more explicit. The father turns to the woman floating above the bed and strokes her hand. It is one of the few obvious gestures of affection in Andrei Tarkovsky's œuvre. The woman says 'it's as though I'm floating in the air.' She looks dreamy, or post-orgasmic, lying on her side, her body twisted, her hair floating behind her.

The scene is made clearly erotic by the moment that precedes it: Maria has just killed a cockerel. She stares into the camera and smiles wickedly, evilly, triumphantly. Her face is lit starkly from below, accentuating the sockets of her eyes, recalling the manic stares of Stanley Kubrick's alter-egos. This is how Maria looks at the viewer in *Mirror* after her act of violence. The wall behind her drips with water, recalling the hair-washing scene earlier, depicting the child's confused view of the sexual relations between his mother and father. Maria is transfigured – into a wraith. If ever the look of a castrating phallic mother or Medusa was portrayed in cinema, this is it. The sense of this complex montage is ambiguous. Certainly it's about violence, sex, blood, illness and heightened states of perception. The taunting look of Maria just after she's killed the cockerel suggests she's just killed her husband, or his sexuality, or his potency, or his identity, or her memory of it all. She kills the cockerel and it is an act of supremacy. The symbolism of the cockerel is, traditionally, solar, fertile, masculine and phallic.

Decapitation and castration are symbolically and mythopœically equivalent. The poetic implications of this scene are thus clear. Here the woman is mythicized as a monstrous other, the castrating Goddess, the *vagina denta* or 'phallic mother' of psychoanalysis.

Andrei Tarkovsky was unhappy with the scene: he wanted to cut it because it was too obvious what was going on (ST, 109-110). But it's been known all through the movie that the woman Maria (like Natalia, her modern-day counterpart) has been much more powerful, more independent, more dignified, and more valuable than her husband. When the father returns from the war he stands meekly with his children (he's given nothing to 'do' by the director); Maria, meanwhile is a restless, dynamic character. The first time Maria's seen in *Mirror* she is sitting on the fence; then she walks to the house; then she stands in the corner of the room; she walks about; sits and stares out of the window; goes out to the fire. She is not 'motherly' in the usual, stereotypical, traditional sense of the term. She is not shown doing domestic chores, or talking to or cuddling her children (or even being much aware of them). It is the aunt, not the mother, who picks up and looks after the children. The mother is restless, dissatisfied, sometimes portrayed as beautiful, other times as unkempt and ugly. Part of her remains other, a mystery to her children.

In *Solaris,* Hari and Kelvin float languidly together to the strains of Johann Sebastian Bach's music. But this is a rather chaste scene, and Kelvin and Hari aren't entangled in an erotic embrace. Earlier, Hari had appeared as a dream-made sprite, a succubus out of fairy tale and mythology. Kelvin sleeps and Hari arises out of his unconscious. Outside the ship is the giant unconscious, the Ocean. Hari appears framed against the dazzling white circular window of the space ship. The movie is a network of circles. The circle represents the Ocean – on ancient maps, seas were circular, enfolding the known land masses. The circular window also stands in neatly for the planet the space ship orbits above, and for all things to do with space travel. Hari encircles Kelvin – and soon he's orbiting around her, psychologically. In traditional symbolism, the circle is time, eternity, change, cyclical processes (Kelvin repeats his response to his wife to the new Hari, as if he's caught in a circle of repetition, a time loop, a karmic wheel, and the film thus has a tragic, fatalistic aspect to it. Kelvin seems doomed to commit the same mistakes *ad infinitum*).

The second time Hari appears in *Solaris* is also erotic: she cuts off her dress with scissors and embraces Kelvin in bed. Later, Hari writhes on the floor, nipples visible under her wet shirt as she resurrects in an erotic epilepsy. Hari's fit is later replayed by the Stalker's wife, and by Adelaide, the mother in *The Sacrifice*. Instability in women and female identity in Tarkovsky's cinema is equated with sexual arousal. When Eugenia berates Gorchakov in *Nostalghia* she bares her breast. (Tarkovsky is no different from so many filmmakers, who sexualize women through their breasts.)

Andrei Tarkovsky's female characters are seldom seen as independent, completely free of men (unlike art film contemporaries like Ingmar Bergman, Jean-Luc Godard, Margarethe von Trotta, or Pedro Almodóvar, Tarkovsky never made a film with a woman in the lead role). Rather, Tarkovsky's women are always shown in relationship to men, as mothers, wives, daughters, lovers (and occasionally sisters: Tarkovsky's sister figures, in *Ivan's Childhood* and *Mirror*, for instance, barely make an impression they're so under-written).[1] But Tarkovsky's male characters need their women – whether it's poor Ivan dreaming about his mother, or the Stalker coming back to his wife. In *Solaris*, Kelvin will give up his life back on Earth to be with his wife Hari, knowing full well she is a replica created from neutrinos by an alien intelligence.

Mothers and sons is the more common relationship in Andrei Tarkovsky's cinema than fathers and son (fathers tend to be alienated from their sons, or absent, or dead). The mother can be an idealized figure (as in *Ivan's Childhood*), but also somewhat distant and unaffectionate (as in *Mirror*), and occasionally given to hysterical outbursts (in *Stalker* and *The Sacrifice*). There is also a hint that Tarkovsky would prefer women to stay in their roles as nurturing mothers, and not to have a life outside of that.[2] If they do, it is threatening and disruptive (Eugenia in *Nostalghia*, for instance, is not a nurturing mother or passive wife figure, and Gorchakov doesn't know how to treat her).

Tarkovskyan women are sometimes wild, strange, other, with magical powers, only half-understood. Yet Andrei Tarkovsky also shows that men living without women are only half-alive (in *Nostalghia*, for instance). Tarkovsky goes along with the Renaissance alchemist of Prague,

Paracelsus, who said that the second, spiritual birth had to occur in the Mother; one has to die to/ in the Mother first. The same idea occurs in Johann Wolfgang von Goethe's *Faust*, which is a key reference point, philosophically, for Tarkovsky's cinema. All of Tarkovsky's movies can be analyzed as investigations into the anxieties of accomplishing the spiritual rebirth, because each of Tarkovsky's characters is struggling to rebirth themselves, to achieve a second growth after the journey into adulthood, a poetry of sacrifice and transformation, in an alchemical, spiritual and magical fashion. The movies are full of the neuroses, anxieties, doubts, confusions and pains of rebirth, of loss and renewal, of lack and desire.

In the cinema of Andrei Tarkovsky, the women are often on top or above the men, like Tantric Goddesses, like Isis hovering over the dead god Osiris (and being impregnated beyond the grave), like the Madonna in Piero della Francesca's two paintings, the *Madonna della Misericordia* and the *Madonna del Parto*, where the Mother of God shelters, nurtures and mothers humanity below. To simplify things, Tarkovsky shows that if the feminine is not integrated, people are not 'whole', in the Jungian sense, or the integration of *yin* and *yang* in Taoist philosophy. The feminine is essential, and this is embodied in the heterosexist relations in Tarkovsky's visions (and most cinema and art). Men must live with women, as D.H. Lawrence put it, and this is the only erotic relationship fully sanctioned and sanctified by social institutions such as the church, government, law, marriage, and the family (what feminists such as Adrienne Rich termed 'compulsory heterosexuality').

Andrei Tarkovsky's cinema does not challenge any of these received notions (or even subtly modifies them). His depictions of women simply exaggerate neuroses in different ways, a little differently from mainstream international cinema, but not much. (But it's the same with art cinema generally: although it appears to be 'cool', 'progressive', more 'liberal' or more culturally 'advanced', it usually promulgates precisely the same gender and sexual relations as mainstream cinema. Or, to put it another way, Jean-Luc Godard, Michelangelo Antonioni and Wim Wenders aren't that much different from George Cukor, Richard Attenborough or Anthony Mann).

In Andrei Tarkovsky's cinema, sexuality is restrained, like all emotions. As Tarkovsky remarked in *Sculpting in Time*: '[f]or me the most interesting characters are outwardly static, but inwardly charged with energy by an overriding passion' (ST, 17). Tarkovsky's cinema is firmly sited within patriarchal, masculinist discourse. The gaze, narrativity, image and subject-object relation in his cinema uphold the patriarchal status quo. Tarkovsky may not be a macho 'men's men' director, like Howard Hawks,

Sam Peckinpah or John Ford, but his gender politics aren't a lot more developed (indeed, one could say that the movies of a director like Hawks or Ford have a more sophisticated view of women than Tarkovsky).

Andrei Tarkovsky includes beds in his pictures, which might suggest eroticism (the big iron-framed beds of *Stalker, Mirror* and *Nostalghia*) but the sheets are crumpled as after sleep not sex. The married couple at the beginning of *Stalker* sleep in the same bed, but they have their child between them, and judging by the way they lie awake, and later on argue, they don't seem particularly affectionate, and are not a loving couple.

Only once or twice is Andrei Tarkovsky's cinema explicitly erotic. In Gorchakov's dream, Eugenia sits above him, and his hand clutches the mattress. But this is more maternal than erotic, for Eugenia is whispering to him, comforting him in his nightmares, rather like the way the witch in *The Sacrifice* comforts Alex (however, Eugenia's hair is down – a sign of sexuality in Tarkovsky's cinema – and she doesn't look particularly 'motherly'). Just before this shot there's the ambiguous embracing of Eugenia and Gorchakov's wife. It is a fantasy of Gorchakov's of Russia embracing Italy, a reconciliation of nations and homelands. It is more a gesture of feminine and national solidarity than lesbian eroticism, as when Adelaide embraces the maid in *The Sacrifice* (the two women hugging next to the bed in *Nostalghia* recalls a scene in Ingmar Bergman's *The Silence,* where the two sisters, Anna and Ester, embrace beside a window and sitting on a bed).

Illustrations

Making Mirror with Tarkovsky (centre) and his mother (left).

Kolya Burlyaev in Ivan's Childhood

Ivan's Childhood

Roublyov and the fool (played by Tarkovsky's wife, Irma Rausch)

Poster for Andrei Roublyov

The prodigal son's return in Solaris

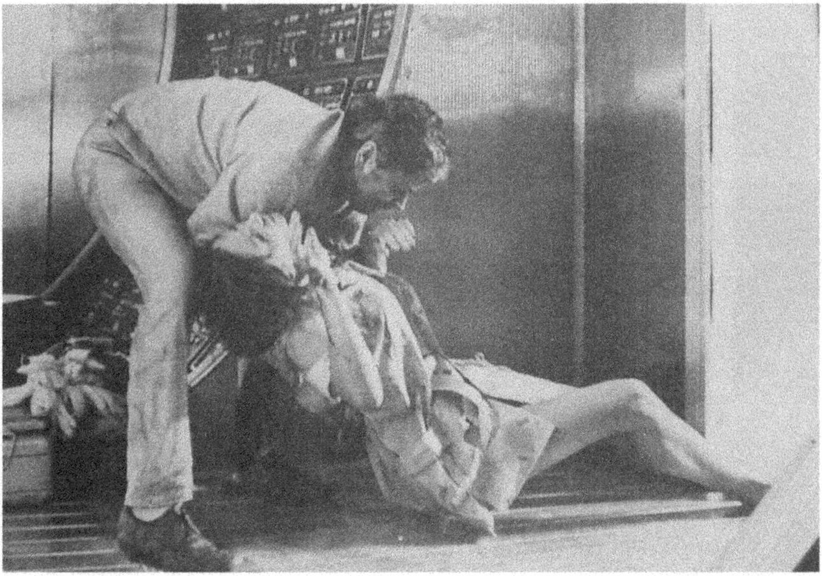

The wonderful Natalia Bondarchuk as Hari in Solaris

Solaris, when it reaches the space station, is harsh and empty, full of white spaces, hard edges, metal, and synthetic materials (plastics, PVC). The long curving corridor, the silvery metal doors, the rows of round windows (one large, with smaller ones on each side), the small shiny mirrors, with the Ocean beyond.

There are two main corridor sets in Solaris: the red one (above), lined with doors to the living quarters, and plastic buttons and boxes, and the white one, with the large circular windows, upright metal cabinets leaning over, and doors leading to the laboratories.

Tarkovsky on the set of Mirror

Leonardo da Vinci, Portrait of Ginevra Benci, 1474

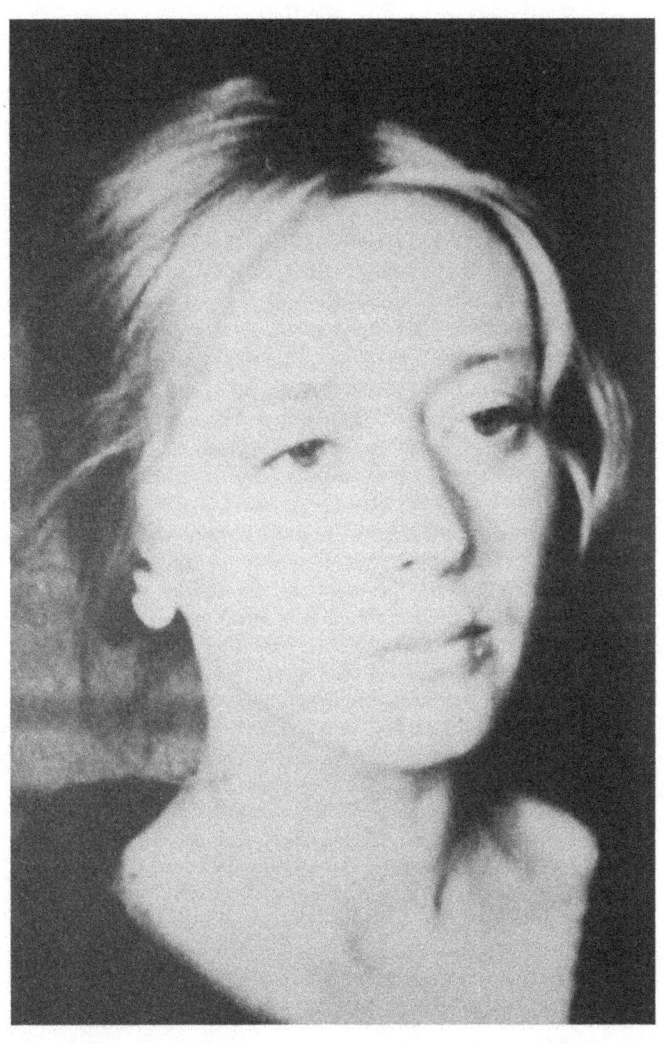

Margarita Terekhova in Mirror, one of the great close-ups in cinema, modelled after Leonardo da VInci

Poetic spaces in Mirror. The apartment scene (below)
wasn't used in the final cut.

Childhood as a visionary dream – the burning barn in Mirror (above).
The fusion of three generations in the final scene of Mirror (below).

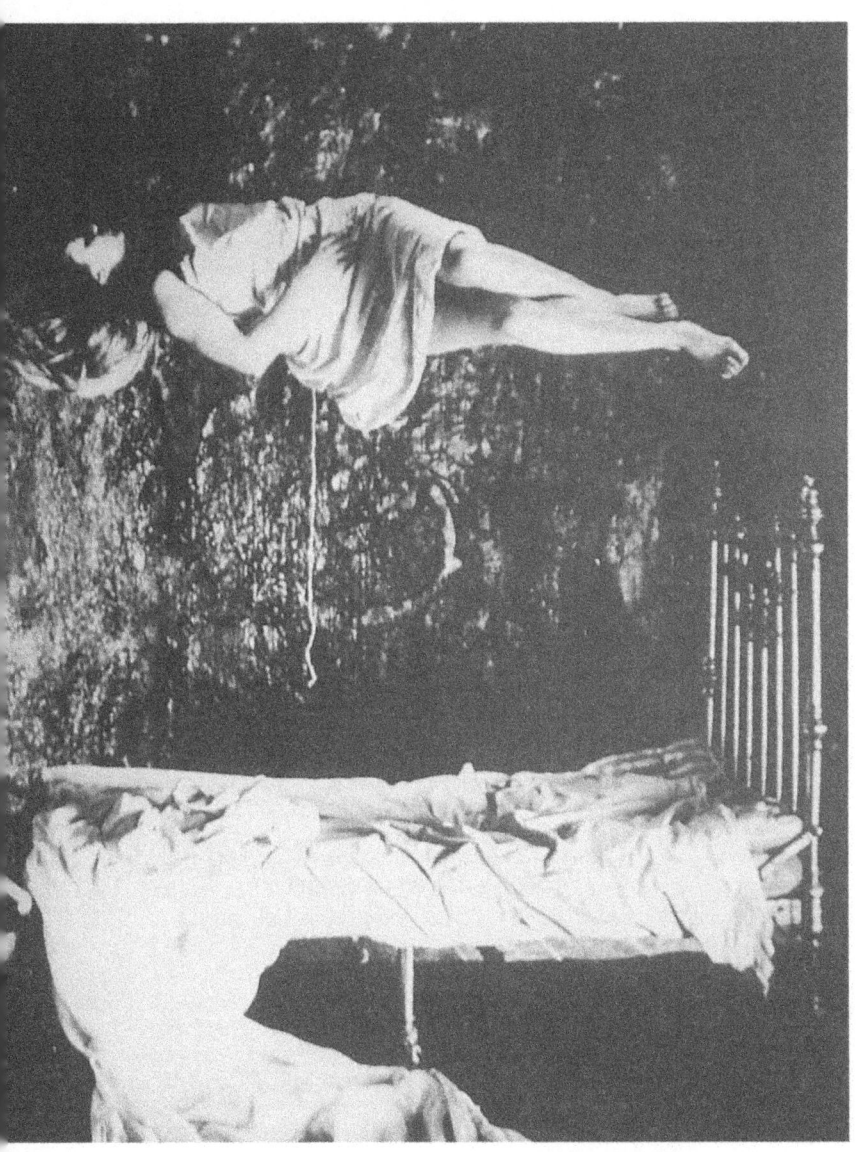

Classic Tarkovsky in Mirror: love as flying, a post-orgasmic experience of levitation, complete with highly stylized art direction on the wall, and a metal frame bed.

Classic Tarkovskyan imagery in Stalker:
a pool, a dog and a dreamer.

Stalker's finale: outside the Room at the quest's end

A brilliant performance as the Stalker by Alexander Kaidanovsky

Natasha Abramova in Stalker (1979).

Domenico's water-logged realm in Nostalghia

Nostalghia

The ending of Nostalghia.

A slow zoom out from M.S. to a wide shot of Gorchakov sitting on the grass next to a pool in front of the Russian house, looking into camera. (There was a house brought into Loreto cathedral, supposedly it was from Nazareth – the house where Jesus was born). Trees in the background. The dog sits next to him. At the end of the lengthy zoom snow starts to fall in the Italian cathedral. A dog is heard barking. The camera lingers on this scene as the Russian folksong fades. The snow continues to swirl; other filmmakers would probably have cut the shot much earlier. A dedication over the shot reads: 'To my mother'. Fade to black.

Tarkovsky does Ingmar Bergman – agai. The Sacrifice.

The finale of The Sacrifice

The final, ecstatic sequence that closes The Sacrifice.

PART TWO
THE FILMS

THIRTEEN

Ivan's Childhood

What's striking about *Ivan's Childhood* (*Ivanovo detstvo*; *My Name Is Ivan* in the U.S.A., 1962) is that it is such an accomplished debut feature movie. Like many other first features, it has elements of a young graduate filmmaker trying to prove himself, a certain flamboyance and self-consciousness (the complex deep focus compositions, for example, or the 'poetic' slow motion in the dream sequences). However, there is far less of this than in many debuts which are intended by the production team to act as a 'calling card' for Hollywood (on the other hand, Tarkovsky wasn't that young – he was thirty when the movie was released, married with a child, and had studied at the national film school for six years). Tarkovsky was aware wanting to test himself, though, of using the making of *Ivan's Childhood* to find out if he could be a film director: it was 'specially important. It was my qualifying examination', he commented later (ST, 27). Tarkovsky said he deliberately 'left the reins slack', and 'tried not to hold myself back' (ST, 27).

Ivan's Childhood is a superb depiction of the loss of innocence in childhood, how youth is robbed of childhood, how the sins of the fathers utterly wreck a young soul. It's also a war movie, and offers a poignant evocation of how war ruins lives. The movie lyrically individualizes war, depicts how wars happen to individuals, not just nations or cultures.

Ivan's Childhood is an absolute gem of a movie, with a very strong central performance from Kolya Burlyaev. In many respects it's the easiest of Andrei Tarkovsky's movies to watch: it's not too long for a start (95 minutes); it has a linear, easy-to-follow narrative; the predicament of the main character is easy to identify with (not so easy for audiences to hook into Andrei Gorchakov's life in *Nostalghia*, for instance); it has an impressive look (with not too many distracting quirks); and it's very moving (it's unusual for a film with a child in the lead role for the character to die. *Home Alone*, *E.T.* or *Harry Potter* this isn't).

Ivan's Childhood launched Andrei Tarkovsky's career with a bold start when it won the Golden Lion award at the Venice film festival in 1962. Also showing in Venice were movies directed by Bernardo Bertolucci (*The Grim Reaper* – his first feature), Frank Perry (*David and Lisa*), and Roman Polanski (his debut, *Knife In the Water*). *The Sacrifice* won awards at Cannes, Guldbagge and BAFTA. *Solaris* and *Nostalghia* also won awards at Cannes.

Ivan's Childhood was based on Vladimir Bogomolov's novella *Ivan* (1957). Originally, the Mosfilm production was going to be directed by Eduard Abalov, who had already shot some scenes, but Mosfilm halted the project in October, 1960 (footage apparently no longer exists of the first version of *Ivan's Childhood*). Part of the budget had thus already been spent, and Mosfilm were going to write off the production. The film eventually came in 24,000 roubles ($95,000) under budget. It was shot in late 1961, on the River Dnieper, at Kanev, with shooting finishing by January 18, 1962 (most of the movie was shot on location, but the chief set – the church crypt – was built in the studio). By March 1, 1962, *Ivan's Childhood* had been examined thirteen times by various artistic councils at Mosfilm.

One of the original writers (Mikhail Papava) had given *Ivan* a happy ending, with the young military scout surviving the war and having a family; Vladimir Bogomolov and Andrei Tarkovsky kept the tragic ending, with Ivan becoming another of the thousands of casualties of war. Bogomolov, who had been a military scout himself in the war, disagreed with Tarkovsky about the director's treatment of his novella, particularly the love story, and how Tarkovsky had downplayed the military aspects.[1]

Andrei Tarkovsky and his screenwriting collaborator, Andrei Konchalovsky (who appears in a cameo as a bespectacled soldier who meets up with the doctor Masha in the movie), altered writers Vladimir Bogolomov and Mikhail Papava's treatment, adding four dream sequences (AT, 67-68), which focussed the film on Ivan's psychological state. (Bogolomov agreed to Tarkovsky's addition of the dreams, even though they significantly transformed his novella. But he did argue with Tarkovsky and co-writer Konchalovsky about the way Tarkovsky wanted to depict wartime. Bogolomov was anxious to have the military aspects accurate to his own memories of WWII. But Tarkovsky wasn't interested in delivering a documentary-style depiction of child spies in the war. Some of the arguments between Bogolomov and the co-writers were 'extremely heated').[2]

Mosfilm's executives and advisors requested minor and major changes in *Ivan's Childhood*; one of the objections (inevitably) was the sight of the remains of Joseph Goebbels and his family at the end (from a newsreel). In

Sculpting in Time, Andrei Tarkovsky discussed the problems of literary adaptions (he made three: *Ivan's Childhood, Stalker* and *Solaris*): some works were fully formed, he said, and thus are difficult to film. Other prose works (usually minor ones, not literary 'classics') can contain ideas which are not so æsthetically developed, and have space allowing for cinematic adaption (ST, 15-16). One can see how novels such as *Wuthering Heights, Tess of the d'Urbervilles* or *War and Peace* are so complete in themselves, they seem to resist film adaption. One can see how a director like Tarkovsky would prefer a more open approach to literary adaption, allowing him to explore his own preoccupations (this is what Andrei Tarkovsky and his co-writers did on *Ivan's Childhood, Solaris* and *Stalker*, altering the plot and treatment to suit his own ends, sometimes to the authors' annoyance). (That Tarkovsky made three literary adaptions out of his seven feature movies is a reminder that Tarkovsky wasn't wholly a writer-director hyphenate who directed movies only from his own original scripts, and he wrote with other authors).

Andrei Tarkovsky was drawn to Vladimir Bogomolov's *Ivan*, he said, by the story of the young scout; and by the character of the boy, tragically denied a proper childhood. The lack of military action and exploits also intrigued him: instead, *Ivan* was about an interval in between forays that had a 'disturbing, pent-up intensity' (ST, 17). *Ivan's Childhood* takes place in the interlude between Ivan's scouting missions behind German lines: at the start of the movie he crosses the barbed wire and the flooded forest, moving from enemy territory to the Russian field station after swimming across the river; at the end of the film, he is escorted back through the swamp.

Ivan's Childhood portrays, confidently and poetically, a bleak, war-torn world, of swamps and rivers, muddy tracks, barbed wire, deserted forests, dishevelled people and tired soldiers, ruined buildings, destroyed remains of military hardware (a crashed German plane looming over a riverbank, canons), rain, drifting mist and smoke, fizzling flares descending out of leaden skies. Solitary figures in sodden, broken landscapes strewn with wreckage, the machines of warfare. Roads churned up into mud.

The world of *Ivan's Childhood* is not the brightly-lit, heroic battlefields of Hollywood's World War Two movies of the same era, but a dark, sombre, stark and brutal world, recalling films such as Andrzej Wajda's 'Polish School' trilogy, *A Generation, Canal* and *Ashes and Diamonds* (1954-58), made a few years before Tarkovsky's *Ivan's Childhood* (which Tarkovsky had seen at VGIK; Wadja's trilogy is a film school favourite). The tracking shots in the trenches in *Ivan's Childhood* recall the lengthy, *virtuoso* shots in the anti-war movie *Paths of Glory* (Stanley Kubrick, 1957). One sequence, where Galtsev and Kholin talk, seems particularly inspired by *Paths of Glory*: they walk along a trench, with the camera first in front of them, then, as they pass it, dollying behind them, all done in a continuous take. (*All Quiet On the Western Front* [1930], may have been another influence – that famous war film has bravura shots where the camera cranes along the top of trenches).

After the opening dream sequence, DP Vadim Yusov establishes the war-time setting of *Ivan's Childhood* with some very stylized, Expressionist shots: Ivan waking up in a windmill, a building out of Gothic horror movies and Northern European painting, portrayed with wide angle, tilted shots. As Ivan walks away from the windmill, Tarkovsky uses another bravura image: Ivan walking into the sun on a barren hillside (Maya Turovskaya related the apocalyptic imagery of the sun and sunsets in *Ivan's Childhood* to examples in the poetry of Alexander Blok, Sergei Urusevsky and Mikhail Sholokhov). The images of the bleak, smoky landscape are accompanied by edgy, foreboding music of drums and brass. (Many another debuting film director might have loaded the opening section with some big scenes, putting the budget and production values up on screen. Tarkovsky has the confidence to leave that out, putting it into a much later scene, when Lt-Col Gryaznov talks on the telephone at the HQ and trucks and extras are glimpsed in the window behind him.)

The German enemy is rarely seen in *Ivan's Childhood*; instead, gunshots and explosions are heard, plus the signal flares which fall throughout the movie against leaden grey skies. In fact, German soldiers are only shown once or twice – in the night crossing of the swamp, for example, and in the newsreel footage of Berlin. However, the Germans are unambiguously loathed, especially by Ivan. For the boy, the Germans are the enemies of art and culture. As he looks at some Albrecht Dürer woodcuts in a large art book (having already read all of the magazines and articles that Galtsev has saved), he remarks that it reminds him of the barbaric Germans, who burn books (Ivan sees a figure riding a horse in Dürer's prints and it reminds him of a German on a motorcycle. Ivan seems to ignore the intense stylization of Dürer's prints, and accepts them as documentary evidence).

Instead of the action-adventure predominating in Hollywood depictions of the Second World War, Andrei Tarkovsky's film is full of scenes of near-silence and people waiting. As one of the characters says, the sound of silence is the sound of war. An eerie, unnerving silence, punctuated by sudden bursts of gunfire and explosions (of course, that makes the movie a lot cheaper to produce, because the war can be suggested through a library of sound effects. Many filmmakers have resorted to the same devices. There are, though, some combat scenes in *Ivan's Childhood*: a series of explosions, for instance, when the Germans start to bomb the Russians. There's a beautiful moment when the bombardment ceases, and birds start singing again over a memorable shot of dust swirling around a cross stuck in the ground, the light behind it creating a halo effect).

Many of Andrei Tarkovsky's familiar motifs appear in *Ivan's Childhood*: rain, fires, trees, tracking shots over water, sounds of dripping water, birds (the sound of birdsong in the dreams; the cockerel who belongs to the old man), dream sequences, long takes, dream images of mothers, doors opening and closing on their own, references to fine art (the icon of the Madonna and Child; Ivan looking at woodcuts by Albrecht Dürer).

Visually, *Ivan's Childhood* is a stunning achievement, with Andrei Tarkovsky and the team conjuring memorable images: Ivan in the flooded forest lit by flares; the handheld shots of the birch wood; the ruined buildings and the mud; the apples spilling over the beach (in one of Vadim Yusov and Tarkovsky's very best shots, the swooping crane shot down to the sand); the snow on the river; the cross in the sun in the dust; Ivan 'flying' in the opening dream sequence. Religious imagery is present in *Ivan's Childhood* in the Virgin and Child icon, the Albrecht Dürer wood prints, and the windmill silhouetted against the smoky sky like a cross. Note that Tarkovsky chose Dürer's *Four Men of the Apocalypse* (c. 1497-98) as the main visual art reference, with its suitable Biblical resonances of devastation (and aligning the Germans with the horsemen who bring ruin to the world: they destroy everything, Ivan complains, including burning books in a town square. Throughout the movie, Ivan has to remind the young lieutenant Galtsev that he has already seen terrible things in the war, even at his young age, including one of the Germans' death camps).

Although rated 'PG' by the British Board of Film Classification, *Ivan's Childhood* contains some disturbing imagery: the charred remains of Joseph Goebbels, for example, and a row of his poisoned children. There is another family shown dead in documentary footage. And in the execution room, in the basement of the bombed German building, is a row of ropes, for hanging prisoners, plus a guillotine. The sight of the guillotine motivates a short montage or vision, for Galtsev, of Ivan's demise, with shots of Ivan rolling over and over, as if he's just been guillotined. (Ivan is definitely dead: a Russian soldier sifts through documents about prisoners, merely grimly noting if they were hanged or guillotined. Galtsev (now scarred and looking much older, and the only survivor among the characters), recognizes Ivan in a photograph, which's shown to the viewer in C.U.). Black ash drifts down from burning papers.

Much of the visual style of *Ivan's Childhood* uses deep focus, wide angle photography, recalling German Expressionist cinema, and movies such as *Citizen Kane* (which had impressed Andrei Tarkovsky, as it has affected so many filmmakers). Like Orson Welles and Gregg Toland, Tarkovsky and cameraman Vadim Yusov created complex compositions in deep focus, with action in the foreground and middle distance (sometimes racking focus between actors, and often having an actor in a big C.U. in the foreground, listening to an out-of-focus actor in the background). For the single take scenes, Tarkovsky and the A.D. Georgi Natanson orchestrated the actors meticulously, so they sometimes move into close-up, or into the distance. The scenes in the military post are perhaps the most obviously Expressionist, with Tarkovsky exploring the ways in which the most mundane and common of dramatic scenes – people talking in a room – can be livened up.

The first shot of Andrei Tarkovsky's first feature movie was echoed in the last shot of his last feature film: a young boy at the base of a tree, with the camera slowly craning upwards into the branches. This shot in *Ivan's Childhood* is an unusual opener: the crane shot is typically an establishing shot at the beginning of a scene, and usually starts high, with a view of the landscape of the movie, craning down to show the protagonist. Here, it cranes up and away from the lead character (the shot also has one of Tarkovsky's favourite devices – the double or stand-in to place a character simultaneously in the foreground and the background). The camera movement upwards relates to the joyous atmosphere of the first scene of *Ivan's Childhood*, where the motion upwards culminates in Ivan seeming to fly. In *The Sacrifice*, too, the crane up shot indicates bliss and transcendence.

The climax of *Ivan's Childhood*, in terms of action, is the night crossing of the river. In a Hollywood war movie, this scene would be played for maximum suspense. In the 1962 movie, the suspense is still there, but much more muted; and the sequence veers off into poetic cinema (with lengthy shots looking down at the water sliding past the boat). (Note how the narrative of *Ivan's Childhood* occurs between Ivan's two expeditions into enemy territory: a Hollywood movie would probably want to show at least one of these adventures).

Ivan is portrayed throughout the movie as a combination of the innocent and cynic, the vulnerable and the tough. There are touching moments, such as when Ivan uses seeds, nuts and leaves he's collected to explain the German positions on a piece of paper. The apparently childish use of leaves and seeds is mitigated by the fact that in this scene Ivan is wrapped in a blanket, with a blackened face, in a field station, just arrived from a military mission. There is nothing childlike about Ivan's occupation.

Andrei Tarkovsky didn't want to romanticize or sentimentalize Ivan or his predicament. Ivan mustn't be the 'pride and joy of the regiment,' Tarkovsky explained, 'he must be its grief'.[3] For Tarkovsky, Ivan's tragic situation was a child who was living as an adult, a child who was caught up in adult life (the war). But he was still a child, and the film had a scene where Ivan was shown to be a child (the scene where he plays at war, on his own in the base).

Nikolai Burlyaev, who plays Ivan, is immensely impressive; convincing at all times, unlike many child actors (a world away from the usual Hollywood child actors). Burlyaev conveys a mixture of innocence and cynicism, enthusiasm and weariness, belief and pessimism. In the dream sequences Burlyaev's Ivan is full of light – clean, mobile and joyful; in the war zone scenes, he is tough, vulnerable, sullen, aggressive, sporting old clothes (speckled grey sweater, black hat, old black pants), dishevelled hair, and a muddy face. (*Ivan* wasn't Kolya Burlyaev's first movie – he had already appeared in four films by then).

Ivan's Childhood garnered many favourable reviews, including five front page reviews during 1962. Jean-Paul Sartre came to *Ivan's Childhood*'s defence when it was criticized by the Italian Communist Party newspaper *Unita* for being 'petit bourgeois'. *Ivan's Childhood*, Sartre wrote, used 'socialist surrealism' to portray a 'Soviet tragedy'; Ivan was a combination of 'monster' and innocent, driven by vengeance for his mother's death (1965). Antoine de Baecque saw Ivan as a victim, saint and martyr (1989, 53-54). Like other children in Tarkovsky's cinema, Ivan is linked with the infant Christ. Revisiting *Ivan's Childhood*, Maya Turovskaya remarked that it was 'balanced and complete, with each strand of the plot, every visual and other motif carried through to its logical conclusion in total clarity' (95).

One of the remarkable elements of *Ivan's Childhood* are the four dream sequences. The dreams are quite separate from Ivan's real life; there is no bridge or interface between the two worlds; instead, there's a gulf which Ivan cannot fuse.[4] And each dream starts out positively, but ends badly. Andrei Tarkovsky told Mikhail Romm that Ivan dreams of the life, the normal childhood, he's 'been robbed of' (CS, 57). The first dream sequence begins with a medium close-up of Ivan (wearing only shorts), the sound of a cuckoo, and the slow crane shot up the tree. Images of a sunlit natural world follow: a goat, a butterfly, trees. As he starts to 'fly' (apparently standing on a camera crane), he laughs happily; the music emphasizes that this is meant to be an ecstatic, transcendent sequence. After showing Ivan rising up into the leaves, there is a helicopter long shot, followed by a long panning medium shot along a wall of cracked earth and roots, ending on a pensive Ivan.

Ivan's fourth dream ends the 1962 Mosfilm production, with shots of Ivan by a dead tree, raising his arm; then the final shot, a track into the tree trunk, so that it obscures the lens. The fourth dream appears at first to be the happiest in the film; it doesn't end with gunshots and the death of his mother, but with ominous drumbeats and shots of the dead tree. However, the viewer knows that Ivan is already dead. As with the endings of *Mirror* and *Nostalghia*, the protagonist is already dead when the dream occurs. In 1962, Andrei Tarkovsky stated that the final (fourth) dream was critical, because the viewer knows now that Ivan is dead, and so it takes on a tragic mood. Although the imagery appeared at first to be upbeat (Ivan running along a riverbank in sunlight), that wasn't the intention at all, Tarkovsky noted. Instead, it was meant to be poignant: 'this is a cinematic-poetic tragedy'.

FOURTEEN

The Passion According to Andrei Roublyov

Andrei Roublyov (1966/ 1971) was the subject of much discussion in the Soviet Union and was withheld by the authorities for years. It was Andrei Tarkovsky's most controversial movie, and retains its power to startle viewers. It's easily Tarkovsky's most visceral and violent movie, by far the most action-packed (and there's plenty of nudity, too). Nowadays, with the many changes in the political and ideological climate (such as *glasnost*, the end of the Cold War, the dissolution of the Soviet Union), some of the political controversies have faded over time. These days, contemporary audiences might find other aspects of *Andrei Roublyov* more unsettling: the treatment of animals, for instance (a cow set on fire, a horse killed on camera), or the images of torture and barbarity. You can slaughter hundreds of actors and extras on screen, but harming animals disturbs many viewers. Feminists might find the treatment of women in *Andrei Roublyov* equally problematic. There are two significant female characters in *Andrei Roublyov*: the pagan woman Marfa that Roublyov possibly sleeps with, and the fool that he adopts. Simplistic second wave feminist film criticism could argue that Roublyov is a 'feminized' character himself (passive, not particularly pro-active).

The movie was defined by a series of negatives by critics and supporters – it was not a historical movie, it was not this, not that (L. Anninsky, 1991). It was partly the film's avoidance of the usual biographical or historical genre features that made it disappoint audiences, who expected something different. Official Soviet critics debated at length whether *Andrei Roublyov* departed significantly from historical genre and Russian folklore and myth. Tarkovsky was taken to task by Soviet critics for what he had left out, for what he had *not* done. For Lev Anninsky in *The Sixties Generation and We*, *Andrei Roublyov* was a typical movie of the 1960s in Russia (perhaps *the* film of the Sixties): it looked forward to the movies of the Russian soil and village life of the 1970s; it explored the individual's relation to society; it rejected stereotypes; it aimed to mix naturalism with poetry; and it was a 'national film'.[1] The actor who played the Duke twins and the military instructor in *Mirror*, Yuri Nazarov, remarked (on the British DVD of the movie) that *Andrei Roublyov* was to Russian cinema what *War and Peace* was to Russian literature. (I would say that *War and Peace*, the 1967 mega-production, is *the* movie of the 1960s in Russia. *War and Peace* is possibly the biggest movie ever made – including *Cleopatra* and *Intolerance*. The scope of some of the battle scenes in *War and Peace* are beyond belief).

Andrei Tarkovsky worked for over two years on the script for *Andrei Roublyov*, with his friend and fellow VGIK student Andrei Konchalovsky (Konchalovsky was a fairly young writer for such a big film – he was 26 in 1963). Tarkovsky acknowledged that it was the actor Vasil Livanov who had proposed making a movie based on Andrei Roublyov's life, when he, Tarkovsky and Konchalovsky had been working on *Ivan's Childhood*.

The film treatment of *Roublyov* was passed in December, 1963. Critics dubbed the panoramic script 'The Three Andreis', referring to Andrei Tarkovsky, Konchalovsky and Roublyov. The script was published (in the journal *Iskusstvo kino*) before the movie came out, when Tarkovsky began work on it (April, 1964): it contained 12 episodes and two prologues, for two parts. The published script contained a prologue to Part One, which contained 9 episodes: *The Buffoon, Theophanes the Greek, The Hunt, Invitation To the Kremlin, The Passion According To Andrei, The Blinding, The Celebration, The Last Judgement* and *The Attack*. There was another prologue, for Part Two: a peasant trying to fly using wings, followed by three episodes: *Indian Summer, Melancholy* and *The Bell*. The finished film had one prologue and 8 parts, with an epilogue in colour.

One of the major scenes to be cut from *Andrei Roublyov* was the Kulikovo Field battle scene, which depicted the Russians victorious over the Tartars. This was an expensive scene, costed at over 200,000 roubles/ $800,000 (the Kulikovo battle sequence had to be cut (because of cost) before the Mosfilm authorities would green-light *Andrei Roublyov*). 'The Hunt' was also dropped – the hunting of swans by the Duke's brother. 'Indian Summer' was cut, in which the fool gives birth to a half-Tartar, half-Russian child. 'The Field of Virgins', the story of Russian women selling their long hair to save Moscow from the Tartars, which interests Roublyov, was left out. Roublyov's memories of his childhood was cut; another vision of a Crucifixion, which Theophanes sees, was dropped (it took place in a desert-like setting, to contrast with Roublyov's vision of a snowy, Russian Cavalry).

However, although various (mainly budgetary) restrictions forced the cuts, the two Andreis (Tarkovsky and Konchalovsky) to combine elements and scenes. Despite the inevitable compromises on any large-scale undertaking of this kind, Tarkovsky and the team were able to stage some spectacular stuff, including the Tartar raid and battle on Vladimir (which is just jaw-droppingly good), and the eye-opening bell-casting scene, both with thousands of extras, costumes, props, horses, stunts, practical effects, and complex staging. There was also a Crucifixion in the snow and a pagan Midsummer Night festival (St John's Eve) involving many nude extras.

It wasn't as if the restrictions, then, forced Andrei Tarkovsky & co. to completely cut out the epic aspects of their project (the budget for *Andrei Roublyov* only ran to 26 horses; the rest (about 90) were borrowed from a hippodrome). Indeed, *Andrei Roublyov* stands as one of the great epic movies, alongside *El Cid, Ben-Hur, Kagemusha, Lawrence of Arabia, Spartacus, Quo Vadis,* and *Intolerance*. It has everything one could wish for in a grand epic: spectacle in abundance, extravagant visual style, exotic settings, and serious themes. As a combination of the interiorized (small-scale) art film and the blockbuster historical epic movie, *Andrei Roublyov* is remarkable.

It's incredible that this was only Andrei Tarkovsky's second movie. It's quite common to put a young director, with a lot to prove, and bundles of energy, someone eager to please, whom the studio can control, at the helm of a big budget film. There are many striking aspects about *Andrei Roublyov,* including: (1) that Tarkovsky created a total masterpiece after only one feature movie; (2) that Tarkovsky's powers of filmmaking seem totally accomplished and confident – the image-making, the direction of actors, the staging and blocking of the scenes, the complex camera moves; (3) that a historical epic film of this era could have such a quiet, introspective hero – and an artist, not a war hero!; (4) that the themes of the movie could be so unusual, even antithetical to the conventional historical epic (spiritual doubt, artistic integrity, morality and conscience).

Filming on *Andrei Roublyov* began in April, 1965, according to Tamara Ogorodnikova, the producer, and Tatyana Vinokurova, head of archives at Mosfilm (though Maya Turovskaya reckoned production started in September, 1964). Shooting ended in November, 1965, due to snow, and continued on location during April-May, 1966. The budget was originally 1.6 million roubles ($6.4m), but was cut down to one million roubles (JP, 80). The return to the location in 1966 raised the budget by 300,000 roubles ($1.2 million). *Andrei Roublyov* is one of those films about which legends have grown, as with *Apocalypse Now, Heaven's Gate* or *Cleopatra,* so facts and figures merge into myth-making and hyperbole.

There are eight parts to *Andrei Roublyov*, with a prologue and an epilogue (in colour). The main locations are the Andronik Spasa Nerukotvornogo monastery, Vladimir, founded in around 1360., and the environs of Moscow (the movie was shot at the real Andronnikov monastery in Moscow, by the Yaouza River, which now houses the Andrei Roublyov Museum, as well as the Monastery of the Trinity St Sergius in Zagorsk, among other locations).

Andrei Roublyov was subject to much scrutiny by the Soviet film authorities, who demanded many cuts, because it was too violent and too long (at 5,642 metres). Andrei Tarkovsky said in December, 1966 (in a letter to Goskino's chairman, Alexei Romanov), that he had cut out 390 metres (15 mins) in 37 changes, and that he didn't want to make any more, because they would alter the film profoundly (T. Vinokuroya, 65). The movie was seen as too 'naturalistic', especially in its depiction of violence. The authorities also wanted the peasants' appearance to be spruced-up.[2] On December 27, 1966, Tarkovsky agreed to cut out the horse-killing, and make other minor cuts.

When further cuts were requested after the premiere at Dom Kino in late 1966/ early 1967, Andrei Tarkovsky & co. refused to make any more changes. Consequently, the movie was shelved for nearly five years, with Mosfilm, Goskino, the critics and Tarkovsky not agreeing on the film. *Andrei Roublyov*'s release was delayed again and again. The Cannes film festival requested the movie, but the Soviet authorities refused. An unofficial screening was arranged and *Andrei Roublyov* was given the International Critics' Prize. More cuts in the film were requested (in 1970 and 1971). The film eventually opened on general release in Russia in December, 1971.

Andrei Roublyov looks stupendous, at times extraordinary. Many of the shots are beautiful to look at. *Andrei Roublyov* is shot in widescreen and black-and-white by Vadim Yusov. Widescreen is common, black-and-white is less frequent; the two together are rare, and here they're ravishing. Black-and-white was chosen to create the mediæval world of *Andrei Roublyov*, because colour would have been too pretty. The colour used at the end of *Andrei Roublyov*, when *The Holy Trinity* is seen, was to suggest the way art can transform life, Andrei Tarkovsky said. For Anne Lawton in *The Red Screen: Politics, Society, Art in Soviet Cinema*, the colour icon ending is a 'true epiphany of mystical splendour' (1992, 129). Of the final section in colour, Tarkovsky said that he 'wanted to bring the viewer to this work through a kind of dramaturgy of colour, asking him to move from certain fragments towards the whole, creating an impressionistic flow'. It was also meant to be a buffer or interlude, between the movie and the outside world, so that the viewer could make up their mind about the film. 'I think if *Roublyov* had ended immediately following the 'Bell' episode it would have been an unsuccessful film,' Tarkovsky explained. 'We needed to keep the viewer in the cinema at all cost. It was necessary to add some type of continuation of the artist's life to show how great he was'.

There are many memorable images and sequences in *Andrei Roublyov*: the opening flight sequence, the bell-casting, the fires in the snow, the river sequence, the Crucifixion in the snow, the pagan festival, and the birch wood. The battle, where the Tartars invade Vladimir, is tremendously exciting, violent and visceral, with Andrei Tarkovsky moving into spectacle cinema territory more usually associated with David Lean, William Wyler, Sergei Bondarchuk, D.W. Griffith or Cecil B. DeMille (Tarkovsky said he referred to Leonardo da Vinci's *Treatise On Painting* for inspiration on how to stage the battle. That's typical of Tarkovsky: while other movie-makers might refer to earlier movies – a John Ford movie, say – Tarkovsky goes to Leonardo da Vinci!).

Andrei Tarkovsky demonstrated that he can handle a large-scale film, complex set-ups, practical fx, stunts, and sequences that involve hundreds of extras – like *Ben-Hur* (William Wyler, 1959) or *El Cid* (Anthony Mann, 1961). (Big scenes like this aren't directors' scenes so much as reliant on efficient first, second and third assistant directors, production managers, location managers and great second unit teams – Bagrat Oganesyan was second unit director). The battle scene involves masses of people, and when the bell is raised up and blessed and finally rings, there are what seems like thousands of people in the vicinity. Tarkovsky and the team create epic cinema here. Tarkovsky & co. have the confidence to cover many of the big scenes with complex master shots and long takes, very demanding for the crew and the actors, who have to hit marks and rehearse moves, time after time.

The pagan festival, for instance, must have been difficult to shoot: it was shot mainly in the magic hour for a start, which would mean coming back day after day for the light (as well as being a difficult scene to light), there were boats, and water, and people swimming, and stunts, and stacks of practical effects (fires, smoke, torches), and many extras were half or fully naked (and they had to run over rough ground).

Much of *Andrei Roublyov* is shot by DP Vadim Yusov with long lenses, often with a person's head in M.C.U. against activity behind, as in the bell-casting sequence, with the bell-caster Boriska against the smoke, or often shot through the legs of people and horses (as in the Crucifixion in the snow). Many of the shots in *Andrei Roublyov* last more than two minutes, giving the film an elegant, slow, processional pace, even in the scenes of violence. Some scenes are staged as *tableaux*, with the figures arranged within the frame like paintings (and the long lenses squash the planes of focus together, bringing the background and middle ground to the front). But these are not static *tableaux*, because Yusov's camera is always moving.

As Sven Nykvist pointed out, although the compositions in *Andrei Roublyov* often place a figure in the centre of the frame, they are not mundane. In a number of two-shots, such as when Roublyov and Theophanes or Roublyov and Daniil are talking, Vadim Yusov frames one closer to the camera than the other, sometimes they're facing away from each other; the blocking of actors within the widescreen frame is dynamic, always interesting. In the log hut in Part One, Yusov uses a favourite New Wave device: the 360° pan, to show the other people sheltering from the storm, and to show time passing.

The influence of Akira Kurosawa, in movies such as *Throne of Blood, The Seven Samurai* and *The Hidden Fortress,* and the film many directors have cited as an influence, *Rashomon*, can be seen on *Andrei Roublyov*: in the high contrast widescreen cinematography; the warriors on horseback; the mud and water; the rain; the graphic violence; the drifting clouds of mist and fog; and the minimal interiors. The general harsh muddy, rainy, snowy, misty mediæval look of *Andrei Roublyov* is familiar from the movies of Kurosawa and Ingmar Bergman (*The Virgin Spring, Throne of Blood, Rashomon* and *The Seventh Seal*, for example). Sven Nykvist said that *Andrei Roublyov* 'was a true revelation to me when I saw it for the first time. Pure image magic!' Tarkovsky said they were aiming not for ethnographic, archæological or historical accuracy so much as a 'physiological truth', a poetic truth which would hopefully ring true for a modern cinema audience (ST, 78).

Andrei Tarkovsky said he loved *The Seven Samurai* and *Sanjuro*, and reckoned that Akira Kurosawa had achieved more in the historical movie genre than anyone else. But Tarkovsky found the concept of *Throne of Blood* lacking, because it took the story of *Macbeth* and applied it to Japanese history, and missed the profound nature of the tragedy.

Of Akira Kurosawa's historical films, Andrei Tarkovsky said:

one perceives his Middle Ages without any exoticism. He is such a profound artist, he shows such psychological connections, such a development of characters and plot-lines, such a vision of the world, that his narrative about the Middle Ages constantly makes you think about today's world.

Andrei Tarkovsky, in *Andrei Roublyov*, revels in the creation of a rainy, dirty, muddy, snowy, violent, cruel and sometimes bizarre post-mediæval world. *Andrei Roublyov*, wrote Amos Vogel in *Film As a Subversive Art*:

> reeks with the evil odour of the Middle Ages, an era of brutality, human degradation, abject poverty, rape, senseless mass slaughter, mud and pagan orgies, when people were at the mercy of both temporal and 'spiritual' powers. (150)

Andrei Roublyov is not only about one creative personality, but at least two (there are others, such as the other painters). 'I wanted to use the example of Rublyov to explore the question of the psychology of artistic creativity', Tarkovsky commented in *Sculpting In Time* (34). In the figure of Roublyov the artistic journey is from activity to doubt and anxiety, a creative block or impasse, and a self-imposed abstinence. His observation of Boriska's intense struggle with the bell, the workers and the whole project, the movie suggests, is instrumental in inspiring him to start painting again. For Boriska, the creative arc moves from having nothing to gaining everything, doing it all by sheer determination, which seems to come from nowhere. Boriska doesn't know the secret of bell-making (he says his father wouldn't tell him), so he's an example of an artist making it up on the fly: total improvization or spontaneity.

Andrei Roublyov is a passive and often mute personality: a watcher, the observer through whom the events of the film are seen. The meditations in *Andrei Roublyov* are on the role of the artist in society, the artist in relation to the state, to politics, to religion, to God, to sexuality, to purity, to vision, to suffering, to life. Each sequence, each part (from one to eight) illustrates an ideological, moral, artistic, and biographical point. Roublyov frames the film, provides the axis around which the movie revolves. In many ways, *Andrei Roublyov* is the clearest filmed statement of Tarkovsky's position on art and spirituality, and the relation between the two.

His movies were about people who possessed an 'inner freedom', as Andrei Tarkovsky described it, while around them are people 'who are inwardly dependent and unfree' (ST, 181). The apparent weakness of his protagonists was in fact an inner strength, he said.

Art is seen as holy, as holy as religion in *Andrei Roublyov*. Art has a sense of the numinous as powerful as religion. Art is seen as a cult, with fetish objects, monastic precepts, followers like pilgrims and mystics, and images of divinity. Constant connections are made in *Andrei Roublyov* between holiness, madness and creativity, embodied in different ways by the figures of Roublyov, the holy fool and the bell-caster Boriska. These three figures are linked in one scene, as if they are three sides of the same person, the same phenomenon: belief and faith in life, with artistic creativity as the ultimate affirmation of life. The theme of three-in-one or the trinity is taken up by Roublyov and his two companions, Daniil and Kirill; and by the subject of Roublyov's most famous painting, *The Holy Trinity* (later, in *Solaris*, there are three men on the space station, and in *Stalker* three men enter the Zone).

The artists in *Andrei Roublyov* offer different views on one of Andrei Tarkovsky's recurring themes: the problem of the artist and her/ his relation to society. Daniil is the conformist, the follower of social trends; Kirill is the untalented artist, too proud and jealous; Theophanes is a real artist, an older generation. Boriska is the untutored youth, working from an intuition that seems divine. Like Roublyov, Boriska veers from self-confidence to self-doubt, from faith to frustration, from ecstasy to despair (JP, 91). Roublyov is a version of the Tarkovskyan artist: humane, humble, sometimes confused, sometimes difficult, sometimes too passive, but with a fundamental faith.

FIFTEEN

Solaris

Andrei Tarkovsky had developed *Solaris* from early 1968 onwards (Andrei Konchalovsky was going to collaborate on the script, but the two filmmakers disagreed about the adaption). It wasn't his first choice to follow up *Andrei Roublyov* (he wanted to make *Bright, Bright Day*, the script which became *Mirror*), and a movie about his mother (parts of this also went into *Mirror*). Tarkovsky said, before he made *Solaris*, that what attracted him to Stanislaw Lem's 1961 book was the story of a man who can't escape his past, who regrets what he's done, and wants to relive his life in order to make amends for it. It was the morality, psychology and philosophy of the book that appealed to Tarkovsky, not the hard science, the technology, or the conventional sci-fi elements. When he applied for money from Mosfilm, though, Tarkovsky emphasized different aspects of the project: '[t]he plot of *Solaris* is taut and sharp, full of unexpected twists and turns and exciting confrontations...We can be sure from the start that the movie will be a financial success' (M. Turovskaya, 52). Despite the success in the West of movies such as *2001: A Space Odyssey* and *The Planet of the Apes*, sci-fi was still a genre at this time (the early 1970s) that was not a guaranteed box office winner. *Star Wars* and *Close Encounters of the Third Kind* were still some years away.

Andrei Tarkovsky wrote an early draft of the *Solaris* script in 1968 (with Friedrich Gorenstein); the film was cast in May, 1970. The scenes of the *dacha* and environs were shot at Zvenigorod, about 40 miles from Moscow, from March to Summer, 1971. The River Ruza was another location. Vadim Yusov and Tarkovsky chose to shoot some of the scenes in black-and-white (such as Kris burning his papers on a bonfire; though, as these take place, like the others, in the present day, there seems to be no really good reason for using black-and-white). The Japan shoot (consisting of cityscapes and car shots in Tokyo) took place in late September/ early October, 1971. Getting towards the end of cutting the movie, in December, 1971, Tarkovsky said in his diaries he was pleased with some scenes (the suicide, Tokyo, the mother, the lake, the night conversation, Kris's dreams), but wasn't sure if the film would work as a whole (D, 45).

The movie was shown to Mosfilm at the end of December, 1971. Unfortunately, Mosfilm requested many changes (35 in all), and then further changes. The comments from Mosfilm and Goskino, detailed in Andrei Tarkovsky's diary for January 12, 1972, included: produce a clearer image of Earth in the future, including some landscapes; clarify the society of the future, whether it's socialist, communist, and capitalist; drop the concept of God and Christianity; cut out the foreign executives at the conference; delete the mother scene; shorten the Earth scenes; shorten the bed scene; cut out the shots of Kris without his trousers; clarify the time for Kris's journey out and back, and his work; show the space journey; make it clear that Kris completed his mission; the encephalogram should be shown at the end; Gibarin should have committed suicide for the benefit of his friends and colleagues; make the necessity for contact more explicit; Hari 'ought not to become a person', and why does she vanish?; Sartorius lacks humanity as a scientist; put the scene back in of Berton and Kris's father talking about their youth; and clarify Solaris and the visitors (D, 49-50).

The movie was released on March 20, 1972, and was chosen to go to Cannes in May, 1972. After the debacle of *Andrei Roublyov*, *Solaris* received a proper release, which must've gratified the filmmakers. Natalia Bondarchuk remarked that she visited many places to promote the film. (Akira Kurosawa, in Russia at this time, recalled how he and Tarkovsky had gone to a restaurant after a late night screening of *Solaris* in Moscow, drunk lot of vodka, and sang the theme from *The Seven Samurai* together).

Andrei Tarkovsky praised Natalia Bondarchuk in his diaries (D, 46); he had considered using Ingmar Bergman regular Bibi Andersson for the part of Hari (as well as his first wife, Irma Rausch, which would've added another layer of autobiography to the project). But Tarkovsky was unhappy with Donatas Banionis, something of a Method actor, who had to know the motivation for his scenes. This wasn't what Tarkovsky wanted from an actor at all. For him, the actor had to be the servant of the film, to fit in with the grand scheme of the film. Tarkovsky didn't want to spend too much time going through explanations or motivations. The idea of working with actors like Robert De Niro or Dustin Hoffman, performers who spend weeks preparing and researching and practising for a role, would be anathema to Tarkovsky.

Solaris was Andrei Tarkovsky's first feature movie in colour (*The Steamroller and the Violin* had been shot in Sovcolor). Tarkovsky said he wasn't entirely happy with his use of colour in *Solaris*, and one can see that in some scenes, where the colour is not as controlled as in the later films (the use of the widescreen format, though, is excellent). After *Solaris*, however, Tarkovsky's films were mainly in colour, though with many black-and-white sequences, and many in the twilit borderland between full colour and black-and-white. (The use of colour is not tied in to the psychological narrative in the film, as it would be in *Mirror* and later films, and the switches to black-and-white seem somewhat arbitrary).

The dichotomies in *Solaris* are between the present and the past, the past as it really was and the past as one'd like it to be, the human and non-human, age and youth, reality and wishes and dreams, inside the station and outside, the individual's unconscious and the Ocean, Earth and Solaris.

It was the 'moral problems' in Stanislaw Lem's novel that attracted Andrei Tarkovsky, not the technology, the science or speculative questions (D, 362). For Tarkovsky, Khari (Hari) represented Kelvin's conscience. As Tarkovsky put it:

> in simple terms, the story of Khari's relationship with Kelvin is the story of the relationship between man and his own conscience. It's about man's concern with his own spirit, when he has no possibility of doing anything about it. (D, 363)

The whole point was that Kelvin wasn't able to do the right thing even when he had a second chance, Tarkovsky explained. Because if he had been able to live the second time around differently, he wouldn't have been guilty the first time (D, 363).

Kris begins *Solaris* detached from people, his face blank, unresponsive, apparently uncaring; his emotional trajectory in the movie is towards love, sympathy, conscience. He comes back to life. The tragedy of *Solaris* is that, by the time Kris has learnt to become more fully human, or human once again, it is too late. He repeats the same mistakes in his relation to the Ocean-made Hari that he made with the real person.

Andrei Tarkovsky fused mother and wife, as he would do to even greater lengths in *Mirror*. Both Kris's mother and wife are depicted in similar ways, as distant, beautiful, blank (with the Leonardo da Vinci Smile). They share the same patchwork dresses and shawls.

Solaris's a slow movie. At the beginning, there's no dialogue until nearly three minutes from the end of the credits. There's no exposition or real conversation for 6 minutes. The exposition of the video tape playback lasts up until 20 minutes (it's far longer and talkier than a contemporary Hollywood movie, which would want to move the story along much swifter;

a Hollywood screenwriter might also be encouraged to find a more compelling method of delivering the scientific exposition. It's as if Andrei Tarkovsky and Friedrich Gorenstein are simply getting the sci-fi bit out of the way, and being deliberately dull in doing so). *Solaris* doesn't reach the space station until some 36 minutes.

The Earth scenes were meant to be beautiful and mysterious, to represent what Kelvin is leaving behind (and revealing his homesickness). For Akira Kurosawa, the early scenes on Earth haunted the rest of the film with their beauty: 'they almost torture the soul of the viewer like a kind of irresistible nostalgia toward mother earth nature, which resembles homesickness'.

The 1972 movie, when it reaches the space station, is harsh and empty, full of white spaces, hard edges, metal, and synthetic materials (plastics, PVC). (The design is still late 1960s – the high-key lighting, the Minimal decor; as in films like *The Knack, THX-1138* or *2001: A Space Odyssey,* or John Lennon's *Imagine* music video, rooms are painted all in white). The long curving corridor, the silvery metal doors, the rows of round windows (one large, with smaller ones on each side), the small shiny mirrors, with the Ocean beyond.

Memory and the past is a recurring theme in *Solaris*, mediated through the modern technology of sci-fi, the video tape (in the book, the video tapes are written reports). There are three video tapes: the account of Berton's visit to Solaris; Gibarin's suicide note to Kris; and Kris's father's home movies. (The home videos are pretty accomplished, with slick camerawork – these are not amateur movies). The home videos include images of Kris's mother in a fur coat, in the snow, and later beside the lake; Hari at the *dacha*, waving to the camera (and dressed in her familiar shawl and beige and brown dress); Kris as a five year-old boy, and very briefly as a teenager.

The ending of *Solaris* looks like this: on the spaceship Johann Sebastian Bach's organ music starts up. Zoom in to Kris's little plant, set against the white circle of the window. This is a poetic link to the opening shots of the film, of the reeds in the river. Then Kris is seen beside the lake, as at the beginning of the movie. It is now wintry, though (the lake is frozen – a wonderful touch, but apparently not intentional). Dead, bare trees. Mist. The *dacha*; the dog; the fire (which's still burning, as if Kris hasn't been away for long). The music ends. Kris approaches the house and looks inside. His father is there, lost in himself, sorting through books and papers. It is raining on him (but he doesn't notice), steam rising from his shoulders. Kris's father sees Kris staring in at the window, and goes to the front door: Kris kneels before him and embraces him, just as he did with his imagined wife. The scene conflates issues such as love, family, œdipal relationships, dreams, memories, wish-fulfilment, patriarchy and death. The scene recalls the Biblical Prodigal's Return (as in Rembrandt's famous 1669 painting in the Hermitage). The ending was partly about, Tarkovsky explained, returning to the source, to the cradle, to home, to the place that can never be forgotten (D, 364). And it has even more significance for Kelvin, because he has travelled so far on the road of technological progress to reach that realization.

The final shot of *Solaris* (actually three shots blended together): in extreme wide angle, a crane up away from and above the house and the embracing father and son. Two dissolves: to a helicopter shot of the house, rising away from it; then to a very distant visual fx view of the house, the lake and the island amid the green Ocean. The electronic music reaches a crescendo, the frame goes white, then fades to black – credit: 'the end'. It is a stunning ending, bigger indeed than *2001: A Space Odyssey.* At the end of *2001: A Space Odyssey*, humankind is reborn as a superbeing, but for what purpose? The ending of *Solaris* is deeper: humanity is shown as being on the point of learning that its purpose is really love, to love and be loved. This is what Kris concludes, or that the movie concludes for him. It is one of Tarkovsky's central messages.

Kris imagines and 'makes' Hari, the 'wife' made of neutrinos. She becomes more human, more like his vision, his version of reality – or, rather, of what he would like reality to be. His wish kills him; desire is a killer. *Solaris* is based on a classic idea in science fiction, but also a classic idea in Western literature. The movie works with mythic, archetypal elements. This man has been encountered a billion times before. He is single, heterosexual, white, bourgeois, highly educated, disenchanted, an outsider. He voyages into the unknown, in true heroic fashion, to solve a mystery. Kris is a protagonist that embodies significant aspects of the modern world: he's, appropriately, a psychologist (the postmodern shaman, the psychologist as a technological witch doctor). (One could see *Solaris*, as Maya Turovskaya does [123], as the only occasion in which Andrei Tarkovsky explored a love story. But it's more like going over the remains of a ten-year-dead love relationship, and when Kris revives the emotional bond with Hari, it is deeply ambiguous. Not least because the rational part of Kris realizes that his beloved is created from neutrinos by an alien presence).

For some critics, *Solaris* is a disappointing movie – as an Andrei Tarkovsky film, or as a sci-fi film. Perhaps if *Solaris* had been conceived and lit and set in a *Stalker*-sort of future world – in a run-down, shabby space station, it might have been better for those critics and viewers expecting that. The actor who plays Kris, Donatas Banionis, is the weakest central performance in Tarkovsky's cinema; unfortunately, so much depends upon his performance – to carry the philosophical and spiritual weight of the movie.

Andrei Tarkovsky and Friedrich Gorenstein added a new character, Maria, Kris's wife, in scenes set on Earth. Stanislaw Lem's novel took place entirely on the space station. Lem rejected Tarkovsky and Gorenstein's first script, in which some two-thirds of the film would be set on Earth. While Lem's book emphasized that human values and emotions are dwarfed by the immensity, indifference and hostility of the cosmos, Tarkovsky's movie enshrined those human qualities to the maximum, clinging onto them up until the last shot. Tarkovsky and Gorenstein added many of their own references to Lem's novel, too: to *Faust* (the scientist Satorius); Fyodor Dostoievsky; Leo Tolstoy; Miguel de Cervantes (*Don Quixote*); Greek mythology (the myth of Sisyphus); and Pieter Brueghel. *Solaris* is in part a compendium of Tarkovsky favourites from high Western culture.

After he'd completed it, Andrei Tarkovsky said he was pleased with *Solaris*, preferring it to *Andrei Roublyov*: '[i]t's more harmonious than *Rublyov*, more purposeful, less cryptic. More graceful, more harmonious than *Rublyov*' (D, 53). His adaption of Lem's novel couldn't be faithful, Tarkovsky asserted: 'I attempted to put on screen my own reader's version of *Solaris*. In order to remain faithful to the author I had to deviate from the novel now and then in search of visual equivalents for certain themes'.

Andrei Tarkovsky said he was intrigued by the idea that Kelvin was an average guy, so ordinary he was also a bore, but something happened to him on Solaris, when he encountered Hari. Unfortunately, Stanislaw Lem didn't share Tarkovsky's take on the story: 'as soon as he [Kelvin] begins to feel something or suffer – he becomes a human being. And this was leaving Lem completely unmoved. Totally unmoved. And I was deeply moved by this'.

Solaris is sometimes mentioned in books on science fiction and fantasy films, and aligned with sci-fi films of the same era – *2001: A Space Odyssey*, obviously, but also quirky *Dark Star* (John Carpenter, 1974), bleak, brilliant *THX 1138* (George Lucas, 1971), environmental odyssey *Silent Running* (Douglas Trumbull, 1973), consumer fantasy *The Cars That Ate Paris* (Peter Weir, 1974), and dystopian *Westworld* (Michael Crichton, 1973).

Solaris is nearly always compared unfavourably with *2001: A Space Odyssey*, although Andrei Tarkovsky was keen to distance himself from MGM's movie, and *Solaris* clearly had very different aims and themes. *The*

History of the Movies guidebook offered a typical view: that it 'was an error for Tarkovsky to have attempted to follow *2001: A Space Odyssey*, a cinematic cul-de-sac, especially with a less dramatic use of decor and technology' (1988, 419). David Thomson was scathing of *Solaris*: '[a]n episode of *Star Trek* explored this theme with more wit and ingenuity, less sentimentality, and a third of the length' (in ib., 419). For Thomson, the 'visualisation of *Solaris* is as senselessly elaborate as in *2001: A Space Odyssey*, and the philosophy as mediocre' (1978, 597).

THE 2002 REMAKE OF *SOLARIS*

There were rumours in 2000 of James Cameron (*Titanic, Terminator, Avatar, Aliens*) being involved in a remake of *Solaris*. The idea of Cameron, of all people in Hollywood, directing a remake of an Andrei Tarkovsky film was depressing for Tarkovsky fans (and not just remaking a Tarkovsky movie, but a very good film, and a classic science fiction film). Somehow, the fusion of the brash, Republican showman of Hollywood blockbusters and a holy icon of art cinema seemed unlikely and unwelcome (my first reaction was: get your filthy hands off Tarkovsky!). Subsequent reports (in early 2001) had director Steven Soderbergh (*Sex, Lies and Videotape, Erin Brockovich, Ocean's Eleven*) attached to the project. The movie emerged from 20th Century Fox in late 2002, with Soderbergh directing and writing, and Cameron, Rae Sanchini and Jon Landau producing. George Clooney and Natascha McElhone starred, with Jeremy Davies, Viola Davis and Ulrich Tukur supporting.

20th Century Fox's *Solaris* was the first Andrei Tarkovsky movie to be remade (although the producers insisted their film was a new and different approach to Stanislaw Lem's novel from the 1972 Mosfilm movie). Indeed, the 2002 *Solaris* was a very different animal: it was a dissection of a love affair between Chris Kelvin and his wife Rheya, containing numerous flashbacks which depicted the various stages of the romance, up to Rheya telling Chris she had been pregnant and had aborted the child, unsure how he would react. The 2002 *Solaris* kept the film at the level of a psycho-drama between two people, while Tarkovsky & co. had moved towards moral, ethical and philosophical explorations.

All fears of Hollywood tarnishing the legacy of Andrei Tarkovsky with a tacky remake were allayed: the 2002 *Solaris* was a smart, minimal take on the novel, but wasn't a patch on the 1972 movie (like Steven Soderbergh's other films, the *Solaris* remake came across as a filmed treatment of what the final movie would look like, a script in progress, rather than a rounded, accomplished film on its own). And it didn't dent Tarkovsky's reputation one bit.

SIXTEEN

Mirror

MIRROR AND POETRY

Mirror (*Zerkalo* or *The Bright, Bright Day*) is a poem. This is the key to understanding the movie. It is a *ciné*-poem, complete with metaphors, allusions, references, historicity, lyricism, concrete and abstract images, a number of voices, motifs and symbols, autobiography, stanzas and refrains. Some images correspond to a line in a poem, while the refrains and links are the shots of fire which fade to black. If one thinks of *Mirror* poetically, then the form – the overlapping, the montages, the merging of imagery and events from the past and present – becomes clear. The spectator has to make an effort to unravel the components of the piece, has to fill in gaps and re-order the events, but it makes sense in the end.

Mirror begins with one of the most poetic ten or fifteen minutes in cinema: from the moment where Maria is sitting on the fence, to the house on fire, then after that to the hair-washing and rain-filled room sequence. There is so much going on, so much that is startling. Only a few movies – like *The Magnificent Ambersons* or *Akira* – have a similarly miraculous first reel. Oliver Assays reckoned (in 1997) that the post-credits sequence is 'one of the most beautiful things I had ever seen in the movies' (1997, 24). Absolutely.

Mirror is Andrei Tarkovsky's beloved project, one he (seems to have) wanted to make for a long time (it remained his favourite movie, and closest to his concept of cinema [CS, 255]). It is loosely autobiographical, and combines many elements, from poetry read in voiceover by the director's father Arseny Tarkovsky, to dream sequences, flashbacks, newsreel and mnemonics (memory devices). The movie is a poetic exploration of childhood: the long dolly shots around the old house in the country and the Moscow apartment explore the spaces of childhood, the geography of memory: the table was there, the chair was here, the window was there, and so on. A movie of acutely remembered places. Film as personal psychogeography, self-reflexive, even indulgent, recalling Federico Fellini's *Otto e Mezzo* (1963) and *Amacord* (1973), classics of the autobiographical or personal movie genre (*Ulysses' Gaze* (Theo Angelopoulos, 1995) is another). For Oliver Assayas, *Mirror* was about film perception, a film which went *beyond* cinema, into 'issues of memory and remembrance, and the relationship between memory and perception' (1997, 24).

One of the fan letters (which Andrei Tarkovsky quoted in his diary) enthused about *Mirror*:

> it is your best film, it is a film about life, the most truthful and realistic film of life that we have ever seen. How is it that you have such amazingly subtle understanding of all the confusion, complexity and splendour of life? (D, 213)

'I believe if one tells the truth, some kind of inner truth, one will always be understood', Andrei Tarkovsky commented, *pace Mirror*. In cinema, Tarkovsky said he wanted both the documentary, factual approach, in which every detail must be accurate, and the emotional, subjective, inner truth.

(But although *Mirror* would be 'a film built in its entirety on personal experience [D, 13], it wouldn't, as Andrei Tarkovsky maintained in *Sculpting In Time*, be Andrei Tarkovsky talking about himself. It was, rather, ultimately a movie about feelings: about his feelings towards his loved ones and relatives, and about his own inadequacy – 'my feeling of duty left unfulfilled' [ST, 134]).

In a 1975 interview, Andrei Tarkovsky said *pace Mirror* that 'there are no entertaining moments in the movie. In fact I am categorically against entertainment in cinema: it is as degrading for the author as it is for the audience.' That's a typical Tarkovskyan comment (but he's totally, utterly wrong about entertainment, I think). Tarkovsky also took a dim view of art's ability to educate, too: 'art cannot teach anyone anything, since in four thousand years humanity has learnt nothing at all' (ST, 50). Art shouldn't explain, or prove, or answer questions, Tarkovsky said (ST, 54).

According to Andrei Tarkovsky's diary, *Mirror* was allocated 622,000 roubles (a small budget; about $2.5 million) and 7,500 metres of Kodak film. Filming began in September, 1973 and finished in March, 1974. *Mirror* was not sent to Cannes (Tarkovsky and co-writer Alexander Misharin blamed Filip Yermash, Goskino's chairman, for this). It was released in the Soviet Union in early 1975 at a third (then second) distribution category.

The 1975 film had a number of titles. It was *The Bright, Bright Day* (or *The White, White Day*) for a long time (this title comes from one of Arseny Tarkovsky's poems). In February, 1973 Tarkovsky wrote: 'I don't like *The Bright Day* as a title. It's limp. *Martyrology* is better, only nobody knows what it means; and when they find out they won't allow it. *Redemption* is a bit flat, it smacks of Vera Panova. *Confession* is pretentious. *Why Are You Standing So Far Away?* is better, but obscure' (D, 69). It's not just in pre-1989 Soviet Russia where filmmakers were forbidden to use a title by state institutions. In the West, titles are not copyrighted (at least in the UK), but it would be a foolish company, however, that tried using names such as 'Disney', 'MacDonald's' or 'Coca Cola' on a product or service, those corporations being notorious for the number of litigations they pursue). But Tarkovsky is not to referring to another studio, company or artist who might prevent him from using a title, but to the Soviet authorities.

Mirror started to take shape around 1968, when Andrei Tarkovsky worked with his co-writer, Alexander Misharin (Tarkovsky had asked Misharin to help him edit the script of *Andrei Roublyov*, which Misharin had been reluctant to do, because Andrei Konchalovsky was the writer, but wasn't around at the time. Misharin helped Tarkovsky to cut out a whole section of *Andrei Roublyov*).

Andrei Tarkovsky had originally planned filming interviews with his mother with a concealed camera, using questions such as 'when did you begin smoking?', 'do you like animals?', 'are you superstitious?', 'are men or women stronger, do you think?', 'do you ever have friends outside your circle?', 'do you always speak the truth?', 'what would make you especially happy now?', 'have you ever envied youth?', 'which are your favourite poems?', 'are you capable of hatred?', 'which part of your life would you say was happy?', 'what do you think about space travel?', 'do you like Bach?', 'what do you remember about the war with Spain?', 'what was the funniest thing that ever happened to you?', 'are you a good swimmer?', 'do you remember the day when you sensed you would become a mother for the first time?', 'which is your favourite season?', 'have you ever starved?', 'what do you think about war?', 'what is freedom?', 'how many years did you work at the printers?', and 'are you scared of the dark?'

Mirror, according to the script *A Bright, Bright Day* (Mosfilm, 1973), was going to have less documentary footage and more memories of Tarkovsky's childhood. The narrator was going to quote from Aleksandr Pushkin's 'The Prophet' (a favourite Tarkovsky text) and walk past a funeral at a cemetery, encouraging the narrator to muse on life and death.

The Bright, Bright Day screenplay had opened with a scene in a cemetery, and a funeral. Scenes included the demolition of a church in

1939; the mother selling flowers in a market; a horse riding lesson; a scene at a ractrack; and a forest scene at night (M. Turovskaya, 63).

> I wanted to tell the story of the pain suffered by one man because he feels he cannot repay his family for all they have given him [Tarkovsky wrote in *Sculpting In Time*]. He feels he hasn't loved them enough, and this idea torments him and will not let him be. (133-4)

The Mosfilm movie would be about a mother, Andrei Tarkovsky said: 'any mother capable of arousing an interest in the authors,' Andrei Tarkovsky and Alexander Misharin wrote in their proposal for *Mirror* (when the film was called *Confession*): 'as all mothers, she must have had a full and fascinating life. This must be the ordinary story of a life, with its hopes, its faith, its grief and its joys' (CS, 257). The concept, according to Misharin and Tarkovsky, was to trace the 'spiritual organization of our society' through 'the rightful fate of one person; a person whom we know and love, who is called Mother' (CS, 258).

The narrator in *Mirror* is strictly a *narrator*, in the technical, literary sense of the term. Rather than being the narrator of a novel, however, *Mirror*'s narrator is the narrator of poetry, because *Mirror* is a *ciné*-poem, rather than the cinematic adaption of a novel. (And, to reinforce that, *Mirror* quotes from poetry far more than novels). So, although he is heard off-screen, interacts with characters (chiefly with Natalia), and is glimpsed briefly on his death bed, he is still not really meant to be a flesh-and-blood character like Maria, Ignat or Natalia. He is the narrator of the poem that is the movie.

The script continually evolved, with daily rewrites (that's normal on many movies, but *Mirror* had a loose structure, which could accommodate all sorts of additions or alterations.[1] As Andrei Tarkovsky wrote in *Sculpting In Time*, 'a great deal was finally thought out, formulated, built up, only in the course of shooting' [131]). Tarkovsky acknowledged that *Mirror* was the most complex of his films structurally and dramatically. The stuttering and hypnotism scene (which opens the film) was probably going to be put somewhere in the middle of the film, because the twelve year-old Ignat is seen turning on the television in the present-day Moscow apartment. Ignat would thus have been introduced differently. A likely opening of *Mirror* would have been: (1) the titles followed by (2) the long tracking shot around the narrator's apartment, establishing the present-day location, and the narrator, then (3) the printing works scene, then (4) the mother and doctor scene in the field.

The post-production of *Mirror* was troublesome because the first rough cuts of the movie didn't work (and it wasn't simply a case of the filmmakers hating the first rough cut, as they so often do). *Mirror* was '*extremely difficult* to edit', Andrei Tarkovsky confessed (my emphasis). The movie, as Alexander Misharin noted, had too many scenes and too many themes, and they couldn't be arranged by editor Lyudmilla Feiginova into a form that satisfied everyone. If the scenes were arranged in a particular pattern, Misharin said, some other scenes would be left out. There was a moment of revelation when the 34 or so scenes fell into the final form. As Misharin told it, Tarkovsky's wife Larissa had sewn a kind of sack with pockets in it, which they hung on the wall and placed the scenes in each pocket. As if by a miracle, Misharin remembered, both he and Tarkovsky had seized the scenes at the same time and shuffled them into the same order. After that, the post-production of *Mirror* continued without problems.

Alexander Misharin recalled that the writing process on *Mirror* had been intense for a time: he and Andrei Tarkovsky had shut themselves away for three or so weeks and wrote every day. They employed a common practice among co-writers: they wrote scenes on their own, then swapped them and edited the other's scenes. Misharin said people reckoned they knew which were the scenes Tarkovsky had written and which were his, but often the opposite was the case. *Mirror* was not only about Tarkovsky's past and family; there was plenty of Misharin's background in there, too. Misharin recalled that he and Tarkovsky only fell out seriously once or twice.

The newsreel footage in *Mirror* is a substantial element in the movie. It is gathered from all sorts of sources, the result of anonymous camera teams, and from so many places – throughout Russia, but also in China, in Berlin, in Spain, in Prague, and in Hiroshima. A lot of the footage is familiar from the countless documentaries on World War Two, on Russian history, on Nazi Germany, and on 20th century history (there are whole cable and satellite channels now dedicated to airing this kind of material).

But Andrei Tarkovsky deploys it in quite different manner from the typical TV documentary. There are no captions and no voiceovers identifying the many images and historical events. And none of the characters in *Mirror* refer to the footage, or even to the events depicted in the newsreels. Instead, Tarkovsky relies on the viewer's knowledge of history to fill in the gaps. Some of the newsreel will be familiar (the nuclear bomb explosions require no gloss). But much of it will be unknown to many in the audience. At the same time, viewers will not need to know where and when some of the newsreels were shot. The remarkable footage of the Soviet balloonists, for example, or the moving images of soldiers trudging doggedly through mud and water do not require the viewer to know all the details. (Editor Lyudmilla Feiginova does employ one of the standard devices of TV news and documentaries: she and sound man Semyon Litvinov add studio sound effects to footage that was shot silent (as a lot of it was).)

Some viewers and critics were confused by the use of the same actors for different roles in *Mirror* (even though this is is a not uncommon strategy: it's used in the *Back To the Future* series [1985-90], for instance, and other time travel movies. A famous instance occurs in *The Wizard of Oz* [1939], although that's not time travel).

Part of the point of using the same actors and actresses for the mother/ wife and narrator/ son is to show that the past and present are connected and interfuse. The present exists beside the past, not only in dreams and memories, but also in people, in their faces, personalities and actions. There is a historical, social and personal continuity. One cannot escape the influence of the past, and the same situations are re-enacted (for example, the 1930s family is broken, and the present-day husband and wife have parted). Cinema works at the point of viewing in a continuous present, yet it is always, as Jean Cocteau said, 'filmed death'. The past and present are bound up tightly together in the last shot of the film: Maria is there, and Maria as an old woman with Maria's two children (the old woman doubles as a grandmother). Matriarchy and female solidarity is affirmed, as is generation-to-generation continuity, ambiguity and sadness.

'I should like to ask you all not to be so demanding, and not to think of *Mirror* as a difficult film', Andrei Tarkovsky asserted in 1975. It is no more than a straightforward, simple story. It doesn't have to be made any more understandable.

Structurally, there are two moments in the past that are explored in *Mirror*: 1935-36, 1942-43, and the present (*c.* 1974). The movie principally takes place in these *three* time zones (discounting the newsreels), and in, primarily, *two* locations: a modern day apartment in Moscow, where the narrator lives (but is not seen); and the *dacha* (house) in the country, where the narrator lived as a boy with his mother, while his father was away at war or in the services. Characters are compared to each other, while others are irreconcilably opposed. (The newsreels, though, are roughly chronological).

Past (1935 and 1942)		Present (about 1974)
Maria, the mother	>	Natalia, the modern wife/ mother
Children's grandmother	>	Maria as an old woman (*and the narrator's mother*)
Aleksei, aged 5		
Aleksei, aged 12	>	Ignat, aged 12
Father (soldier)	>	Aleksei, the narrator

The mother and the boy of the past also dwell in the present. There are further complexities: Andrei Tarkovsky's real father reads his own poems (but the poetry in the movie is not identified as by Arseny Tarkovsky), while Tarkovsky's own mother appears as the grandmother (Maria as an old woman), *and* the grandmother in the 1935-36 scenes (or she is Maria as an old woman transposed to the past).

Pier Paolo Pasolini had cast his mother to play the aged Virgin Mary in *The Gospel According To Matthew* (and Martin Scorsese liked to use his mother in minor roles). Andrei Tarkovsky's own step-daughter was the red-haired beloved of the teenage Aleksei, and Tarkovsky's second wife, Larissa Tarkovskaya, played the doctor's wife. The *dacha* of the past is built on (the foundations of) Tarkovsky's real childhood home (it was important for Tarkovsky to build his childhood home in the *exact* spot it had once stood). The movie is one long evocation of one person's childhood. It might have turned out self-indulgent and pretentious. Instead it is magnificent and profound.

MIRROR AS SPIRITUAL (AUTO)BIOGRAPHY

The function of the image, as Gogol said, is to express life itself, not ideas or arguments about life. It does not signify life or symbolise it, but embodies it, expressing its uniqueness.

Andrei Tarkovsky, *Sculpting In Time* (111)

As an evocation of childhood, the yearning, mystery and pain of it, *Mirror* is unsurpassed in cinema. True, Andrei Tarkovsky does simplify things by missing out the agony of adolescence. Instead he chooses two ages, five and twelve, in which children are still children, and not restless, disaffected, disappointed teenagers. The movie could be extended indefinitely through a variety of age ranges: 2, 8, 15, 19, 26, and so on. Tarkovsky also excludes a crucial part of childhood – education and school; also, the child's relations with other children. By leaving out school and friends, Tarkovsky presents a highly selective view of childhood. For Tarkovsky, childhood is largely a lonely experience, with parental affection a rarity.

Mirror also acts as the spiritual biography of an age: the eras of 1935-36 and 1942-43 are so poignantly evoked by the newsreels. These images, seemingly a world away from an intimate portrait of childhood, fuse beautifully with the rest of the film. There are moments of forced symbolism – the narrator releasing the bird, for instance, which is intended to relate to his death. It is a motif out of the dumbest pop promo (don't Queen have a video where Freddie releases a white dove?). The movie, though, soars above pretension and artifice by the magnitude of its passion. There is no denying the lucidity and poetic authenticity of these mnemonic images. *Mirror* is the closest thing in cinema to a poem by Rainer Maria Rilke, Arthur Rimbaud or C.P. Cavafy, those masters of the poetry of nostalgia. Like the poems of Rilke, Cavafy and Rimbaud, *Mirror* is a dense mesh of constellations of images and memories, a veritable mnemonic banquet. It is a movie of fierce self-reflexive intensity – something like Rimbaud in his poem of childhood 'Le Poëtes de sept ans'. Among the thousands of mainstream (Hollywood) movies that try to depict children and childhood, very few come close to the luminous authenticity of *Mirror*. Yet *Mirror* never slips into easy sentimentality (although it does come close once or twice). It never becomes complacent or banal. It is marvellously self-reflexive, yet avoids all the traps of inwardly-looking art. Though unashamedly introspective, *Mirror* virtually achieves a universal transcendence.

CRITICS ON *MIRROR*

Michael Dempsey called *Zerkalo* 'intractable', 'ineffable' and 'enigmatic' (1981). 'Enigmatic' *Mirror* certainly is. Some critics said it was 'a crossword puzzle'. Herbert Marshall reckoned in a 1976 article that *Mirror* was very unusual in terms of mid-Seventies Soviet cinema, and was difficult for Soviet critics to understand (95). Nothing like it had been seen in Soviet cinema before, Marshall asserted. *Mirror* is not only told entirely subjectively, but from a subjective point of view at different periods of life both in reality and in memories and dreams, from a boy, a teenager, to a man, the director himself, and his father and mother. Such a film has hitherto never been seen on the Soviet screen. (ib., 95).

According to John Dunlop, *Mirror* 'encountered a wall of opposition on the part of the Soviet film industry'.[1] Some critics (Maya Turoskaya, T. Elmanovits, Mikhail Bakhtin, V.I. Solovyov) saw *Mirror* as the record not of one's person's life, but of a generation. V.I. Solovyov caught the spirit of the movie right when he said in *Novoye russkoye slovo* that *Mirror* seemed to be portraying 'not film images but *my* thoughts, *my* memories' (1989, 11). Maurice Clavel wrote of *Mirror* that there is 'no other film like it. One can see how little subjectivist this film is. Perhaps it itself is sacrificial, like Russia according to Pushkin'.[2]

Viewers wrote to Andrei Tarkovsky about how much *Mirror* had affected them. Tarkovsky subsequently quoted some of these letters in *Sculpting in Time*. For Leonid Bakhtin, part of *Mirror*'s power is precisely its puzzling, mysterious elements. Jacques Grant noted that *Mirror* is not so much an anti-Marxist as an 'a-Marxist' movie; Tarkovsky avoids confronting politics; Grant saw the motif of the mirror as a barrier, 'placed by the filmmaker between himself and a world which he refuses to see and to discuss' (1978, 68). That's a common criticism among film reviewers, castigating the director for *not* making the movie they thought he should have made. Why *should* a personal movie be about memories of childhood deal with politics or the so-called 'real' world? But of course, Tarkovsky *does* address social, historical and political issues throughout *Mirror*, not only by including the many newsreel images, but also evoking a moving scene of Stalinist repression. There are many other movies of childhood which completely avoid references to historical events. In fact, *Mirror* is *very* unusual in being both a film of personal memories *and* wider historical and social issues.

---

[1] In A. Lawton, 1992, 241.

SEVENTEEN

Stalker

ON *STALKER*

Stalker's *mise-en-scène* is roughly-hewn, broken-down, burnt-out and long-forgotten: buildings and machines lie derelict, areas are grassed-over, distinctly post-apocalyptic (or at least – at best – post-industrial). The Stalker's home is a derelict place, with bare floorboards, sparsely furnished, the daughter's crutches lean against a wall, pills and a glass of water on a round bedside table, and lightbulbs that burn out. In the last shots, hundreds of books on shelves are shown in the Stalker's bedroom. The preamble text, after the opening credits, tells how the Zone was caused by an alien presence. The movie may be taking place in some present or near-future, but the post-industrial desuetude could be 1879 or 1939 or 2079, as well as 1979, when the film was released (and it could be set, like *The Sacrifice*, with not that many changes, in A.D. 85, as well as 1979 or 1985). The landscape of *Stalker* is, as usual in Tarkovsky's cinema, not confined to any particular time frame.

Critics have aligned the world of *Stalker* with Stalinist Russia. For Balint Anrdás Kovács and Akos Szilágyi, the Zone represents the secrets a society withholds to maintain itself. It's an area of the past (and collective memory) which's officially closed off (except to the outsiders who have to explore it continually). Reviews in the U.S.A. (such as by Janet Maslin and Vincent Canby) were much less excited than European critics (by the time of *Stalker*, the Andrei Tarkovsky cult was growing in Europe). Maya Turoskaya spoke of *Stalker*'s 'minimal' look (1989, 109). For David Wingrove, in *Science Fiction Film Source Book*, the Zone is 'the spiritual heartland, the imagination, life itself in the midst of non-life', whose sinister, alien nature is suggested with no visual effects at all, making *Stalker* true science-fiction, as well as

> pure cinema – a wonderful succession of multiple expressive images which accumulate in the viewer's mind and attain deep significance...

not merely an exceptional science fiction film, a great work of art, and perhaps the most memorable experience in sf [sci-fi] cinema. (1985)

Scott Bukatman in *Terminal Identity* linked the Zone with other sci-fi zones, such as the 'Interzone' of William Burroughs, the zonal geography in Jean-Luc Godard's movie *Alphaville*, and the segmented Germany in Thomas Pynchon's *Gravity Rainbow* (1993, 163). John Moore asserted that *Stalker* is 'arguably the most sophisticated science fiction film to be made to date' (1999, 121).

When Andrei Tarkovsky got his hands on the *Stalker* project, Maya Turovskaya remarked, the sci-fi element was pruned back to just a few elements (the Zone, the daughter, the journey, the wishes). 'Nobody now died, nobody reached their goal, nobody even crossed the threshold' (107). In the original proposal, there were two stalkers – 'Carrion Crow' and 'Red' (the latter was basis for the Stalker in the film). Inside the Zone there were visions of people who were caught in time-warps, mirages, dangerous marshes. and the Writer wanders into a house and decides to stay there (CS, 378).

The dangerous aspects of the Zone exist primarily in the Stalker's dialogue: the Writer and the Professor and the viewer do not get to *see* what the Zone can do. The threats, the traps, the hardships seem to exist only in the Stalker's mind. The Writer and the Professor only have his word to go by. Only rarely does the Zone actually offer something dangerous, and even then it is ambiguous: when the Writer approaches the Room via a direct route, a voice calls out to him, telling him to stop and go back. But even this may just be a Wizard of Oz moment, because it's only a voice, and nothing more, which threatens the Writer. There's nothing tangible (no sci-fi monsters here, no arrows, no gunshots). And even this voice, it is suggested, could have been produced by the Writer himself.

But the Stalker walks about as if he's being watched all the time, as if he's in someone's gun sight, as if the Zone will sprang a new trap at any moment. The Stalker's behaviour is paranoia encapsulated: he's always telling the other two not to touch things, or to stay away from certain areas.

Stalker was intended to have a unity of time and space and action, Andrei Tarkovsky said, to take place within a space-time close to real time (ST, 193). 'I wanted it to be as if the whole film had been made in a single shot', Tarkovsky wrote in *Sculpting In Time* (193). David Russell remarked that Tarkovsky's movies together make 'one great film', which motifs, images, events, characters and themes echoing each other.[1]

According to Anne Lawton (1992), *Stalker* was seen by three million people in a year, while *Moscow Distrusts Tears* (Vladimir Menshov, 1980), which won Best Foreign Film Oscar, was seen by 75 million (three million may be a small audience for a Russian movie in its homeland, but that's not a complete flop – especially since *Stalker* was really an art movie. A typical Hollywood film might be seen by 30 million viewers after it's finished its cycle through theatrical, satellite, airlines, pay-TV, cable, DVD and video, network and syndicated television markets). Tarkovsky said *Stalker* wasn't his favourite film: 'it was very difficult to make it, almost impossible to edit it'.[2] At other times, the maestro said he was very pleased with it.

The locations for *Stalker* included: Dolgopa in Russia; Tallinn in Estonia; Isfara in Tajikistan; and Chernobyl / Pripyat in Ukraine (the whole movie was going to be shot in Tajikistan at one time – but an earthquake scuppered that idea). *Stalker* was shot twice. The problems with the imported Kodak film stock were sensed from day one of the shoot (the editor, Lyudmila Feiginova, explained that Russian labs were not so good at processing Kodak stock. Three other films had problems with the faulty film stock). *Stalker* was shot in 1.37:1 aspect ratio. Andrei Tarkovsky had to wait some time before he saw the rushes, and shooting continued until the fault was made official. By that time, about half of the film had been made, and two thirds of the budget had been spent. Tarkovsky said in his journal that the footage shot at Tallinn had to be scrapped twice – because of faulty equipment as well as Mosfilm's laboratory processing (D, 146). A later diary entry had the film being defective three times (D, 154).

Accounts differ on exactly how the movie was closed down and re-started a month later. Andrei Tarkovsky apparently used the technical fault to stop the shoot and rethink the film – it wasn't the total disaster it might have been to other filmmakers. If Tarkovsky had been *really* happy with the film as it was being shot, he would have kicked up a big fuss if the stock was faulty. Goskino was considering writing off the film as a 'creative accident'; Tarkovsky was happy to write off the film already shot, but wanted to begin again from scratch. He got his way. (The clashes with collaborators may have been more damaging than the technical set-backs).

Goskino and chairman Filip Yermash gave the green light for the maestro to start over – if he agreed to make *Stalker* as a two-part project (which he did); it was a way of exploiting the technicalities. And it meant that Andrei Tarkovsky could rewrite the film (which he did), hire a new cinematographer (Georgy Reberg was out, Leonid Kalashnikov was in), and a new set designer (Alexander Boym was out, and Shavkat Abdusalamov was in). (Tarkovsky had had problems with both his DP and set designer, both crucial roles on a Tarkovsky production. Odd, because Tarkovsky had got on with Reberg during *Mirror*, which had been one of the happier shoots for Tarkovsky; and Reberg's contribution to *Mirror* is immense. But Tarkovsky had also replaced his regular cinematographer for *Mirror*, Vadim Yusov. Even so, some of the scenes that Reberg shot – such as the waterfall scene – made it into *Stalker*'s final cut, according to editor Feiginova, DPs Reberg and Knyazhinsky and actor Kaidanovsky).

So shutting down *Stalker* was also a way of hiring new crew members, as well as rewriting the script. There were eventually some ten versions of the script, according to actors Alexander Kaidanovsky and Nikolai Grinko. It also meant new money, and more raw stock.

The crew had been shooting in Estonia for some three and a half months (from May to August, 1977) before the production was halted. The budget for *Stalker* was originally (in 1977) planned to be 650,000 roubles according to some estimates (about $2.6 million). It went up to a million roubles ($4m).

Shooting continued in late August, 1977. When the movie was planned again, this time as a two-part project, it was put into the 1978 slate of productions, and shooting resumed in June, 1978, in Tallinn. A third DP was hired (Alexander Knyazhinsky), with Andrei Tarkovsky now taking over as production designer. Post-production continued through December, 1978 into early 1979, with Goskino accepting the movie in May, 1979 (and – a first for Tarkovsky – no major cuts or alterations were requested). (Tarkovsky fired some of the *Stalker* crew, such as Alexander Boym and Shavkat Abdusalimov, but some – like Leonid Kalashnikov – had walked out.) The Soviet authorities (including military officials) didn't like the movie, and it had a limited release (only 196 prints were struck, for instance). Within Russia, *Stalker* was negatively reviewed in general – or simply ignored. Its positive reputation in the West – to the point of now being a cult movie – really began with a showing at Cannes in 1980.

A. Merkulov also remarked that the budget of the second movie (300,000 roubles/ $1.2m) only covered the first part, so that the production team had to stretch the budget for half of the film over the whole movie. Merkulov noted how, a year earlier, they had had many tanks and vehicles for the scene in the Zone, but had to make do with three tanks second time around. Merkulov spoke movingly of how devastating it must have been for Tarkovsky when the film shot was ruined. But set-backs, projects begun and uncompleted, projects that never get past the script stage, are common occurrences for the professional movie-maker. It wasn't the first time that a film was shot then abandoned, but the fact that it was a technical fault with experimental film stock must have seemed frustratingly stupid (and avoidable) to Tarkovsky and the production team.

Merkulov even suggested that the film stock may have been deliberately wrecked.

Despite the financial and logistical difficulties, the personality clashes, the hirings and firings, the stops and starts, and the lengthy production cycle, *Stalker* wound up as one of Tarkovsky's most accomplished and hypnotic movies.

Stalker was based on the Strugatsky brothers' novel. (Andrei Tarkovsky said that Georgy Kalatozisvili had considered making *Roadside Picnic* into a movie, but hadn't been able to come to an agreement with the Strugatsky brothers.) The Strugatskys' books (Boris, b. 1931, and Arkady, 1925-1991) were concerned with issues such as technology, social change, nuclear power, relativity, and how science affected the individual. Their work included *Destination: Amaltheia, Far Rainbow, Second Invasion, Monday Begins On Saturday, Tale of the Troika, Snail On the Slope,* the *Maxim Trilogy, Definitely Maybe* and *The Ugly Swans*. The Strugatskys' novels, including *Roadside Picnic*, explored social and individual morality.[3]

Most of the script collaboration on *Stalker* was between Arkady Strugatsky, Boris having withdrawn from the project (not everyone could work with Andrei Tarkovsky; Arkady Strugatsky said that Tarkovsky would work on the script late into the night, then shoot the next day). The break on *Stalker* after the film stock was ruined gave Tarkovsky & co. an opportunity to rewrite the movie yet again. Tarkovsky took out the references to multiple zones in the book, the detailed descriptions of the zones, and the precise explanations of them; he altered the character of the stalker (called Red in the book; Tarkovsky toned down his more ruthless personality); Tarkovsky also lost the Golden Ball, the object of the quest in the Zone (which grants wishes); Monkey is more mutated in the book (her mutations are caused by Red's journeys in the Zone, and Red's wish is for his daughter to be cured).

But Andrei Tarkovsky did keep plenty of elements from the book (such as the 'Plague Quarter' borders around the Zone, the gun, the nuts thrown to test the terrain, the trains and flatcars, and the fundamental narrative of the quest to the heart of the Zone). An early draft of (entitled *The Wish Machine*) had the Stalker going into the Zone to ask for a cure for Monkey.

The Stalker, the spiritual as well as physical guide to the Zone, explains the Zone: how it's difficult to traverse it; how direct routes are not always the best or quickest; how new traps are created and old ones abandoned; how one can't go back the same way; how one mustn't go into the Zone with the wrong intentions (such as bringing a weapon); how the wretched, those who have lost all hope, are let through. The Stalker explains the Zone all the way through the movie, not just in a preliminary piece of exposition.

It's his favourite subject of conversation, he reveres it as well as being terrified of it.

Andrei Tarkovsky stressed the physical, non-allegorical nature of the Zone, saying it didn't stand it for anything else; it was not a metaphor. But it's totally metaphysical and allegorical! The Zone is clearly a 'mindscreen', to use Bruce Kawin's term (1978), but it is also the 'mindscreen' of the Writer and Scientist as well as the Stalker, and also a collective mindscreen. It is a mysterious, dystopian, forbidden and forbidding place. Critics have linked *Stalker*'s Zone to Chernobyl, the site of the 1980s nuclear accident; to Mayak, the guarded radioactive city; and to the Gulags (the Stalker looks like a Gulag or concentration camp inmate). The Stalker was related by critics to an inmate (a 'zek') of the labour camps, and the Zone to the camps, the Gulag, to Russia, and to the Eastern Bloc nations.

In "The Thing from Inner Space", Slavoj Zizek said the Zone in *Stalker* might have five possible meanings for a Russian audience: a prohibited area; a Gulag or prison; land poisoned by technology (such as nuclear or biological warfare, Chernobyl); forbidden foreign territory (like Berlin within the GDR); or a meteorite impact zone (like Tunguska in Siberia).

Certainly the Zone evokes nuclear disaster areas (the Stalker throws metal nuts to uncover radioactive waste), but it is not any specific site. It could be the site of any disaster (such as a virus or plague, or a former war zone). The tiled floor and hypodermic needles evoke 'an abandoned laboratory of deadly experiments'.[4] It seems to post-industrial, a one-time factory or power plant; but it might also be a scientific research centre. There are few dramatic spaces in *Stalker*: the Zone, the Stalker's home, the bar, the factories where they climb aboard the railway truck.

Cleverly, the filmmakers have the Zone appear a more complicated place than it at first looks. There is a gulf between the Zone as it appears to the viewer and as the characters (particularly the Stalker) react to it. The camera pans to a waterfall and a great surge of white water – one imagines it to be deep and dangerous. But then the actors step through it: it's only ankle-deep. The pipe (called the 'meat-grinder' by the Stalker) seems innocuous enough, but the Stalker is terrified of it (and his fear infects the others). In the script, the pipe scene is only 3/8ths of a page (CS, 405); in the movie, it's a major sequence. In *Stalker*, it becomes wearying just to walk a few yards. This is a wasteland in miniature.

One might see the *Stalker* landscape as Freudian and over-eroticized: the long tunnel, for instance, which can be seen as a vaginal image, followed by the flooded room at the end of it, which is suitably uterine. The Room itself, the goal or Grail of the whole film, can also be seen as a womb motif, recalling mythological motifs of plenitude, such as Eden or Paradise, or the Holy Grail and the Celtic cauldron over-flowing with life. (Tarkovsky's films contain many elements of mythology and Classic Greek tragedy, which enable them to transcend their eras.) The climax of the movie has the protagonists sitting down on the floor of the Room. There is a pool in front of them, and the major element in the climactic shot is rain falling. The imagery of the rain, the pool and the Room can be seen as relating to rebirth, women's mysteries, a 'return to the Mother', and natal themes (rain as life-giving, orgasmic *jouissance*, the re-affirmation of primal, natural reality). The rain shatters the mirror of the pool, which has reflected back the protagonists' male narcissism and fantasies for much of the movie. The shattering of the mirror destroys the men's slide into narcissistic fantasy, abstraction and idealism, and restores the real, mobile, changeable, transient natural world. But it could have any other interpretation: the never-ending nature of a quest, say, or that the travellers can't avoid bringing their own neuroses and worldviews with them which are reflected back at them. (In the script of *Stalker*, the climax is only a quarter of a page of stage directions [CS, 414]).

Stalker is the first movie of Andrei Tarkovsky's late, mature style, which's marked by the long, slow sequence shot, the long and slow zoom in or tracking shot. Time expands softly, slowly. The film itself is long (some 160 minutes), but contains only about 142 shots, an extraordinarily low number for a film of the late 1970s (and this is even more amazing, because it's 142 shots in a film of two hours and forty minutes, not a conventional one hour and thirty or forty minute feature movie). This makes an average shot length of over a minute (the equivalent in a Hollywood movie from the 1970s onwards would be less than four or five seconds). A typical Hollywood feature of the time might have 800-1,000 shots (or more, in a movie of 2 1/2 hours-plus). By the 1990s and 2000s, 1,500 was not uncommon.

So *Stalker* is a movie constructed from lengthy sequence shots, many lasting several minutes. The camera tracks just above surfaces: a sewer pipe strewn with refuse, a water-logged interior, the human body as a landscape. The shots dazzle with their dynamic cinematography, and they fit together seamlessly. The tension in each shot seems to hang precariously on the edge of something – as if something extraordinary or puzzling is going to happen, or as if the film itself is going to burn in the projector, as in a candle or a fire. Or perhaps it might be swept away or dissolved by the dripping water. Tarkovsky's later films have this quality of being on the edge of destruction – or transfiguration. A film in the process of melting away into itself. A film burning to ashes like the book of poems in *Nostalghia* or the house in *The Sacrifice*, or melting into a clear mountain stream. Nothing left in the darkness but the sound of running water. The movie ends, you shut your eyes in the dark – but still hear running water.

Most of the sets in *Stalker* appear to be adaptions of existing locations (Tarkovsky is credited as art director – after two previous designers had been fired. Rashit Safiullin was set decorator. In the Hollywood system, the production designer, prop master and the art director are not the same people as the ones who actually dress the sets). High on the list of props and equipment on *Stalker for* the art department and the physical effects crew must have been hoses, rigs and trucks for rain and creating puddles, smoke and fog machines, greens (plants), scrapped military vehicles, and the entire contents of junkyards and cast-offs from factories and hospitals, for the machinery and detritus strewn over the Zone (the newspapers, the cables, the bits of metal, the trash of whole towns). At times, the dressing of the sets in a Tarkovsky film looks as if a flood or tidal wave has receded, leaving pools of brackish water, grass permanently damp or dewy, and garbage strewn everywhere.

When the travellers halt in the middle of the 1979 Russian movie, they lie or sit beside a shallow pool; the Stalker is isolated on a little island, his hand lying in the water. (Sometimes the water in *Stalker* looks stagnant and lifeless, appropriate for the post-apocalyptic environment of the story). As well as pools in *Stalker,* there are rivers, lakes, flooded warehouses, dripping tunnels, rooms of water, and waterfalls. The only obviously artificial set, and the least successful example of production design, because it looks so self-consciously 'futuristic' or weird, is the room of mounds of sand (Tarkovsky designed this set).

Musically, *Stalker* focusses on one of Eduard Artemiev's compositions: the lyrical, haunting flute theme (also known as the Stalker's theme). There was plenty more music written by Artemiev for *Stalker*, but editor Lyudmila Feiginova and Andrei Tarkovsky opted not to use it. The idea of using classical music behind the sound of the train, in the Stalker's house scenes that open and close the movie, derived from Tarkovsky telling Artemiev that he heard music behind the rhythmic sounds of trains. Thus, Ludwig van Beethoven and Maurice Ravel can be discerned underneath the rattle and rumble of the train. (Using classical music was also part of Tarkovsky's project of grounding cinema in something historically recognizable to the audience. The same approach was used in *Star Wars*).

Stalker is a movie, like *Nostalghia*, in which hardly anything happens. There is no 'action' in the traditional, Hollywood sense of the term. *Stalker*'s 'action' is deeply interiorized and contemplative, bordering on the mystical. No car chases, multiple explosions, drugs, gadgets, spaceships, special effects, techno-fetishism, fist fights, sex scenes, or 500 uses of the word 'fuck'.

The movie is itself (and for its maker) a religious quest. Making the film becomes a prayer and re-making the film (on viewing it) becomes a pilgrimage. The quest of the three main protagonists is also religious (or at least philosophical). As in fairy tales and mediæval pilgrimages, characters set out to find what they've always desired (or feared). As the Stalker puts it, what you've desired brings you most pain in life. Your desire defines your life. As Tarkovsky rightly realizes, it is not the goal, not this or that particular sacred site or Holy Land that matters to the pilgrims, but the journey itself. Each traveller has different motives and goals, and each re-evaluates their lives by the end of their journey near the end of the film (the Writer seems to be re-evaluating his goals throughout the film. Unlike the others, the Writer is continuously psychoanalyzing himself – and everything else around him). *Stalker*, Tarkovsky said in *Sculpting In Time*, was about 'human dignity, and how a man suffers if he has no self-respect' (ST, 194).

The three men can be seen as:

Art	Science	Religion
Writer	*Scientist*	*Stalker*
Poetry anti-rationalism/ cynicism	rationalism/ unbelief/ industry/ war	magic pure faith intuition

Only the Stalker can see (or feel) the danger in the Zone (but when the others disobey his orders, they don't seem to suffer any significant consequences). He has faith/ belief/ God. He believes, wholeheartedly. He does not question his belief, nor the Zone and its properties. The other two veer from naïve, ever-hopeful primitive belief, to world-weary cynicism: at times they despise the Zone and their reasons for being there. Sometimes both the Writer and the Professor offer bored cynicism in response to the Zone, but they also fear it, and respond swiftly to the Stalker's awed reaction to the Zone.

As in *Nostalghia*, there are the familiar Tarkovskyan motifs in *Stalker* of a dog, fire, water, birds, milk, and so on. There are many passages of near-silence. There is less and less dialogue as the movie progresses. (The family members may also represent principles: Monkey is the mystical, the Stalker is the religious or spiritual, and the Stalker's wife is the social or ethical principle). In the script, the Professor tells the Writer that the

Stalker was crippled in the Zone by a bad accident, and has been in prison twice (CS, 397). He also used to work for the Professor as a lab technician.

There are Christian themes in *Stalker*: aside from the religious nature of the quest and the 'miraculousness' of the Zone, the Stalker himself is linked with Christ. He looks like a suffering saint and martyr; he is called 'one of God's fools'; he quotes, in voiceover, from the *New Testament*, and is associated with Christ at Emmaus. In one shot, the Stalker's voice is heard over a shot of the prone Stalker by the waterfall; a cut shows the other two listening with eyes closed; the camera pans from the Scientist to the Writer, who rests leaning on him; the Writer opens his eyes, looking at the Stalker; the camera pans back to the Scientist, who is also now looking at the Stalker, whose further Christian affinities have been revealed. At the end of the 'telephone room' scene, the Writer mocks the Stalker's religiosity by putting on a crown of thorns (and the Stalker asks him to desist).

Desire is a recurrent theme in *Stalker* – note that one of its titles was *The Wish Machine*. The Stalker tells the other two that their dreams and their desires will come true when they reach the Room. *Stalker* is all about desire, and the desire to desire, the daring to desire. Gradually the motivations for each character are developed, from the superficial to the more profound. When they reach the room next to the Room, the Stalker says that it is the greatest moment in their lives, when their deepest wish will come true. *Stalker* has affinities with many quest narratives, including the important notion that when the endpoint is attained, each individual's desires have been changed by the journey, and the goal of the quest is not what they expected at all.

CONCLUSION

At the end of the movie the Stalker is changed most. He frets and groans about the intelligentsia, the faithless. His own faith has been shattered. He goes through an Existential crisis. His wife nurses him like a Madonna in *Pietà* paintings, with the dead Christ at the foot of the Cross. She says she'd like to go into the Zone, but this doesn't pacify the Stalker.

The Writer remains as cynical as ever. He says soul-searching is an invention of the mind. He puts a Crown of Thorns on in the Zone and mocks the Stalker and his faith. He says the Stalker is like a shaman, enjoying the sense of power, of being able to order people about, to say who lives and who dies in the Room or the Zone (the power of a deity). The

Writer is halfway between the Stalker's position (maximum faith) and the Scientist's (total disbelief). The Writer wants to believe, but is severely disappointed when the pilgrimage fails to deliver. The Scientist says he doesn't understand anything anymore. Andrei Tarkovsky explained that his interpretation of Fyodor Dostoievsky's *The Idiot* would be about someone who wanted to believe, but could not. For Tarkovsky, Dostoievsky 'dealt with the tragedy of the loss of spirituality. All his heroes are people who would *like* to believe, but cannot'.[1]

The movie ends with a transference of power, like *The Sacrifice*: from the Stalker to his daughter. It is a religious ending, the hopeful image of the child, the future, of the cyclical nature of life. Note that the two main scenes with Monkey – Monkey on the Stalker's shoulders, which begins with a close-up of Monkey in her golden headscarf, and the last table scene – are both in full colour, suggesting hope, a way out and transformation from the squalor of the black-and-white scenes. Only the two scenes with the Stalker's daughter are in colour, outside of the central scenes set in the Zone, suggesting that Monkey has a magical connection with (the powers of) the Zone. (Three endings to *Stalker* were shot, and each was included in the film, though not in the way originally scripted. The Stalker's wife's monologue, for instance, was going to occur in the bar, to the three men. Tarkovsky and editor Lydumilla Feiginova shifted it to the Stalker's house, which alters its resonance. The magical act of Monkey's and the lament of the Stalker were added to the script later).

The 1979 Mosfilm movie is perfectly circular: at the beginning the Stalker gets out of bed, pulls on his trousers, talks to his wife, then leaves. At the end these actions are precisely reversed. In *Stalker* Andrei Tarkovsky makes an unambivalent statement about faith and belief over cynicism and unbelief, of love and relationships over hatred and chaos, of hope and the future over despair and death. (But it is also ambiguous: the three men appear in the bar in the same positions, as if they haven't been anywhere; their journey has been psychological and spiritual. Similarly, the events in *The Sacrifice* might all have been a dream of Alex's, a product of the insanity which overwhelms him at the end. And Kelvin, at the end of *Solaris,* seems to have travelled back to Earth and been reunited with his father. But, as the camera flies higher and higher, it's revealed that, no, he is still on the planet Solaris after all, and his journey has been into the interior).

EIGHTEEN

Nostalghia

TARKOVSKY IN ITALY

Andrei Tarkovsky might have gone the whole way in his new (Italian) spelling of the word *nostalgia*: he included the 'h'. Including the 'g' turns the word into its Greek original: *gnostalghia*, which means 'homing-pain': *gnostos* = home, and *alghia* = pain. The film is full of gnostalghia; mainly for Russia, Russia in Italy.¹ The story concerns a man in exile, adrift from his homeland and family life. The situation echoes Tarkovsky's exile at this time (late 1970s to early 1980s). 'I wanted to make a film about Russian nostalgia,' Tarkovsky explained, 'about the particular state of mind which assails Russians who are far from their native land' (ST, 202). And at times that nostalgia, that inability to escape from the past, can seem like a sickness (ST, 206).

Nostalghia was produced by Manolo Bolognini, Franco Casati, Renzo Rossellini, Daniel Toscan du Plantier for Opera Film (Rome)/ RAI Television Rete 2 and Sovinfilm.

Nostalghia works on many levels, and there are many components in this seemingly sparse movie. There is the sexual antagonism between Gorchakov and his wife; between Gorchakov and Eugenia; between Eugenia and her past; there are the symbols of fire and water; the letter of Pavel Sosnovsky; the poetry of Arseny Tarkovsky; the dream sequences; Eugenia's nightmare; the model landscape in Domenico's house; the setting of the Bagno Vignoni, with the objects of civilization being dredged up; the Cathedral; Piero della Francesca; childbirth; poetry and translation; Russia and Italy and exile; and spiritual bankruptcy.

Nostalghia came about partly because Andrei Tarkovsky wanted make a movie in Italy (which he had visited a few times), and because of his friendship with Tonino Guerra, Michelangelo's Antonioni's regular screenwriter (Antonioni himself had visited the Moscow film festival in 1975). Guerra had met Tarkovsky in 1962 (at the time, he was married to a

Russian, Lora Yablochkina).

Andrei Tarkovsky had previously made a documentary on Italy, *Tempo di Viaggio* (*A Time To Travel*), which he created with Toninio Guerra, who scripted *Nostalghia*. Many of the places Tarkovsky filmed in the 63-minute Italian television documentary were used in *Nostalghia* (including the St Catherine Pool, the region around Piero della Francesca's *Madonna del Parto* at Monterchi near Arezzo, and the hotel room). In writing his Italian travel film, Tarkovsky said he wrote the script in Russian, then had Guerra's Russian wife translate them into Italian for Guerra; he would rewrite them, then Yablochkina would translate them back into Russian for Tarkovsky (D, 194). This would be one of the sources (like other elements in *Time To Travel*) of the translation theme in *Nostalghia*.

In the documentary by Donatella Baglivo about the making of *Nostalghia* (*Andrei Tarkovsky Directs Nostalghia*, a.k.a. *Un Poeta nel Cinema*, 1983, CIAK; which's essential viewing for Andrei Tarkovsky), the maestro is shown at the height of his powers, but on foreign soil, surrounded by an Italian crew and shooting in the heart of Italy. Interpreters were required on set at all times – not just to translate from Russian to Italian, but also from Russian and Italian to English. The three lead actors of *Nostalghia* were different nationalities: Oleg Yanovsky was Russian, Erland Josephson was Swedish, and Domiziana Giordano was Italian. A script reading, for example, between Tarkovsky and his three leads, required a translator to go from Russian into Italian, and another interpreter to translate that into English (for Josephson's benefit). Yankovsky seems to have been one of Tarkovsky's few Russian speakers on set. Sometimes, although there were many reasons for Tarkovsky's exile from Russia, it appeared as if Tarkovsky was deliberately creating challenges for himself. From the documentary one can see that some of the Italian crew had difficulty adapting to the working methods of the Russian genius, just as he had trouble working in the Western, European film industry.

In *Andrei Tarkovsky Directs Nostalghia*, one sees Andrei Tarkovsky taking great care with every detail of the shoot: he's often at work around the set, adjusting a drape, arranging candles, re-adjusting the lighting, and so on. He's seldom seen losing his temper or acting the prima donna, and appears to have infinite patience with the technical process of filmmaking. He will wait and wait until he gets exactly what he wants. Tarkovsky appeared to be actually a relatively quiet presence on set, not loud or joking or acting the clown or the dictator. However, it is always clear who is boss, who is requesting this or that from the crew or the actors, and who is driving the show.

The painter in Andrei Tarkovsky comes to the fore in the *Nostalghia* documentary – so many of Tarkovsky's shots are constructed like paintings (still life paintings, or portraits, or landscapes). Tarkovsky is shown adjusting props and sets as if he's art directing the location or set to look like some vision in his head. Tarkovsky told his co-writer Tonino Guerra that

> starting with *Solaris*, and then in *Mirror*, and in *Stalker* there are the same objects, always the same. Certain bottles, certain old books, mirrors, various little objects on shelves or on windowsills. Only that which I would like to have in my home has the right to find itself in a shot of one of my films.

Although *Nostalghia* focusses on three main characters, and appears to be a 'small-scale' movie, there are quite a few big scenes: the speech in the square in Rome, and the procession of religious devotees in the church, for instance. These scenes demanded a good deal of organization, animals and extras to look after, and plenty for the first and second assistant directors to do. The evocations of Russia were also elaborate scenes, requiring smoke, rain, wind and complex lighting, as well as extras and animals.

In Donatella Baglivo's documentary, Andrei Tarkovsky is seen patiently working with his actors, going over lines and actions, rehearsing action, or showing his actors what he wanted by stepping in and performing the blocking himself. In the scene where Eugenia has a long speech in the hotel bedroom, actress Domiziana Giordano took a while before she understood what Tarkovsky wanted and was able to deliver it. Tarkovsky took lots of time to go over the kind of thing he was after and shot take after take until Giordano's performance came close to his vision. Giordano later said that she was nervous about working with Tarkovsky, but that he was actually pretty easy to act for. She remarked that he had tons of ideas about how to shoot a scene, but would often compress those ideas, cutting out variations, when it came to shoot. Tarkovsky was absolutely meticulous in terms of paying attention to every aspect of filmmaking, Giordano said. (Tarkovsky considered casting Jill Clayburgh in the lead role in *Nostalghia* (she had starred in *La Luna* (Bernardo Bertolucci) the previous year, which Tarkovsky had hated).)

Andrei Tarkovsky found it a little difficult to adapt to working conditions in the Western movie industry (and the Italian film industry has its own particular modes of operating. Some other visiting filmmakers have found it exasperating and corrupt). *Nostalghia* caused problems also because the Russian genius worked slowly, and didn't like to keep to the agreed schedule.

Andrei Tarkovsky's *Tempo di Viaggio* consists largely of Tarkovsky and Tonino Guerra travelling around Italy visiting sites that Guerra introduces to Tarkovsky with a view to including them in the movie *Nostalghia*. Tarkovsky and Guerra visit Ravello, Lecce, San Sepulchro, St Catherine Baths and the Amalfi coast, among other Italian spots. These location scouting trips are intercut with conversations between Tarkovsky and Guerra in what is presumably Guerra's home in Rome. Tarkovsky and Guerra discuss their film project, Tarkovsky's favourite filmmakers, fiction films, and Tarkovsky offers advice to young filmmakers. Although there's plenty in *Tempo di Viaggio* to interest a Tarkovsky fan, it isn't a particularly distinguished work. It doesn't really get to grips with his subjects – Italian art and culture, the differences between Italian and Russian culture, being an exile or visitor from Russia in Italy, and so on. *Tempo di Viaggio* seems rushed, unfinished, messy, and confused.

In *Nostalghia,* the central character, Gorchakov, a Russian, goes to Italy to research an 18th century musician called Pavel Sosnovsky (that's just the pretext for the visit, and it's not particularly important). He meets an Italian interpreter, Eugenia, and the religious fanatic, Domenico (Domenico in the movie was meant to be a teacher of mathematics from a village in Tuscany. Domenico's character was developed and strengthened during shooting, Andrei Tarkovsky said at Cannes). All the time he yearns for Russia. Gorchakov cannot relate to the people around him in Italy, nor can he share his impressions of the new country with them (ST, 202). And he cannot escape his own past. *Nostalghia* is unequivocally a film about alienation: it is about 'someone in a state of profound alienation from the world and himself' (ST, 204).

There are two places and two main time zones in the movie: past and present, Russia and Italy; that is, sepia-and-white dream/ memory sequences of rural Russia of the past (and also Domenico's past); and the colour present day Italian sequences. To confuse things, Italy is also shown in sepia-and-white, as if in the past, but actually these are dream, fantasy or memory sequences. Andrei Tarkovsky said in an interview in *American Film* that he was searching for a kind of montage which had the subjective logic of dreams or memories or thoughts. Hardly anything is said: the film is even more spacious than *Stalker* or *The Sacrifice*. The film is full of a soft light and mist.

Most of the shots in *Nostalghia* are slow tracking shots, either forwards or backwards, or sideways. The Baths are filmed with crabwise dolly shots, low down, with the wall that surrounds the pool moving across the bottom of the frame. There are many interiors, too, of corridors: hotel corridors, the arcades of the churches; and the Milan hotel courtyard. At times the sepia-and-white and colour shots merge: it's difficult to tell which is which. The mist smooths over the jumps between the two (Tarkovsky fills his visions of both Russia and Italy with mist).

When the movie was being set up with RAI TV in Italy, three months of preproduction, two months of shooting and three months of post-production were being talked about. Part of the film was going to be shot in Russia (the Russian flashbacks/ dream sequences), but that was logistically too difficult. The Soviet authorities dragged their feet, and were reluctant to co-operate with RAI TV. The deal was eventually set-up between RAI, Gaumont/ Italy and Sovinfilm.

In the first draft of the script for *Nostalghia*, Eugenia and Gorchakov were in Venice, in a boat; there were Russian scenes, in snowy St Petersburg and Moscow; Gorchakov speaks to his wife by phone and argues with her; and there's a scene from *Crime and Punishment* (between Svidrigailov and Raskolnikov). *Nostalghia* would thus contained many scenes straight out of Fyodor Dostoievsky's *œuvre*, and in some ways it's Andrei Tarkovsky's most Dostoievskian movie (Tarkovsky was still very keen on making *The Idiot* at this time).

In the script, Gorchakov is still alive after the candle-carrying scene – he's checking out of his hotel, and talking with Eugenia, who's in Rome, on the phone; she tells him about Domenico's demonstration (CS, 498f). The movie alters the sequence of events: Gorchakov dies in the screenplay from a heart attack in the hotel. After his death, he dreams of being with his family in Russia, and waking them up to see the moon rise. After that came the final scene, of the Russian *dacha* in the Italian Cathedral. The moonrise sequence was put earlier in the film (with Gorchakov dreaming of it, but not appearing in his dream), and only the Cathedral scene followed Gorchakov's death. It makes more dramatic sense to cut straight from Gorchakov dying at the end of the candle and baths scene to the final dream.

FURTHER THOUGHTS ON *NOSTALGHIA*

Critic Neya Zorkaya suggested that Gorchakov was not just rejecting Eugenia because of indifference or fear of her sexuality, but because she embodies the past (the glory of the Renaissance in particular, in her affinity with Renaissance madonnas), but without the all-important spirituality.[1] She represents material beauty without the spiritual underpinnings. Eugenia thus embodies the spirituality that Gorchakov is searching for (which has also gone from his homeland, Russia).[2]

Andrei Tarkovsky recognized just how deeply *Nostalghia* reflected his situation, and felt uneasy about that. For some critics, that was part of its problem: *Nostalghia* was too self-indulgent, too much of Tarkovsky going the Federico Fellini route of mythologizing one's own life. 'I love and admire the filmmaker Tarkovsky, and believe him to be one of the greatest of all time', Ingmar Bergman confessed. 'My admiration for Fellini is limitless,' Bergman continued, 'But I also feel that Tarkovsky began to make Tarkovsky films and that Fellini began to make Fellini movies. Yet Kurosawa has never made a Kurosawa film'.[3] Certainly a few film critics have also viewed Fellini's later movies as self-parodies (Tarkovsky said much the same), as Fellini 'doing Fellini' (and filmmakers such as Steven Spielberg and George Lucas are routinely accused of rearranging collections of their greatest hits). In some respects, Tarkovsky hadn't made enough films to be guilty of that kind of regurgitation, but one or two critics (including Tarkovsky's fellow filmmaker Andrei Konchalovsky), have seen Tarkovsky's later movies (they are referring specifically to *Nostalghia* and *The Sacrifice*) as Tarkovsky 'doing Tarkovsky'.

NINETEEN

The Sacrifice

THE WORLD OF *THE SACRIFICE*

The Sacrifice (a.k.a. *Offret* or *Sacrificiatio*) takes place in the present (1985) on the coast in Sweden. It is set before what is taken to be a limited nuclear war (i.e., a conflict that escalates to nuclear attacks, but not a full-scale nuclear exchange). The middle-aged hero, Alexander, bargains with his life, makes a pact with God to sacrifice himself so as to avoid the catastrophe. But Andrei Tarkovsky seems to have forgotten, or not taken into account, that Sweden, like Switzerland, is one of the nations best prepared for a nuclear attack.[1] There are hints in the movie, such as references to missile bases, that this isn't Sweden (Sweden doesn't have missile bases, but Russia at the time – as now – has plenty). There are 5.5 million shelter places for the 8 million souls in Sweden. If *The Sacrifice* was really a factual, rather than a spiritual or metaphysical, film, then the people in the country house would almost certainly be sheltered. Victor, being a doctor, would be part of a priority relief system. The TV announcement is inaccurate – the Swedish government is much better prepared than that. Further, as the mainstream nuclear films demonstrated, a nuclear attack coming so suddenly and unexpectedly, without a build-up of conflict, is highly unlikely.

But it doesn't matter: Andrei Tarkovsky's is a spiritual movie, and the nuclear catastrophe is a dramatic means of having someone's life thrown upside-down, forcing an ontological re-evaluation (and Tarkovsky is not interested in the details of a limited nuclear war). A nuclear war is a very extreme narrative device. In literature it is often an individual's murder (in André Gide, Albert Camus, William Shakespeare or Sophocles), or a suicide (in Fyodor Dostoievsky), or love-making (in Thomas Hardy), or loss of love (in Francesco Petrarch).

Andrei Tarkovsky is deliberately ambiguous about the oncoming holocaust: it would have made the movie silly if it was totally clear that

Alexander had saved the world via a prayer and sleeping with the 'witch' Maria. Then it would be relatively easy for anyone to save the world. (Some people would be queuing up to sleep with a witch. But that's a different movie). At the same time, the atomic onslaught cannot entirely be seen as a dream of Alexander's, or a group dream involving the main protagonists at the house, because it makes the actions in the later part of the film motiveless and confused. Alexander's going to extremes (burning down the house) is rendered pointless if his 'dark night of the soul' has all been a dream. Alexander's conscious act of despair in a way proves (or demonstrates) his religious faith (P. Christensen, 1987). *The Sacrifice*'s narrative is metaphorical and metaphysical, because an unethical (and un-Christian) act such as sleeping with Maria cannot save the world in conventional terms. However, if the events seen are 'real', then making love with Maria rescues the planet, and burning the house saves Alexander's soul (ibid.). Producer Anna-Lena Wibom said of *The Sacrifice* that it was 'clear as daylight and quite obvious in its message to contemporary people everywhere'.

Sven Nykvist was a major contributor towards *The Sacrifice*. He had also been offered *Out of Africa*, directed by Sydney Pollack. Nykvist said that Tarkovsky wasn't much interested in lighting: 'of primary importance were composition, camera movements, the literally moving image'. Nykvist said it could take hours for Tarkovsky to decide how to shoot a scene when he first visited a location. Only when he had made his decisions could Nykvist come in to light the scene. This could also take a long time because many of the set-ups were lengthy tracking shots (which can often be tricky and time-consuming to light).

Anna-Lena Wiborn produced *The Sacrifice* for the Swedish Film Institute. Andrei Tarkovsky complained that the movie production process in Sweden treated filmmaking like going to an office, where all that mattered was starting and finishing shooting at particular times, whereas for Tarkovsky filmmaking was an artistic undertaking (D, 342). Wiborn found Tarkovsky's working methods difficult to deal with. He really wasn't used to working with a Western crew, in the Western film system. For instance, Tarkovsky had a habit of ordering rehearsals or improvisations which weren't agreed beforehand in the budget and schedule. He could be vague about exactly what he required, and wouldn't stick to agreements already made. There were clashes, inevitably, but in the West, the movie director is usually king (on the film set, if nowhere else) – and Tarkovsky was also a renowned director.

There are many Christian images and references in *The Sacrifice*: Alex is a troubled saint or mystic, suffering a Dark Night of the Soul. His journey is like the mythic hero's: from pain to enlightenment. He visits a Goddess – incarnated in the 'good witch', Maria. There is a mythic return – not in the saint/ father/ artist, but the pupil/ neophyte/ initiate, Little Man. Maria is explicitly linked with Mary Magdalene, while other names, such as Martha, speak for themselves.2 Maria represents dark, nighttime, the feminine, menstrual creativity, witchy powers; while Adelaide is bright, daylight (i.e. known), ovulatory (maternal) domesticity. Maria's quiet sexuality and self-containment is opposed by Adelaide's loud hysteria, the mother as smotherer. Maria is the strongest woman in the film, though she lives alone; Adelaide, surrounded by people, is the weakest. Maria and Alex are linked visually: they both wear black garments with white patterns: Alex has his *yin-yang* sign on a dressing gown; Maria her patterned headscarf (their task is to become whole, to unite the dichotomy of black and white).

Adelaide is Maria's opposite in the struggle for Alex; but Maria's other opposite is Martha (Adelaide's daughter): it is the virgin/ whore dichotomy. Both women undress, both sleep with their men: Alex on screen with Maria; Martha (perhaps) off-screen with Victor. Victor injects Martha and Adelaide, mother and daughter, with his science, with tranquillizers. The injection is phallic, and also shows how he exacts his patriarchal authority over them. Later, mother and daughter argue over Victor going to Australia. (Adelaide is an unflattering portrait of what Tarkovsky described as a self-assertive, aggressive woman, someone who wants to smother and dominate other people, who won't allow them individuality or independence, and whose lack of spirituality enhances her destructiveness [ST, 223]). Some critics saw Adelaide as an unflattering portrait of Tarkovsky's wife, Larissa.

The autobiographical elements in *The Sacrifice* have been pointed out by critics: the resemblance of Adelaide to Tarkovsky's wife Larissa, for instance (both have a daughter from a previous marriage), or the links between Alex and Andrei Tarkovsky, or the similarity of the *dachas* in *Solaris* and *Mirror* and *The Sacrifice*, or Little Man's affinity with Tarkovsky's own child, Andrei, who at the time wasn't allowed to join his family outside Russia.

The characters are aspects of Alex, the actor/ writer. Victor, the doctor, is the rationalist/ scientist, the public voice of reason; he is opposed by Otto, who is something of a jester, a fool, something of a historian and mystic, and something of an occultist – he collects supernatural tales. The opposition of Victor and Otto recalls the Stalker and the Professor in *Stalker*. Adelaide is, like Victor, part of Alex's public persona – and is also linked to his past, his work in the theatre. Adelaide is shown as standing outside the trinity of women figures: Martha, Maria and Julia (the maid).

Inner/ magical/ secret world		Outer/ scientific/ public world
Otto		Victor
Maria	Alex	Adelaide
boy		Martha
		Julia

Alex is stuck in the middle of these characters and tensions. Throughout the movie he associates himself with the pagan and magical characters, Maria, Otto and the boy (Maria and the boy 'move in a world of the imagination, not that of 'reality'', Andrei Tarkovsky asserted; their world is 'filled with unfathomable wonders' [ST, 228]). He moves away from the public/ social/ rational/ reasonable people, Victor and Adelaide, towards the præternatural, possessed souls. His descent into madness is outwardly destructive, but inwardly regenerative.

One reading of the form of the 1986 film is structured around a classic narrative, with semblances of acts and rising action:

1. Vague but deep-seated dissatisfactions which
2. Crystallize suddenly and violently when the End of the World is announced, forcing
3. The pact with God and the journey towards the total sacrifice after
4. Various thresholds have been crossed, resulting in
5. Death of the self, and
6. Finally, after so long, rebirth.

The Sacrifice contains the whole portfolio of Andrei Tarkovsky's motifs: fire, milk, candles, icons, water, glass, magical objects, childhood imagery, floating, hysteria and decay. There are the typical Tarkovskyan cultural references – to Johann Sebastian Bach, Leonardo da Vinci, Friedrich Nietzsche, William Shakespeare and Fyodor Dostievsky. The bicycle is another connecting object: each of the three main people of the central quest (the quest to sleep with a witch and save the world) ride on the bike: Otto at the beginning (the messenger who brings/ sets the quest); Alex in the middle, the (anti)hero riding out on the quest, like a knight of Arthurian romance; and Maria at the end, the object of the quest/ the saviour/ magical agent. In this film horses are absent (except the wild horses of Leonardo's *Adoration of the Magi*).

STYLE/ SPACE/ SOUND

The external world of history, the personal past and culture in *The Sacrifice* come into the house (and Alex's world) from clearly marked outside culture bearers: Victor brings Alex a book of icons; Otto brings the map and telegrams. They are both kings, Magi to Alex's Christ. The Leonardo da Vinci painting is a central emblem in the movie. The picture frightens Otto, who prefers Piero della Francesca. The whole film is shot by Sven Nykvist in a Leonardo *sfumato* style, where objects are shrouded in shadows. The Leonardo print is seen in a dim room. When Alex and Otto discuss it they are shot against the light, their faces, like Leonardo's faces, melt into the darkness.

The house in *The Sacrifice* is a Leonardo da Vincian world. Objects are seen in a new way: things become sinister – like the cupboard door that creaks, or the glass that rattles. The filmic darkness also recalls the Early Netherlandish painters, particularly the dark but luminous interiors, the detailed and shiny surfaces in the paintings of Rogier van der Weyden, Hans Memling, Jan van Eyck, Petrus Christus and Quentin Massys. Anna Asp said the house in *The Sacrifice* was designed to be timeless, as if the movie could have been set in the 19th century or in the future; there was a 'God's face' on one side of the house (comprising windows for eyes and a door for the mouth); the interior was twice the size of the exterior; Asp said that they 'agonized about whether this would be a problem; but ultimately, no one who saw the finished film commented on it' (P. Ettedgui, 115). Tarkovsky was incredibly particular about the design and decoration of the house, Asp explained. 'He wanted to discuss every detail, for example, the distance between the top of a chair to the sill of a window' (ib., 114).

Objects are beautiful in *The Sacrifice*. Andrei Tarkovsky's sense of space and surface is sublime here. His grasp of space, light, volume and mass is highly developed. Cinema has never been so beautiful. Tarkovsky controls movements, colour and sound so dynamically. He is a Prospero, charming the viewer with cinematic enchantment, orchestrating his angelic/ dæmonic devices like a Renaissance wizard. The sound of fighters overhead, for instance, is a roar that fills up all the frequencies, from the lowest to the highest (the sound was created from a combination of a number of Swedish military aircraft, plus some low rumbles and other noises). The wind noise in the trees is another mysterious expression, of a Total Other. Alex sits in the Baudelairean 'forest of symbols'. The wind is a mass of voices, stretched out into breaths of sound.

Owe Svensson was part of the sound team on *The Sacrifice* (he had worked with Ingmar Bergman, Bo Widerberg, Liv Ullmann and Jan Troell, among others). The sound in *The Sacrifice*, Svensson pointed out, was more subtle and multi-layered than in Russian movies of the time, which tended to be stripped-down and rather heavy-handed. Russian movies (and Italian) tended to add music and only a few heavy sound effects, rather than building up atmospheres with a range of sound fx.

Owe Svensson recalled that Andrei Tarkovsky wanted to find some old recordings of cow herding calls (O. Svensson, 2003). He didn't want songs that had been set to music, and eventually Svensson found a shepherd's recording that had been recorded on a wax cylinder, via a telephone link from Rättvik in rural Sweden to Swedish Radio in Stockholm. (As the quality of the recording was poor, reverb was added, and the song was mixed with outdoor sounds.) Tarkovsky asked Svensson to mix the cow songs with the Japanese flutes (taken from a vinyl album). Foghorns (some from ships, some from lighthouses) were also added.

ENDINGS

In his contract, Andrei Tarkovsky had agreed with the producers (Anna-Lena Wibom and Katinka Farago) to bring *The Sacrifice* in at 2 hours 10 mins, but he wanted it to be 149 minutes (and that's how long the movie finally was. The first rough cut was 190 minutes). Editing *The Sacrifice* didn't mean simply joining together all of the long takes (there were only 120 cuts in *The Sacrifice*). It meant six months of very difficult work, according to Michal Leszcylowski. Each cut was 'subject to deep critical scrutiny'.[1]

The Sacrifice ends on a note of extraordinary beauty, profundity – and optimism. Despite being a difficult film for some to sit through (except for art film addicts), and despite the gloomy plot and the dark *mise-en-scène*, it is a supremely positive, life-affirming movie. The last scene is a pastoral one: the herd of cows, the grass, the ululations of what sounds like a shepherdess, the bright sky, images recalling Classical/ Greek pastoralism and Arcadia. (No surprise that the cow is, symbolically, the great Moon Goddess, a symbol of procreation and plenty, the sacred animal of India, a powerful image of the matriarchal and feminine realm.)

With the sublime, abstract music of Johann Sebastian Bach swelling (the music contributes *a lot* here), and the slow crane-shot up the tree, and the imagery – of the tree against the sky, against the sun shining on the glittering sea, the spectator seems to be rising bodily into Heaven. The crane shot points the spectator towards heaven, quite literally and physically, just as at the end of Dante Alighieri's *Divina Commedia*, or Francesco Petrarch's *Canzoniere*. In mediæval times the glorification was of Christ and the Virgin Mary; in Andrei Tarkovsky's cinema, in this last scene of *The Sacrifice,* the apotheosis lies in Maria, in the cows, in the pastoral imagery, in the tree, in the ocean. The achievement is of life itself, life and death, the whole of existence and experience. So it is *life itself* that is being glorified – not the viewers, not the boy, not nature, but life as a whole. This is why *The Sacrifice* is one of the most joyous of movies. Few movies are as exhilarating as this.

TWENTY

Critical Responses to Andrei Tarkovsky's Cinema

CRITICAL RESPONSE

The critical response to Andrei Tarkovsky's movies has been varied. For some Tarkovsky is a genius, and his films are some of the finest in cinema; for others, his films are pretentious, boring, indulgent, irrelevant and obscure. Jay Leyda, in *Kino,* his magisterial history of Soviet cinema, said that Andrei Tarkovsky learned to bypass the mass audience, making beautiful puzzle films from which 'each flattered spectator could take away his interpretation as the only possible one' (403). Certainly, Tarkovsky flatters his audience, as well as exasperating them. I have said throughout this study that one of the most important aspects of Tarkovsky's films is their openness, enabling the viewer to manœuvre.

Andrei Tarkovsky wanted his movies to be seen and admired: an audience was essential for the artist 'to fulfil his personal spiritual mission', as he grandly put it (ST, 165). Although he did not deliberately try to please his audience (in the Hollywood manner), and hated the commercial pandering to their tastes (ST, 174-5), he also hoped 'fervently that my picture will be accepted and loved' (ST, 170). Of course, that's what most artists want (and especially with something like a feature film, which can soak up years of a filmmaker's life).

Andrei Tarkovsky's view of criticism was that it was too often illustrating an idea, or confirming an opinion or private aspiration or personal position of the critic (ST, 46). To grasp an artwork properly, the viewer should cultivate 'an original, independent, 'innocent' judgement' (ibid.). (Tarkovsky spoke dismissively of the people who study to become movie directors and actors – i.e., who become critics – but who are destined to wind up on the edges of the industry, lacking the strength to give up and start another profession [ST, 88]).

Because cinema is an art, Andrei Tarkovsky maintained, it's wrong to expect it to be easy to understand. 'Nobody demands that of the other arts', Tarkovsky said.[1] Tarkovsky and his co-writers sometimes appeared wilfully obscure – in not providing clear information on characters or events, or signposting clearly what are dreams, memories, wishes, and other kinds of realities. Sometimes it's not clear *who* is having the dreams or memories (in *Nostalghia*, for instance, Gorchakov seems to dream from Domenico's memories). For Tarkovsky, it doesn't always matter whose mindscreen the sequences represent – it's the images and sounds that count.

For Ivor Montagu, writing in 1973, Andrei Tarkovsky is 'one of the best things to happen in world cinema for a long time'.[2] Giovanni Buttafava called Tarkovsky's movies 'complex heterodox individual works', 'a series of films that turned the ambiguity of everyday life into the subject of severe subtle investigation'.[3] Of Tarkovsky's *œuvre*, Peter Green wrote in 1987: 'this handful of completed works is individually of such weight and vision that each one of them alone might have secured him a place in film history' (1987). Maybe not *Ivan's Childhood*, but any one of Tarkovsky movies from *Andrei Roublyov* onwards would guarantee him a place in the cinematic pantheon. This sentiment was typical of the obituaries British critics wrote, such as Ian Christie and David Robinson. They waxed lyrical about Tarkovsky. In "Raising the Shroud", Christie noted, though, that 'there is an urgent need now to resist a premature canonisation' (38). (Obituaries for Andrei Tarkovsky appeared in January, 1987 in *Pravda, Literary Gazette* and *Soviet Culture* in the USSR, written by Goskino and the Filmmakers' Union).

Andrei Tarkovsky's movies were often dismissed as élitist puzzles by the Soviet authorities and critics: his were regarded as films for minorities. Nikolai Sizov, director of the Moscow Film Studios, said *Mirror* was 'too complex'.[4] For the movie-maker V.N. Naumov, *Mirror* was 'un-understandable' (ibid.). Sergei Gerasimov, the veteran director who was for years chief of the Joint Acting and Directing Workshops at VGIK, where Tarkovsky studied, said that Tarkovsky was 'a man of very serious talent' (ibid.). Of *Mirror*, Herbert Marshall wrote in 1976 that it was very sophisticated and new:

> Such a film has hitherto never been seen on the Soviet screen... here for the first time is the 'subjective history' of a Soviet filmmaker in his own film. (ib., 95)

When Soviet movies of the time were expected to be 'social realist', it's understandable why *Mirror* should have seemed so radically different.

(Some Russian critics – and filmmakers – couldn't quite accept the idea that Andrei Tarkovsky was making a movie about his own life, rather than a larger, social subject).

Up until the mid-1990s, Andrei Tarkovsky was usually given a few lines in histories and encyclopaedias of cinema, but not much more than that. Tarkovsky was usually placed next to Sergei Paradjanov and his *The Colour of Pomegranates* in movie guides (but being put beside Paradjanov means being in very good company indeed). Usually *Andrei Roublyov* was discussed (it was probably the Tarkovsky film that created the most fuss in the Soviet Union). *Mirror* was the next film cited in the film guides and history books, but the rest of Tarkovsky's cinema was rarely analyzed.

In critical books on cinema, Andrei Tarkovsky often emerges as a talented but obscure or minor figure: *The Oxford Companion to Film* said Tarkovsky's movies 'are intense, personal works, often disconcerting in the violence they portray' (L. Bawden, 679). In the British Film Institute's *Encyclopaedia of European Cinema*, the entry on Tarkovsky described him as 'a filmmaker's filmmaker'; *Mirror and Stalker* were classed as 'two deeply personal and somewhat obscure movies, which were partly autobiographical'.[5] For *The Film Handbook*, *The Sacrifice* suffered from 'a somewhat contrived religiosity and a morbid disenchantment with human aspiration and achievement'.[6] Tarkovsky has a sizeable entry in the weighty *International Dictionary of Films and Filmmakers*, in the *Directors* volume. G.C. Macnab stated that his work 'can verge on the inscrutable. Too opaque to yield concrete meaning, it offers itself as sacral art, demanding a rapt, and even religious response from its audience' (L. Hillstrom, 1997).

In *Halliwell's Film Guide*, one of the popular British cinema guides, *The Sacrifice* was described as a 'brilliantly filmed but obscure and confusing parable that does not easily yield its meaning', and *Nostalghia* was an '[i]ndescribably doomladen, occasionally beautiful, stylistically interesting and for the most part very boring parable of a kind unique to its director' (L. Halliwell, 1993). *Solaris* for Leslie Halliwell was 'heavy-going but highly imaginative', technically superb but 'the whole thing is rather humourless' (L. Halliwell, 2000). Reviewers for the London listings magazine *Time Out* have generally been big fans. Tarkovsky was given just a few lines in *The History of the Movies*, mentioning *Nostalghia* and *The Sacrifice* only (A. Lloyd, 1988).

Vincent Canby, reviewing *Nostalghia* for the *New York Times*, called Andrei Tarkovsky a 'film poet with a tiny vocabulary' (quite a few of the US movie critics found *Nostalghia* disappointing, a repetition of Tarkovsky's established symbols and themes: 'flawed plot', 'overloaded metaphors', 'banal and lofty generalization', 'a kind of theatre of gibberish', 'heated melodrama').

In *Elliot's Guide To Films On Video*, *The Sacrifice* was seen as 'mostly an intense examination of various angst-ridden obsessions, and is sustained by excellent performances, Sven Nykvist's outstanding camerawork and some truly memorable sequences', while *Nostalghia* was 'an oppressive and doomladen meditation, sustained by a few images of great beauty and opaque symbolism, but too stylized and sluggish to be really effective' (J. Elliot, 1993). Another popular film guidebook, by Leonard Maltin (one of the better US reviewers), was a fan: *Mirror* was 'superbly directed'; *Nostalghia* was 'a provocative, insightful epic, lovingly rendered by one of cinema's true poets'; and *Andrei Roublyov* was a 'magnificent film worthy of comparison with the best of Sergei Eisenstein's historical dramas' (L. Maltin, 2000). While Maltin acknowledged that films like *Solaris* and *The Sacrifice* were not for all tastes, they were *tour-de-forces* from the director.

Geoff Andrew wrote in *The Film Handbook* that Andrei Tarkovsky's later movies are 'deeply flawed by self-indulgence [and] tend towards obscurantism and a cold, intellectual aloofness' (280). There is some truth in this: Tarkovsky's films, despite their intense poetry, can seem cold. But he is not intellectual: he is very anti-intellectual (Tarkovsky wasn't a fan of intellectualized or literary filmmaking, *mise-en-scène* and staging which illustrates an intellectual or literary idea). He makes few concessions to his audience, however. He forces the viewer to work – suffer even, but in most cases his artistic rigour is justified.

The Bloomsbury Foreign Film Guide claimed *Nostalghia* contained 'scenes of an almost perverse obscurity and the final sequence is tedious beyond belief' (R. Bergan, 411). The final sequence, the nine-minute take, is either fabulous or monotonous for the viewer: it either works or it doesn't: if the viewer doesn't identify with Gorchakov's fate, and the big themes of the movie, the whole sequence is pointless.

Many critics have disliked the length and slowness of Andrei Tarkovsky's movies (reviewers hate long movies, for good reasons), the pomposity and self-indulgence of his art. But there have been many self-indulgent filmmakers (such as Charlie Chaplin, Orson Welles, Alfred Hitchcock, Jean-Luc Godard, Maya Deren and Walerian Borowczyk. However, Tarkovsky has usually made much longer films than those directors. On the other hand, he only made seven features, far less than Hitch, Godard or even Welles).

In the British 1982 *Sight & Sound* critics' poll, *Andrei Roublyov* was joint tenth (with *2001: A Space Odyssey*); above *Andrei Roublyov* in the poll were the usual 'classic' films: *The General* and *The Searchers* (joint 8th);

Vertigo, The Magnificent Ambersons and *L'Avventura* (joint 7th); *Battleship Potemkin* (6th), *8 1/2* (5th), *Seven Samurai* and *Singin' in the Rain* (joint 3rd), *The Rules of the Game* (2nd), with *Citizen Kane* at the top. (But that was Tarkovsky's only appearance in the *Sight & Sound* top ten movies). Twenty years later, in 2002, Tarkovsky wasn't on the list of movies, or of the top ten movie directors. The filmmakers topping the list, polled from film directors (not critics) were Orson Welles, Fellini, Akira Kurosawa, Coppola, Alfred Hitchcock, Kubrick, Wilder, Ingmar Bergman, Scorsese, Lean and Renoir). The favourite movies of film directors in the same poll were the usual suspects: *Kane, Godfather, 8 1/2, Lawrence, Strangelove, Bicycle Thieves* and so on).

The Hollywood trade magazine *Variety* raved about *Andrei Roublyov*, calling it 'brilliantly-fashioned' from a director of 'exceptional talent' (D. Elley, 1996). *Ivan's Childhood* was sympathetically reviewed ('lyrical', 'flamboyant', 'rich use of camera'), as was *Solaris* ('Tarkovsky spins a strange, slow but absorbing parable'.) The visual fx may not have been spectacular for *Variety*, but the 'playing is intense and effective'.

Although Andrei Tarkovsky said in his writings that he hated much of (particularly American) contemporary culture, of the mass-produced MacDonald's, Coca-Cola, Disney kind, he could, according to Layla A. Garrett, 'talk for hours about *The Terminator*' (1997). (Tarkovsky's interest in the Arny flick *The Terminator* was partly, according to Garrett, because of his interest in time travel. It's no surprise that Tarkovsky could discourse at length on cyborg fantasy movies like *The Terminator* – one reason is that, although he said he wasn't that interested in science fiction, he was a director who made not one but two science fiction movies. Two out of his seven feature films were sci-fi. That's a big proportion).

David Cook noted in his excellent *A History of Narrative Film* (still the finest single bok on cinema) that *Nostalghia* was 'perhaps Tarkovsky's most mysterious and inaccessible film, but it was a great success at Cannes in 1983' (1990, 769). Cook added that 'to many Western observers even [Tarkovsky's] films made abroad bear the marks of careful, covert Soviet censorship' (770). Many critics have been sympathetic to the humanism underlying Tarkovsky's poetic, determinedly non-social-realist movies. David Quinlan in *The Illustrated Guide to Film Directors* said that *Solaris* was 'really a plea for love and peace under its enigmatic surface' (1985), while Jack Ellis said that *Ivan's Childhood* has 'a strong and clear humanist message carrying along its unusual display of technical virtuosity' (344).

In another doorstop guidebook to cinema, *The Story of Cinema*, David Shipman admitted he was sent to sleep by Andrei Tarkovsky's movies, and left the cinema showing both *Solaris* and *Mirror* before an hour was up. Of *Ivan's Childhood*, Shipman said that its 'exquisite photography… represents nothing but exquisite photography', and the often-used story of a young boy being taught by an older solder 'has never been so unfeelingly projected' (1048). Shipman reacted even more violently to *Mirror*, which he said contained no plot, 'nor the slightest resemblance to human behaviour or connection with imaginative thought' (1049); an extraordinary view. For Shipman, Tarkovsky was cultured but not necessarily intelligent enough to make a successful movie.

After his death in 1986, retrospectives of Andrei Tarkovsky's films were organized in Moscow in 1987. There have been Tarkovsky movie seasons (and Tarkovsky conferences) since then, not only in Moscow and St Petersburg, but in many major cities. Tarkovsky's version of Modest Mussorgsky's opera *Boris Godunov* (1872) was staged in London in the mid-1980s and in St Petersburg in 1990.

All of Andrei Tarkovsky's films have been available on video and DVD for many years. Tarkovsky is a significant presence on the internet. There's a Tarkovsky Society (founded in 1989, at the time of the first Tarkovsky International Symposium), a Tarkovsky Prize for filmmakers, and a Museum of Andrei Tarkovsky opened in 1996, based in the house where Tarkovsky lived. Andrei Tarkovsky turns up in some unusual places. For instance, in a 1998 book on animation in cinema by Paul Wells, Tarkovsky is quoted at length on poetry.[7]

CRITICS ON ANDREI TARKOVSKY'S CINEMA'S RELIGIOUS DIMENSION

Few critics have seriously addressed the religious content of Andrei Tarkovsky's cinema. Yet it is at the religious level that Tarkovsky wished to be understood most clearly. The religious, ethical and emotional level is Tarkovsky's cinematic province. Critics and filmmakers have all talked about the beauty of Tarkovsky's images. Critics gushed wildly about Tarkovsky's visuals, using similar terms as art historians did about the paintings of Caspar David Friedrich, Vincent van Gogh and Mark Rothko. Words such as 'tragic', 'serene' and 'magical' are frequently employed.

Some critics said that Andrei Tarkovsky's movies lack an awareness of an ideological structure as do Ingmar Bergman's; Tarkovsky does not seem to consider politics or ideology as important enough to put into his movies. Although historical events such as the Tartar attack on Vladimir in *Andrei Roublyov* or Domenico's speech in Rome in *Nostalghia* could easily be given a political or ideological slant (as they might be if filmed by Sergei Eisenstein), Tarkovsky declines, and, in the case of Domenico's 'demonstration', goes for the Existential and spiritual angle.

Up until Vida T. Johnson & Graham Petrie's excellent 1994 book, there were two book-length critical studies of Andrei Tarkovsky readily available in English, by Mark Le Fanu and Maya Turovskaya. Both were disappointing. Most of the critical articles on Tarkovsky's cinema have been praiseworthy (*reviews* in magazines and newspapers may be negative, but journalists and critics don't usually bother to write an *article* or *essay* which's wholly negative, although sometimes they will to debunk something, or reply to another critic. In other words, if a critic bothers to write about Tarkovsky at all, they're usually fans).

For articles and essays on Andrei Tarkovsky's cinema, please see the bibliography.

ANDREI TARKOVSKY'S STATUS

Among American filmmakers of his generation there are few comparisons to make with Andrei Tarkovsky. Even American directors such as Francis Coppola, Philip Kaufman, Terence Malick, Peter Bogdanovitch, Robert Altman and Martin Scorsese, whose movies sometimes share some similar qualities with Tarkovsky's, are actually a world away from Tarkovsky's cinema.

One could look at the alienation of modern man in contemporary society in, say, 1974's *The Conversation* (Gene Hackman wandering about in a raincoat on his own is a bit of a Tarkovskyan figure) or *Badlands* (Terence Malick, 1973), but it's not really the same cinematic field. On the other hand, one could see the exploration of the darkness at the heart of Western culture in *The Godfather* as far superior in its way than, say, *Nostalghia*. But what American cinema seldom does is tackle the same issues as Tarkovsky – spiritual quests and Existential alienation – or approach cinema in the same poetic fashion.

Andrei Tarkovsky wasn't a fan of the action or adventure type of movie, embodied in American cinema. Rather, Tarkovsky wanted to avoid outward movement, and explore inner worlds (ST, 204). Tarkovsky does seem to be the polar opposite of an action movie director, his conception of the European art film being at odds with films like *Titanic, Jurassic Park, Pirates of the Carribean, Spider-man* or *Men In Black*. There were times, though, when Tarkovsky could have benefited from a greatly increased budget: on *The Sacrifice*, for example, for the apocalyptic scene of the crowd milling around in the courtyard, when there weren't enough extras contracted for the scene, and the crowd looks thin on the ground (literally). And multiple cameras (or more than two) would have helped with the climactic single take of the burning house, so that, if one failed, another might have got the shot.

Orson Welles, D.W. Griffith, Sam Peckinpah, Howard Hawks, Nicholas Ray, Elia Kazan – Andrei Tarkovsky is like few American filmmakers. Like Erich von Stroheim (on *Greed*), Michael Cimino (on *Heaven's Gate*) and Jacques Tati (on *Playtime*), Tarkovsky was sometimes allowed to go over budget, to movie as much as he liked (in general), sheltered by the Soviet movie system. On *Nostalghia*, for example, made outside the Soviet industry, the show was given 150,000 metres of film stock and $1.5 million (the shooting ratio on an average 35mm feature film might be 6:1. A 90 minute film uses 8,100 feet of film, so, shooting at a ratio of 6:1, 50,000 feet of stock would be required. So the 450,000+ feet Tarkovsky had for *Nostalghia* was a more generous shooting ratio. Some directors, of course, still shoot more than that).

Like certain other *auteurs* (such as Woody Allen, Federico Fellini and Bernardo Bertolucci), Andrei Tarkovsky had a knack of getting pretty much what he wanted from his movie deals. Or, if not exactly what he desired, then a lot more production help and artistic control than many film directors. The scale of *Andrei Roublyov*, for example, is amazingly large for a second feature (although it's not uncommon for youngish directors to be given the reins of a big project, which is often really controlled by producers and studios). Like Federico Fellini and Ingmar Bergman, Tarkovsky was allowed to pursue his very autobiographical projects with a relatively large amount of investment and resources (Bergman worked with far less money than Fellini, but he was still able to be very prolific, at least compared to his contemporaries). The budgets Tarkovsky was given for his movies were small by general Hollywood standards: there was no $31 million anti-war extravaganza (*Apocalypse Now*) for him, and no months spent in the Italian countryside making a six-hour Marxist history of Italy (*1900*, Bernardo Bertolucci, 1976).

What is certain is that Andrei Tarkovsky joins the ranks of the Soviet and Russian greats: Alexander Dovzhenko, Vsevolod Pudovkin, Dziga Vertov, Sergei Eisenstein and Lev Kuleshov. Tarkovsky is probably now the most celebrated postwar Soviet/ Russian filmmaker (though not the most representative), rising above Grigory Chukrai, Andrei Konchalovsky, Mikhail Kalatozov, Grigory Kozintsev, Emil Lotianu, Elem Klimov, Alexander Sokurov and even Sergei Paradjanov and Sergei Bondarchuk.

But only time will tell if Andrei Tarkovsky finally enters the hallowed realm of his passionately admired cinematic heroes and gurus: Ingmar Bergman, Robert Bresson, Luis Buñuel, Jean Vigo, Kenji Mizoguchi, Michelangelo Antonioni and Akira Kurosawa.

TEN BEST MOMENTS IN ANDREI TARKOVSKY'S FILMS

1. The first twenty minutes of *Mirror*.
2. The dreams in *Ivan's Childhood*.
3. The bell-casting sequence in *Andrei Roublyov*.
4. The Stalker's dream in *Stalker*.
5. Weightlessness in *Solaris*.
6. The ending of *Solaris*.
7. The witches' procession in *Nostalghia*.
8. The *dacha* in the Cathedral in *Nostalghia*.
9. The closing minutes of *Mirror*.
10. The tree and the boy at the end of *The Sacrifice*.

Notes

INTRODUCTION

LIFE
1. H. Marshall, in A. Lawton, 1982, 179.

THE TARKOVSKY INDUSTRY
1. In V. Johnson, 1994b, 45-46.

THIS BOOK
1. Luis Buñuel, Tarkovsky enthused in *Sculpting In Time*, was a poet of anti-conformism, an uncompromising, furious protest which was expressed in the 'sensuous texture' of his films (ST, 51). Buñuel's approach to cinema wasn't political, or conscious, or cerebral, Tarkovsky maintained, but emotional and poetic. And that, combined with the sensuality of his films, made his works very appealing for Tarkovsky.
2. G. Deleuze, 1989, 68.
3. C. Paglia, "Interview", in K. French, ed. *Screen Violence*, Bloomsbury, London, 1996, 42.
4. In other words, Tarkovsky is valued precisely because his cinema appears to be the opposite of (or a refreshing alternative to) mainstream filmed entertainment: it employs non-Hollywood actors; it has a lack of banal dialogue and didactic (Hollywood) music; it does not seem to compromise; does not pander to or patronize audiences; it doesn't use gratuitous violence or sensation; it's not formulaic; it's not overblown by massive budgets, and so on.
5. I. Bergman, in J. Graffy, 18.
6. I. Bergman, in D. Robinson.

PART ONE: THE ARTIST

ONE : THE POETRY OF CINEMA

THE POETICS OF CINEMA
1. T. Mitchell, 1984, 56.

ANDREI TARKOVSKY AS POET
1. In N. Sinyard, 1992, 47.
2. B. Amengual: "Andrei Tarkovski après sept films", in M. Estève, 1983.
3. In 1947, quoted in H. Chipp, 549,
4. G. Bataille, *Literature and Evil*, tr. A. Hamilton, Calder, London, 1973, 65.

ANDREI TARKOVSKY AND THE HISTORY OF POETRY
1. M. Turovskaya, 15.
2. A. Pushkin, in D. Obolensky, 108.

TWO: THE FILM IMAGE

CAMERAWORK
1. Quoted in J. Boorman, 1997, 128.

THE TRACKING SHOT
1. 1970, in J. Leyda, 35.

DISTANCE AND VIEWPOINT
1. A. Hitchcock, in *Hitchcock On Hitchcock*, Faber, London, 1997, 125-7.

SURFACES
1. In V. Stoichita, 15.
2. P. & L. Murray, *Art and Artists*, Penguin, London, 1976, 256-7.

DECAY AND TRASH
1. The relation between the excremental and the ecstatic realms has been analyzed by writers such as G. Wilson Knight (see Knight's study of Powys, Lawrence, Joyce and other writers in *Neglected Powers*, Routledge & Kegan Paul, London, 1972).

THREE: THE MYSTERIES OF SPACE AND TIME

1. In G. Mast, 76.

TIME IN ANDREI TARKOVSKY'S CINEMA
1. Quoted in P. Strick, 1989.

SCULPTING IN TIME
1. In M. Tarkovskaya, 1983, 233.
2. D.H. Lawrence, *Reflections on the Death of a Porcupine*, in *A Selection From Phoenix*, 456-7.

THE SACRALIZATION OF SPACE
1. P. Klee, *The Thinking Eye*, Lund Humphries, London, 1961, 340.

SPACE AND ABSTRACTION
1. G. Matthieu, *Vers une structuration nouvelle des formes*, Les Études Carmelitaines, De Silea De Bronwer, Bruges, 1958.
2. E. Husserl, *Cartesian Meditations*, Marintus Nijhoff's, The Hague, 1960, 57.

FOUR: SYMBOLS AND MOTIFS

WATER
1. In R. Graves, *The White Goddess*, Faber, London, 1961, 218-19.

FIRE
1. W. La Barre, *Muelos,* ib, 107, 130.

FIVE: THE WORLDS OF ANDREI TARKOVSKY

TARKOVSKY'S WORLDS
1. *Time*, Mch 20, 1978, 20.

LANGUAGE
1. H. Cixous, in V. Conley, *Hélène Cixous*, University of Nebraska Press, Lincoln, 1984, 57.
2. T. Moi, 1988, 99-100.

SIX: SOUND AND MUSIC

SOUND AND SPACE
1. A. Truppin, 237.
2. A. Truppin, 241.

SOUND IN *THE SACRIFICE*
1. Similar off-screen explosions are used in *The Bounty* (Roger Donaldson, 1984, GB), here sounding like canon fire and emphasizing Captain Bligh's rage.

SILENCE
1. J. Ferguson, 171.
2. Samuel Beckett, *The Beckett Trilogy*, 375-8.

CLASSICAL MUSIC
1. P. Kolker, 1985, 61.

SEVEN: PRODUCTION

FAST FILMS
1. Quoted in D. Robinson, Jan 3, 1987.
2. V. Johnson, 1994, 8.
3. J. Leyda, 318.

SHOOTING
1. J. Moreau, 1976, in J. Leyda.
2. D. Bordwell, 1988, 85.

BUDGET
1. T. Mitchell, 1983, 54.

ANDREI TARKOVSKY'S UNMADE FILMS
1. J.-L. Godard, in *Godard On Godard*, 227.
2. In 1969, in J. Leyda, 251.

EIGHT: ANDREI TARKOVSKY AND PAINTING

ANDREI TARKOVSKY AND LEONARDO DA VINCI
1. In V. Stoichita, 10.
2. In H. Chipp, 188.
3. S. Freud, 155.

LEONARDO DA VINCI'S *ADORATION OF THE MAGI*
1. O. Spengler, *The Decline of the West*, tr. C.F. Atkinson, ed. H. Werner, A. Helps, Allen & Unwin, London, 1961, 155.

ANDREI TARKOVSKY AND PIERO DELLA FRANCESCA
1. A. Stokes, *The Stones of Rimini*, in P. Francesca, 1985, 11.
2. R. Vischer, *Luca Signorelli and the Italian Renaissance*, 1879, in ib., 10.
3. R. Alberti, *Tratto della Nabilta dello Pittura*, 1585, in ib., 10.

NINE: PHILOSOPHY AND RELIGION IN ANDREI TARKOVSKY'S CINEMA

VISION QUEST
1. W. La Barre, 1972, 140, 171.
2. J. Leyda, 1977, 346.
3. P. Green, 1985, 54.

RELIGIOUS EXPERIENCE
1. B. Kawin, 1987, 63.

TEN: STRUCTURE AND NARRATION

ENDING IN ECSTASY
1. N. Kagan. *The Cinema of Stanley Kubrick,* Continuum Publishing, New York, NY, 1991/ 1997, 230.

ELEVEN: CHILDHOOD, FAMILY AND CHARACTER

RELATIONSHIPS
1. A kiss is regarded by some people as more intimate than intercourse; in some porn videos actors don't kiss, and focusses on genital contact, whereas in Tarkovsky's work, on a different level of intimacy, the most people do is kiss.

CHARACTER TYPES, ARCHETYPES, STEREOTYPES
1. Hysteria, or womb-madness, is connected with the powers of women during menstruation, according to Penelope Shuttle and Peter Redgrove, powers which men traditionally do not understand, and try to suppress (*The Wise Wound*, Paladin, London, 1986).
2. M. Praz, *The Romantic Agony,* tr. A. Davidson, Oxford University Press, Oxford, 1933, 50, 320.
3. As G. Petrie and V. Johnson point out, the story Alexander recounts in *The Sacrifice* when his sister cut off her long hair 'makes Tarkovsky's own ideas on this subject almost too transparent' (JP, 221).

TWELVE: LOVE, GENDER AND SEXUALITY

1. Tarkovsky had a strained relationship with his own sister, Marina Tarkovskaya.
2. See V. Johnson and G. Petrie, JP, 246.

PART TWO: THE FILMS

THIRTEEN: *IVAN'S CHILDHOOD*

1. Mosfilm, 1962, 39f.
2. M. Turovskaya, 32.
3. Tarkovsky, quoted in M. Turovskaya, 35.
4. M. Turovskaya, 7.

FOURTEEN: *ANDREI ROUBLYOV*

1. L. Anninsky, *Shestidesyatniki i my*, VTPO Kinotsentr, Moscow, 1991.
2. V. Johnson & G. Petrie, 1994b, 12.

SIXTEEN: *MIRROR*

MIRROR AND POETRY
1. The *Bright, Bright Day* version of the screenplay contained scenes which did not make it into the final film (though the ending was much the same): the cemetery scene; the mother selling flowers in the war; the demolishing of a church cupola; the mother and sister at a hippodrome; and the father's description of battle casualties.

CRITICS ON *MIRROR*
1. In A. Lawton, 1992, 241.
2. In J. Passek, 284.

SEVENTEEN: *STALKER*

STALKER
1. D. Russell, *Sight & Sound*, 1990.
2. A. Tarkovsky, in "Ispoved", *Kontinent*, 42, 1984.
3. See C. Pike, "Change and the individual in the work of the Strugatskys", in P. Davies, 1990, 90f.
4. J. Orr, 1998, 50.

CONCLUSION
1. A. Tarkovsky, quoted in M. Turovskaya, xxii.

EIGHTEEN: *NOSTALGHIA*

TARKOVSKY IN ITALY
1 Ian Christie noted that in Russian nostalgia means a longing for home, rather than for the past (M. Turovskaya, 159).

FURTHER THOUGHTS ON *NOSTALGHIA*
1. N. Zorkaya, in JP, 162.
2. V. Johnson and G. Petrie suggest that Eugenia doesn't really work as a character because she has to carry too many concepts: threatening sexuality, the wife and family he's escaped from, contemporary materialism, secular society, the death of spirituality of the past, Gorchakov's self-imprisonment, and his inability to connect (JP, 163).
3. I. Bergman, 1994, 334.

NINETEEN: *THE SACRIFICE*

THE WORLD OF *THE SACRIFICE*
1. See D. Campbell, *War Plan UK*, Burnett, London, 1982, 461.
2. Tarkovsky may have chosen the name Alexander in *The Sacrifice* because it begins with an 'a', like the names of many of his other protagonists. Alexander is also the first name of some of Tarkovsky's cultural heroes: Alexander Pushkin, Alexander Dovzhenko, Alexandre Astruc (there is also Alexander Solonitsyn and Alexander Blok).

ENDINGS
1. M. Leszcylowski, 1987, 284.

TWENTY: CRITICAL RESPONSES TO ANDREI TARKOVSKY'S CINEMA

CRITICAL RESPONSE
1. M. Turovskaya, 69.
2. Ivor Montagu, 1973, 92.
3. In A. Lawton, 1992, 276.
4. In H. Marshall, 1976, 94.
5. G. Vincendeau, 1995, 419.
6. G. Andrew, 1989, 282.
7. P. Wells, *Understanding Animation*, Routledge, London, 1998, 94.

CINEMA IN THE WAKE OF ANDREI TARKOVSKY
1. J. Park, 114.
2. Further correspondences have been noted by John Orr (1998, 55-56).
3. I. Christie, 1998.
4. In A. Lawton, 1992, 243.

Filmography

This is a short filmography of movies directed by Andrei Tarkovsky: there are other, more detailed filmographies available elsewhere.

There Will be No Leave Today
(Segodnya uvolneniya ne budet)

Short made at VGIK in 1959

The Steamroller and the Violin
(Katok i stripka)

Production company – Mosfilm; *script* – Andrei Mikhalkov-Konchalovsky and Andrei Tarkovsky; *photography* – Vadim Yusov in Sovcolour; *editor* – L. Butuzova; art director – S. Agoyan; *music* – Vyacheslav Ovchinnikov; *sound* – V. Krashkovsky
VGIK Diploma project, 1960. Length – 46 minutes
Sasha – Igor Fomshenko; Sergei – V. Samansky; Girl – Nina Arkhanelskaya; Mother – Marina Adzhubey.

Ivan's Childhood (Ivanovo destvo)

Production company – Mosfilm; *script* – Mikhail Papava and Vladimir Bogomolov, based on Bogomolov's book *Ivan*; *photography* – Vadim Yusov in black-and-white; *editor* – G. Natanson; *art director* – Evgeni Cherniaev; *music* – Vyacheslav Ovchinnikov; *sound* – E. Zelentsova.
Released in 1962. Length – 95 minutes.
Ivan – Kolya Burlyaev; Captain Kholin – Valentin Zubkov; Lieutenant Galtsev – E. Zharikov; Corporal Katasonych – S. Krylov; Lieutenant-colonel Gryaznov – Nikolai Grinko; Masha – L.Malyavina; Ivan's mother – Irma Tarkovskaya.

Andrei Roublyov

Production company – Mosfilm; *prodcucer* – Tamara Ogorodnikova; *script* – Andrei Mikhalkov-Konchalovsky and Andrei Tarkovsky; *photography* – Vadim Yusov in Scope and black-and-white, part in Sovcolour; *editor* – Ludmila Feganova; *art director* – Evgeni Cherniaev; *music* – Vyacheslav Ovchinnikov; *sound* – E. Zelentsova.
Production – 1964-66. Domestic release – 1971. UK release – 1973. Length – 185 minutes. Other versions: 146 minutes, and one 6 minutes longer than the previous longest known, shown in Moscow, 1989.
Andrei Roublyov – Anatoly Solonitsyn; Krill – Ivan Lapikov; Daniel – Nikolai Grinko; Theophanes the Greek – Nikolai Sergeyev; mute girl – Irma Raush Tarkovskaya; Boriska – Nikolai Burlyaev; Buffoon – Rolan Bykov.

Solaris

Production company – Mosfilm; *script* – Andrei Tarkovsky and Friedrich Gorenstein, based on Stanislaw Lem's book; *photography* – Vadim Yusov in Scope and Sovcolour; *editor* – Ludmila Feganova; *art director* – Mikhail Romadin; *music* – Eduard Artemiev, J.S. Bach's *Chorale Prelude in*

F minor.
Production – 1969-72. Release – 1972. Length 165 minutes (some versions 144 minutes).

Chris Kelvin – Donatas Banionis; Hari – Natalia Bondarchuk; Snaut – Yuri Jarvet; Sartorius – Anatoly Solonitsyn; Burton – Vladislav Dvorzhetsky; Kelvin's father – Nikolai Grinko; Gibaryan – Sos Sarkissyan.

Mirror (Zerkalo)

Production company – Mosfilm; *producer* – E. Waisberg; *script* – Andrei Tarkovsky and Aleksandr Misharin; *photography* – Georgy Rerberg in Sovcolour and black-and-white; *lighting* – V. Gusev; *editor* – Ludmila Feganova; *art director* – Nikolai Dvigubsky; *music* – Eduard Artemiev.

Domestic release – 1974. UK release – 1980. Length: 106 minutes.

Aleksei's mother/ Natalia – Margarita Terekhova; Ignat. aged 5 – Filipp Yankovsky; Aleksei/ Ignat, aged 12 – Ignat Daniltsev; father – Oleg Yankovsky; print worker – Nikolai Grinko; Lisa – Alla Demidova; military instructor – Yuri Nazarov; passer-by – Analtoly Solonitsyn; voice of Aleksei the narrator – Innokenti Smoktunovsky; Aleksei's mother as an older woman – Maria Tarkovskaya.

Stalker

Production company – Mosfilm; *producers* – Aleksandra Demidova and Willie Geller; *script* – Arkady and Boris Strugatsky, based on their story *Roadside Picnic*; *photography* – Aleksandr Knyazhinsky, colour; *lighting supervisor* – L. Kazmin; *editor* – Ludmila Feganova; *production designer* – Andrei Tarkovsky; *music* – Eduard Artemiev; *sound* – V. Sharun.

First screened – 1979. Length – 161 minutes.

The Stalker – Aleksandr Kaidanovsky; the Writer – Anatoly Solonitsyn; the Scientist – Nikolai Grinko; Stalker's wife – Alisa Freindlikh; Stalker's daughter – Natasha Abramova.

Nostalghia

Production company – Opera Film (Rome)/ RAI Television Rete 2 and Sovinfilm; *producers* – Manolo Bolognini, Franco Casati, Renzo Rossellini, Daniel Toscan du Plantier; *script* – Andrei Tarkovsky and Tonino Guerra; *photography* – Guiseppe Lanci, in Eastman Colour; *editor* – Erminia Marani, Amedeo Salfa; *art director* – Andrea Crisanti; *sound effects* – Massimo Anzellotti, Luciano Anzellotti; *sound mixer* – Danilo Moroni.

Production, 1981-83. Release – 1983. Length 126 minutes.

Andrei Gorchakov – Oleg Yankovsky; Domenico – Erland Josephson; Eugenia – Domiziana Giordano; Gorchakov's wife – Patrizia Terreno.

The Sacrifice (Offret)

Production company – Swedish Film Institute (Stockholm)/ Argos Film (Paris), with Film Four International (London), Josephson & Nykvist, Sveriges Television/ SVT 2, Sandrew Film & Teater, with the participation of the French Ministry of Culture; *producer* – Katinka Farago; *script* – Andrei Tarkovsky; *photography* – Sven Nykvist, Eastman Colour and black-and-white; *editor* – Andrei Tarkovsky and Michal Leszcylowski; *art director* – Anna Asp; *music* – J.S. Bach's *St Matthew Passion*, Swedish and Japanese folk music; *sound* – Owe Svensson, Bosse Persson, Lars Ulander, Christin Lohman, Wikee Peterson-Berger.

Release, 1986. Length – 149 minutes.

Alexander – Erland Josephson; Adelaide – Susan Fleetwood; Otto – Allan Edwall; Julia – Valerie Mairesse; Maria – Gudrun Gísladóttir; Victor – Sven Wollter; Martha – Filippa Franzén; Little Man – Tommy Kjellqvist; Julia – Valerie Mairesse.

Availability

The work of Andrei Tarkovsky is fairly readily available on DVD, video and other formats. There are varations between editions, of course. For instance, the DVD of *Mirror* (from Artifical Eye in the U.K.) contains two different sound mixes (and they are *very* different). In general, the sound mix or dub that was overseen or approved by the filmmakers themselves is the one to go for. And movies are best seen in the original language.

The main distributors of Tarkovsky's works are:
In the U.S.A.: Kino Video. Criterion. Facets.
In the U.K.: Artifical Eye. Criterion. Russico.
In Australia: Shock.

Bibliography

BY ANDREI TARKOVSKY

"Tarkovsky", *Kogda film okonchen* [When the film is finished], *Iskusstvo kino*, Moscow, 1964
interview, *Ekran*, 65, Sbornik, Iskusstvo, Moscow, 1966
"Zapechatlennoye vremya [Imprinted time]", *Iskusstvo kino,* 4, 1967
interview, M. Ciment, *Positif*, 109, Oct, 1969
"Vsesoyuznaya pereklichka kinematografistov" [An All-Union Filmmakers' Discussion]", *Iskusstvo kino,* 4, 1971
"Zachem proshloye vstrechayetsya s budushchim? [Why does the past meet the future?]", *Iskusstvo kino*, 11, 1971
Bely, bely den [Bright, bright day], Mosfilm, Moscow, 1973
"O Kinobraze [About the film image]", *Iskusstvo kino*, 3, 1979
"My delayem filmy [We make films]", *Kino*, Lithuania, 10, 1981
interview, *Time Out*, 568, Mch, 1981
interview, *Time Out*, 686, Nov, 1981
"Between Two Worlds", interview, *American Film,* Nov, 1983
interview, *Time Out*, 729, Aug, 1984
interview, *The Listener*, Aug, 1984
"A Propos du *Sacrifice*", *Positif*, 303, May, 1986
"Entretien", *Cahiers du Cinéma*, 392, Feb, 1987
"Ya chasto dumayu o vas [I think of you often]", *Iskusstvo kino,* 6, 1987
Le Sacrifice, Schirmer, Munich, 1987
"Strasti po Andreyu [The passion according to Andrei]", interview, *Literaturnoye obozreniye*, 9, 1988
Zerkalo [*Mirror*], *Kinostsenarii*, 2, Goskino, 1988
"Krasota spasyot mir" ["Beauty will save the world"], *Iskusstvo kino*, 2, 1989
"Vstat na put [Taking the right path]", *Iskusstvo kino*, 2, 1989
Lektsii po kinorezhissure [Lecture on film directing], ed. K. Lopushansky, Lenfilm, Leningrad, 1989
Martyrolog: Tagebücher, 1970-1986, tr. V. Schutz-Bischitzky & M. Milack-Verheyden, Limes, Berlin, 1989
Sculpting in Time: Reflections on the Cinema, tr. K. Hunter-Blair, Faber, London, 1989
Time Within Time: The Diaries, 1970-1986, tr. K. Hunter-Blair, Seagull Books, Calcutta, 1991
Andrei Rublev, tr. K. Hunter-Blair, Faber, London, 1991
Der Spiegel. Filmnovelle, Arbeitstagebücher und Materialien zur Entstehung des Films, Limes Verlag, Berlin, 1993
Collected Screenplays, Faber, London, 1998
Andrei Tarkovski: Récits de jeunesse, Paris, 2004
Diaries, tr. C. Giroldi, ed. P. Rey, Cahiers du cinéma, Paris, 2004
Instant Light: Tarkovsky Polaroids, Thames & Hudson, London, 2004
Interviews (Conversations with Filmmakers), 2006

OTHERS

N. Abramov. "Dialog s A. Tarkovskim o nauchnoy fantastike na ekrane [Dialogue with A. Tarkovsky about science fiction on the screen]", *Ekran, 1970-1971*, Moscow, 1971
H. Agel. "Andrej Tarkovski", in *Le visage du Christ à l'écran*, Desclée, Paris, 1985
C. Akesson. *The Sacrifice: The Film Companion*, I.B. Tauris, London, 2000
J. Alexander. "Tarkovsky's Last Vision", *Cinema Papers*, Melbourne, May, 1987
Andrej Tarkowskij, Reihe Film, 39, Carl Hanser Verlag, Munich, 1987
O. Assayas. "Tarkovsky: Seeing is Believing", *Sight & Sound*, Jan, 1997
H. Baba. *The Andrei Tarkovsky Films*, Misuzu Shobou, Tokyo, 2002
L. Bawden, ed. *The Oxford Companion to Film*, Oxford University Press, Oxford, 1976
S. Beckett. *The Beckett Trilogy: Molloy, Malone Dies, The Unnamable*, Picador/ Pan, London, 1979,
R. Bergan & R. Karney. *Bloomsbury Foreign Film Guide*, Bloomsbury, London, 1988
I. Bergman. *Bergman on Bergman, Interviews with Ingmar Bergman*, by S. Björkman *et al*, tr. P.B. Austin, Touchstone, New York, NY, 1986
—. *Images: My Life in Film*, Faber, London, 1994
R. Bird. *Andrei Rublev*, BFI, London
—. *Andrei Tarkovsky: Elements of Cinema*, 2008
E. Blank. "*The Sacrifice*, trapped by its monologues", *Pittsburgh Press*, Jan 2, 1987
J. Boorman & W. Donohue, eds. *Projections 7*, Faber, London, 1997
—. *Projections 8*, Faber, London, 1998
D. Bordwell. *Narration in the Fiction Film,* Routledge, London, 1988
—. *Ozu and the Poetics of Cinema*, British Film Institute, London, 1988
F. Borin. *Andrej Tarkovsky*, Venice, 1987
R. Bresson. *Notes on the Cinematographer*, tr. J. Griffin, Quartet, London, 1986
J. Brosnan. *Future Tense: The Cinema of Science Fiction*, St Martin's Press, New York, NY, 1978
—. *Primal Screen: A History of Science Fiction Film*, Orbit, London, 1991
S. Bukatman. *Terminal Identity: The Virtual Subject in Postmordern Science Fiction*, Duke University Press, Durham, NC, 1993
G. Buttafava. *Il cinema russo e sovietico*, Torino, 2000
J. Campbell. *The Power of Myth*, with B. Moyers, ed. B.S. Flowers, Doubleday, New York, NY, 1988a
V. Canby. review of A*ndrei Roublev*, *New York Times*, Oct 10, 1973
H.B. Chipp, ed. *Theories of Modern Art*, University of California Press, Los Angeles, CA, 1968
P. Christensen. "Kierkegaardian Motifs in Tarkovsky's *The Sacrifice*", *Soviet and East-European Drama, Theatre and Film*, 7, 2/3, Dec, 1987
I. Christie. "Raising the Shroud", *Monthly Film Bulletin*, Feb, 1987
—. "Returning to Zero", *Sight & Sound*, Apl, 1998
M. Ciment, ed. *Dossier Positif*, Editions Rivages, Paris, 1988
J. Clute & P. Nicholls, eds. *The Encyclopaedia of Science Fiction*, Orbit, London, 1993
L. Cooke & P. Wollen, eds. *Visual Display*, Bay Press, Seattle, 1995
J.C. Cooper. *An Illustrated Dictionary of Symbols*, Thames and Hudson, London, 1978
A. Crisanti. "Le décor de *Nostalgia*", in G. Ciment, 1988
A. de Baecque. *Andrei Tarkovski*, Cahiers du Cinéma, Paris, 1989
G. Deleuze. *Cinema 1: The Movement Image*, Athlone Press, London, 1989
—. *Cinema 2: The Time Image*, Athlone Press, London, 1989
M. Dempsey. "Lost Harmony: Tarkovsky's *The Mirror* and *The Stalker*", *Film Quarterly*, Autumn, 1981
N. Savio D'Sa. "Andrei Rublev: Religious Epiphany in Art", *Journal of Religion and Film*, 3, 2, 1999
Nathan Dunne, Jean-Paul Sartre & Marc Forster. *Tarkovsky*, 2008
A. Dzenis. "The Passion According to Andrei: *Andrei Rublev*", *Metro*, 110, 1997
S. Eisenstein. *Film Form*, tr. J. Leyda, Harcourt, Brace & Co, New York, NY, 1949
M. Eliade. *Ordeal by Labyrinth*, University of Chicago Press, Chicago, IL, 1984
—. *Symbolism, the Sacred and the Arts*, Crossroad, New York, NY, 1985
T. Elmanovits. *The Mirror of Time: The Films of Andrei Tarkovsky*, Eesti Raamat, Tallinn, 1980
M. Estève, ed. *Etudes Cinématographiques: Andrei Tarkovsky*, 135-138, Lettres Modernes, Paris, 1983

J. Ferguson. *An Illustrated Encyclopaedia of Mysticism*, Thames & Hudson, London, 1976
V.P. Filimonov. *Andrei Tarkovskii: Sny i lav' o Dome*, 2011
L.A. Garrett. "Der rätselhafte und geheimnisvolle Andrej Tarkovskij", *Soviet Film*, 7, 1989
—. "Never Be Neutral", *Sight & Sound*, Jan, 1997
—. *Andrei Tarkovsky: a Photographic Chronicle of the Making of the Sacrifice*, 2011
G. Gauthier. *Andrei Tarkovski*, *Filmo*, 19, Edilig, Paris, 1988
D.J. Goulding, ed. *Five Filmmakers: Tarkovsky, Forman, Polanski, Szabó, Makavejev*, Indiana University Press, Bloomington, IN, 1994
J. Graffy. "Tarkovsky: The Weight of the World", *Sight & Sound*, Jan, 1997
J. Grant. "Andrei Tarkovsky", *Cinéma*, 231, 1978
P. Green. "The Nostalgia of the Stalker", *Sight and Sound*, Winter, 1984-85
—. "Andrei Tarkovsky", *Sight and Sound*, 56, 2, Spring, 1987
—. *Andrei Tarkovsky: The Winding Quest*, Macmillan, London, 1993
N. Grinko. "Talisman Andreya Tarkovskogo [The talisman of Andrei Tarkovsky]", interview, *Sovetsky ekran*, 2, 1990
L. Halliwell. *Halliwell's Film Guide*, ed. J. Walker, HarperCollins, London, 1993
—. *Halliwell's Film Guide 2000*, ed. J. Walker, HarperCollins, London, 1999
S. Hancock. "Andrei Tarkovsky: Master of the Cinematic Image", *Mars Hill Review*, 4, 1996
P. Hardy, ed. *The Aurum Encyclopaedia of Science Fiction*, Aurum, London, 1991
T. Hyman. "*Solaris*", *Film Quarterly*, Spring, 1976
E. Hynes. "Stalker", *Reverse Shot*, Spring, 2004
Iskusstvo kino, 2, 1989
W. Jacobsen *et al. Andrej Tarkovsky*, Munich, 1987
V.T. Johnson & G. Petrie. "Andrei Tarkovskii's Films", *Journal of European Studies*, 20, 3, Sept, 1990
—. *The Films of Andrei Tarkovsky. A Visual Fugue*, Indiana University Press, Bloomington, IN, 1994
—. "Tarkovsky", chapter in D. Goulding, 1994
—. "Ethical Exploration" [*Solaris*]", *Sight & Sound*, 2002
G.A. Jonsson & T.A. Ottarsson. *Through the Mirror: Reflections on the Films of Andrei Tarkovsky*, 2006
W. Kaoru. *St. Tarkovsky*, Japan, 2003
A.H. Karriker. "Patterns of Spirituality in Tarkovsky's Later Films", in D. Petrie, 1990
B. Kawin. *Mindscreen: Bergman, Godard and First-Person Film*, Princeton University Press, Princeton, NJ, 1978
—. *How Movies Work*, Macmillan, New York, NY, 1987
H. Kennedy. "Tarkovsky: A Thought in Nine Parts", *Film Comment*, 23, 3, 46, 1987
K. Kieslowski. *Kieslowski On Kieslowski*, ed. D. Stok, Faber, London, 1993
Kinovedcheskiye zapiski, 9, 1991; 14, 1992
R.P. Kolker. *Bernardo Bertolucci*, British Film Institute, London, 1985
B.A. Kovács & A. Szilágyi. *Les Mondes d'Andrei Tarkovski*, tr. V. Charaire, L'Age d'Homme, Lausanne, 1987
P. Král. "Tarkovsky, or the Burning House", *Screening the Past*, 12, Mch, 2001
J. Kristeva. *The Kristeva Reader*, ed. T. Moi, Blackwell, Oxford, 1986
W. La Barre. *The Ghost Dance: The Origins of Religion*, Allen & Unwin, London, 1972
—. *Muelos: A Stone Age Superstition About Sexuality*, Columbia University Press, New York, NY, 1985
R. Lapsley & M. Westlake, eds. *Film Theory: An Introduction*, Manchester University Press, Manchester, 1988
A. Lawton. *Kinoglasnost: Soviet Cinema in Our Time*, Cambridge University Press, Cambridge, 1992
—. *The Red Screen: Politics, Society, Art in Soviet Cinema*, Routledge, London, 1992
M. Le Fanu. *Sight & Sound*, Autumn, 1986
—. *The Cinema of Andrei Tarkovsky*, British Film Institute, London, 1987
S. Lem. *Solaris*, Penguin, London, 1981
J. Leyda. *Kino: A History of the Russian and Soviet Cinema*, 3rd ed, Allen & Unwin, London, 1983

H. Marshall. "Andrei Tarkovsky's *The Mirror*", *Sight and Sound*, Spring, 1976
—. *Masters of the Soviet Cinema*, Routledge, London, 1983
S. Martin. *Andrei Tarkovsky*, Essential Books, London, 2005
G. Mast *et al*, eds. *Film Theory and Criticism: Introductory Readings*, Oxford University Press, New York, NY, 1992
M. McCormick. *Model of a House: An Essay on Andrei Tarkovsky's The Sacrifice*, 2006
A. Mengs, *Stalker,* Ediciones Rialp, Spain
J.C.J. Metford. *Dictionary of Christian Lore and Legend*, Thames & Hudson, London, 1983
V.I. Mikhalkovich. *Andrei Tarkovsky*, Znaniye, Moscow, 1989
T. Mitchell. "Tarkovsky in Italy", *Sight and Sound*, Winter, 1982-83
—. "Andrei Tarkovsky and *Nostalghia*", *Film Criticism*, 8, 3, 1984
T. Moi, ed. *French Feminist Thought*, Blackwell, Oxford, 1988
I. Montagu. "Man and Experience: Tarkovsky's World", *Sight and Sound*, Spring, 1973
J. Moore. "Vagabond Desire: Aliens, Alienation and Human Regeneration in Arkday and Boris Strugatsky's *Roadside Picnic* and Andrei Tarkovsky's *Stalker*", in D. Cartmell *et al*, eds., *Alien Identities: Exploring Differences in Film and Fiction*, Pluto Press, London, 1999
Sihusei Nish. *Tarkovsky and His Time: Hidden Truth of Life*, 2011
G. Nowell-Smith, ed. *The Oxford History of World Cinema*, Oxford University Press, Oxford, 1996
S. Nykvist. "Entretien" (with H. Niogret), *Positif*, 324, Feb, 1988
—. & B. Forslund. *In Reverence of Light*, Albert Bonniers Publishing Company, Sweden, 1997
D. Obolensky, ed. *The Penguin Book of Russian Verse*, Penguin, London, 1965
J. Orr. *Contemporary Cinema*, Edinburgh University Press, Edinburgh, 1998
J. Panshina. "Rossia v ozhidanii chuda", *Russakaia mysl*, Feb 23, 1978
P.P. Pasolini. *Pasolini on Pasolini*, ed. O. Stack, Thames & Hudson, London, 1969
W. Paul. review of *Andrei Roublev*, *Village Voice*, Nov 1, 1973
S. Petraglia. *Andrej Tarkovskij*, Edizioni A.I.A.C.E., Turin, 1975
V. Petric. "Tarkovsky's Dream Imagery", *Film Quarterly*, Winter, 1990
G. Petrie. "Andrei Tarkovsky", in G. Nowell-Smith, 1996
Piero della Francesca: *The Complete Paintings of Piero della Francesca*, intr. P. Murray, notes by P. de Vecchi, Penguin, London, 1985
L. Yan Pin. "Simvolika Tarkovskogom i daoizma [The symbolism of Tarkovsky and Taoism]", *Kinovedcheskiye zapiski*, 9, 1991
D. Quinlan. *The Illustrated Guide to Film Directors*, B.T. Batsford, London, 1983
M. Ratschewa. "The Messianic Power of Pictures: The Films of Andrei Tarkovsky", *Cinéaste*, 13, 1, 1983
Thomas Redwood. *Andrei Tarkovskys Poetics of Cinema* , 2010
D. Richie. *The Films of Akira Kurosawa*, University of California Press, Berkeley, CA, 1965
C. Rickey. "Starkly, a director explores materialism and spirituality", *Philadelphia Inquirer*, Feb 4, 1987
D. Robinson. "Sculptor in Time, Master of Spirit", *The Times*, Jan 3, 1987a
—. "Testament to a Powerful Will", *The Times*, Jan 9, 1987b
W.H. Rockett. *Devouring Whirlwind: Terror and Transcendence in the Cinema of Cruelty*, Greenwood Press, New York, NY, 1988
J. Romney. "Future Soul [*Solaris*]", *Sight & Sound*, 2002
J. Rosenbaum. "Inner Space: Exploring Tarkovsky's *Solaris*", *Film Comment*, 26, 4, Aug, 1990
T. Sabulis. "Director's final *Sacrifice* truly a gift", *Dallas Times Herald*, Jan 16, 1987
D. Salynsky. "Rezhissyor i mif [Director and myth]", *Iskusstvo kino*, 12, 1989
A.M. Sandler, ed. *Mir i filmy Andreya Tarkovskogo* [*The World and Films of Andrei Tarkovsky*], Iskusstvo, Moscow, 1991
J.P. Sartre. *Situations VII*, Gallimard, Paris, 1965
D. Shipman. *The Story of Cinema*, Hodder & Stoughton, London, 1984
D. Shostakovitch. *Testimony: The Memoirs of Dmitri Shostakovitch*, ed. S. Volkov, tr. A.W. Bouts, Hamish Hamilton, London, 1979
N. Sinyard. *Children in the Movies*, Batsford, London, 1992
Nariman Skakov. *The Cinema of Tarkovsky: Labyrinths of Space and Time (Kino: the Russian and Soviet Cinema)*, 2012)

V. Sobchack. *The Limits of Infinity: The American Science Fiction Film*, A.S. Barnes, New York, NY, 1980
—. ed. *The Persistence of History: Cinema, Television, and the Modern Event*, Routledge, London, 1995
V. Solovyov. "Semeynaya khronika ottsa i syna Tarkovskikh [The family chronicle of Tarkovsky's father and son]", *Novoye russkoye slovo*, 12 May, 1989
V.I. Stoichita. *Leonardo da Vinci*, Abbey Library, London, 1978
P. Strick. "*The Sacrifice*", *Monthly Film Bulletin*, Jan, 1987
—. "Tarkovsky's Lost Minutes", *The Times*, July 12, 1989
—. "Releasing the Balloon, Raising the Bell", *Monthly Film Bulletin*, Feb, 1991
A. & B. Strugatsky. *Roadside Picnic*, Pocket Books, New York, NY, 1978
O. Surkova. "Avtobiograficheskiye motivy v tvorchestve Andreya Tarkovskogo [Autobiographic motifs in the creative work of Andrei Tarkovsky]", *Kino-vedcheskiye zapiski*, Moscow, 9, 1991
—. *Tarkovsky and I*, Zebra E, Dekont, 2002
O. Svensson. "On Tarkovsky's *The Sacrifice*", in L. Sider, 2003
N. Synessios. *Mirror*, I.B. Tauris, London, 2001
P. Taggart. "Weighty Film", *Austin American-Statesman*, April 3, 1987
M. Tarkovskaya, ed. *O Tarkovskom [About Tarkovsky]*, Progress Publishers, Moscow, 1989
Arseny Tarkovsky. *Stikhotvoreniya [Poems]*, Khudozhestvennaya literatura, Moscow, 1974
—. *Poems*, Greville Press Poetry, 1992
—. *Blagoslovennyi svet*, St Petersburg, 1993
—. *Sobranie sochinenii [Collected Works]*, 3 vols, Moscow, 1991-93
—. *Life, Life: Selected Poems*, tr. V. Rounding, Crescent Moon, 1999/ 2008
R. Taylor & I. Christie, eds. *The Film Factory: Russian and Soviet Cinema in Documents*, Routledge, London, 1988
—. et al, eds. *The BFI Companion to Eastern European and Russian Cinema*, British Film Institute, London, 2000
K. Thompson & D. Bordwell. *Film History: An Introduction*, McGraw-Hill, New York, NY, 1994
D. Thomson. *A Biographical Dictionary of the Cinema*, Secker & Warburg, London, 1978
A. Truppin. "And Then There Was Sound: The Films of Andrei Tarkovsky", in R. Altman, 1992
M. Turovskaya. *Tarkovsky: Cinema as Poetry*, tr. N. Ward, ed. I. Christie, Faber, London, 1989
"*Sacrifice* Rolls in Sweden Next May", *Weekly Variety*, Sept 12, 1984
J. Verniere. "A beautiful *Sacrifice*", *Boston Herald*, Nov 7, 1986
G. Vincendeau, ed. *Encyclopaedia of European Cinema*, British Film Institute, London, 1995
T. Vinokuroya. "Khozhdeniye po mukam *Andreya Rublyova* [The tormented path of *Andrei Rublyov*]", *Iskusstvo kino*, 10, 1989
A. Vogel. *Film as a Subversive Art*, Weidenfeld & Nicolson, London, 1974
J. Vronskaya. *Young Soviet Film Makers*, Allen & Unwin, London, 1972
M. Warner. *Alone of All Her Sex*, Picador/ Pan, London, 1985
E. Weiss & J. Belton. *Film Sound: Theory and Practice*, Columbia University Press, New York, NY, 1989
D. Wingrove, ed. *Science Fiction Film Source Book*, Longman, London, 1985
P. Wollen. *Signs and Meaning in the Cinema*, Secker & Warburg, London, 1972
F. Yermash. "On byl khudozhnik [He was an artist]", *Sovetskaya kultura*, Sept 9, 1989 & Sept 12, 1989
Laura Vermon. *A Closer Look Into the Life and Famous Works of Andrei Tarkovsky*, 2012
D. Youngblood. "Post-Utopian History as Art and Politics: Andrei Tarkovsky's *Andrei Roublev*", in V. Sobchack, 1995
M. Zak. *Andrei Tarkovsky: Tvorchesky portret [Andrei Tarkovsky: an artistic portrait]*, Soyuzinformkino, Moscow, 1988
N. Zorkaya. "Zametki k portretu Andreya Tarkovskogo [Remarks towards a portrait of Andrei Tarkovsky]", *Kino panorama*, 2, 1977
—. *The Illustrated History of the Soviet Cinema*, Hippocrene Books, New York, NY, 1990
S. Zizek. *Looking Awry*, Verso, London, 1991
—. *Enjoy Your Symptom Jacques Lacan in Hollywood and Out*, Routledge, New York, NY, 1992
—. "The Thing from Inner Space", 1999

Jeremy Robinson has written many critical studies, including *Hayao Miyazaki, Walerian Borowczyk, Arthur Rimbaud,* and *The Sacred Cinema of Andrei Tarkovsky,* plus literary monographs on: William Shakespeare; Samuel Beckett; Thomas Hardy; André Gide; Robert Graves; and John Cowper Powys.

It's amazing for me to see my work treated with such passion and respect. There is nothing resembling it in the U.S. in relation to my work.
Andrea Dworkin (on *Andrea Dworkin*)

This model monograph – it is an exemplary job, and I'm very proud that he has accorded me a couple of mentions… The subject matter of his book is beautifully organised and dead on beam.
Lawrence Durrell (on *The Light Eternal: A Study of J.M.W. Turner*)

Jeremy Robinson's poetry is certainly jammed with ideas, and I find it very interesting for that reason. It's certainly a strong imprint of his personality.
Colin Wilson

Sex-Magic-Poetry-Cornwall is a very rich essay… It is a very good piece… vastly stimulating and insightful.
Peter Redgrove

ARTS, PAINTING, SCULPTURE

The Art of Andy Goldsworthy
Andy Goldsworthy: Touching Nature
Andy Goldsworthy in Close-Up
Andy Goldsworthy: Pocket Guide
Andy Goldsworthy In America
Land Art: A Complete Guide
The Art of Richard Long
Richard Long: Pocket Guide
Land Art In Great Britain
Land Art in Close-Up
Land Art In the U.S.A.
Land Art: Pocket Guide
Installation Art in Close-Up
Minimal Art and Artists In the 1960s and After
Colourfield Painting
Land Art DVD, TV documentary
Andy Goldsworthy DVD, TV documentary
The Erotic Object: Sexuality in Sculpture From Prehistory to the Present Day
Sex in Art: Pornography and Pleasure in Painting and Sculpture
Postwar Art
Sacred Gardens: The Garden in Myth, Religion and Art
Glorification: Religious Abstraction in Renaissance and 20th Century Art
Early Netherlandish Painting
Jasper Johns
Brice MardenLeonardo da Vinci
Piero della Francesca
Giovanni Bellini
Fra Angelico: Art and Religion in the Renaissance
Mark Rothko: The Art of Transcendence
Frank Stella: American Abstract Artist
Alison Wilding: The Embrace of Sculpture
Vincent van Gogh: Visionary Landscapes
Eric Gill: Nuptials of God
Constantin Brancusi: Sculpting the Essence of Things
Max Beckmann
Gustave Moreau
Caravaggio
Egon Schiele: Sex and Death In Purple Stockings
Delizioso Fotografico Fervore: Works In Process 1
Sacro Cuore: Works In Process 2
The Light Eternal: J.M.W. Turner
The Madonna Glorified: Karen Arthurs

LITERATURE

J.R.R. Tolkien: The Books, The Films, The Whole Cultural Phenomenon
J.R.R. Tolkien: Pocket Guide
Beauties, Beasts and Enchantment: Classic French Fairy Tales
Tolkien's Heroic Quest

Brothers Grimm: German Popular Stories
Sexing Hardy: Thomas Hardy and Feminism
Thomas Hardy's *Tess of the d'Urbervilles*
Thomas Hardy's *Jude the Obscure*
Thomas Hardy: The Tragic Novels
Love and Tragedy: Thomas Hardy
The Poetry of Landscape in Hardy
Wessex Revisited: Thomas Hardy and John Cowper Powys

Wolfgang Iser: Essays and Interviews
Petrarch, Dante and the Troubadours
Maurice Sendak and the Art of Children's Book Illustration
Andrea Dworkin
Cixous, Irigaray, Kristeva: The *Jouissance* of French Feminism
Julia Kristeva: Art, Love, Melancholy, Philosophy, Semiotics and Psychoanalysis
Hélene Cixous I Love You: The *Jouissance* of Writing
Luce Irigaray: Lips, Kissing, and the Politics of Sexual Difference
Peter Redgrove: Here Comes the Flood
Peter Redgrove: Sex-Magic-Poetry-Cornwall
Lawrence Durrell: Between Love and Death, East and West

Love, Culture & Poetry: Lawrence Durrell
Cavafy: Anatomy of a Soul
German Romantic Poetry: Goethe, Novalis, Heine, Hölderlin
Novalis: *Hymns To the Night*
Feminism and Shakespeare
Shakespeare: *The Sonnets*
Shakespeare: Love, Poetry & Magic
The Passion of D.H. Lawrence
D.H. Lawrence: Symbolic Landscapes
D.H. Lawrence: Infinite Sensual Violence
The Ecstasies of John Cowper Powys
Sensualism and Mythology: The Wessex Novels of John Cowper Powys
Amorous Life: John Cowper Powys (H.W. Fawkner)
Postmodern Powys: New Essays on John Cowper Powys (Joe Boulter)
Rethinking Powys: Critical Essays on John Cowper Powys
Paul Bowles & Bernardo Bertolucci
Rainer Maria Rilke
Joseph Conrad: *Heart of Darkness*
In the Dim Void: Samuel Beckett

Samuel Beckett Goes into the Silence
André Gide: Fiction and Fervour
Jackie Collins and the Blockbuster Novel
Blinded By Her Light: The Love-Poetry of Robert Graves

POETRY

Ursula Le Guin: *Walking In Cornwall*
Peter Redgrove: Here Comes The Flood
Peter Redgrove: Sex-Magic-Poetry-Cornwall
Dante: Selections From the *Vita Nuova*
Petrarch, Dante and the Troubadours
William Shakespeare: *The Sonnets*
William Shakespeare: Complete Poems
Blinded By Her Light: The Love-Poetry of Robert Graves
Emily Dickinson: Selected Poems
Emily Brontë: Poems
Thomas Hardy: Selected Poems
Percy Bysshe Shelley: Poems
John Keats: Selected Poems
John Keats: Poems of 1820
D.H. Lawrence: Selected Poems
Edmund Spenser: Poems
Edmund Spenser: *Amoretti*
John Donne: Poems
Henry Vaughan: Poems
Sir Thomas Wyatt: Poems
Robert Herrick: Selected Poems
Rilke: Space, Essence and Angels in the Poetry of Rainer Maria Rilke
Rainer Maria Rilke: Selected Poems
Friedrich Hölderlin: Selected Poems
Arseny Tarkovsky: Selected Poems
Paul Verlaine: Selected Poems
Novalis: *Hymns To the Night*
Arthur Rimbaud: Selected Poems
Arthur Rimbaud: *A Season in Hell*
Arthur Rimbaud and the Magic of Poetry
D.J. Enright: By-Blows
Jeremy Reed: *Brigitte's Blue Heart*
Jeremy Reed: *Claudia Schiffer's Red Shoes*
Gorgeous Little Orpheus
Radiance: New Poems
Crescent Moon Book of Nature Poetry
Crescent Moon Book of Love Poetry
Crescent Moon Book of Mystical Poetry
Crescent Moon Book of Elizabethan Love Poetry
Crescent Moon Book of Metaphysical Poetry
Crescent Moon Book of Romantic Poetry
Pagan America: New American Poetry

MEDIA, CINEMA, FEMINISM and CULTURAL STUDIES

J.R.R. Tolkien: The Books, The Films, The Whole Cultural Phenomenon
J.R.R. Tolkien: Pocket Guide
The *Lord of the Rings* Movies: Pocket Guide
The Ghost Dance: The Origins of Religion
The Cinema of Hayao Miyazaki
Hayao Miyazaki: *Princess Mononoke*: Pocket Movie Guide
Hayao Miyazaki: *Spirited Away*: Pocket Movie Guide
The Peyote Cult
Cixous, Irigaray, Kristeva: The *Jouissance* of French Feminism
Julia Kristeva: Art, Love, Melancholy, Philosophy, Semiotics and Psychoanalysis
Luce Irigaray: Lips, Kissing, and the Politics of Sexual Difference
Hélene Cixous I Love You: The *Jouissance* of Writing
Andrea Dworkin
'Cosmo Woman': The World of Women's Magazines
Women in Pop Music
Discovering the Goddess (Geoffrey Ashe)
The Poetry of Cinema
The Sacred Cinema of Andrei Tarkovsky
Andrei Tarkovsky: Pocket Guide
Andrei Tarkovsky: *Mirror*: Pocket Movie Guide
Walerian Borowczyk: Cinema of Erotic Dreams
Jean-Luc Godard: The Passion of Cinema
Jean-Luc Godard: Pocket Guide
John Hughes and Eighties Cinema
Ferris Buller's Day Off: Pocket Movie Guide
The Cinema of Richard Linklater
Liv Tyler: Star In Ascendance
Blade Runner and the Films of Philip K. Dick
Paul Bowles and Bernardo Bertolucci
Media Hell: Radio, TV and the Press
Detonation Britain: Nuclear War in the UK
Feminism and Shakespeare
Wild Zones: Pornography, Art and Feminism
Sex in Art: Pornography and Pleasure in Painting and Sculpture
Sexing Hardy: Thomas Hardy and Feminism

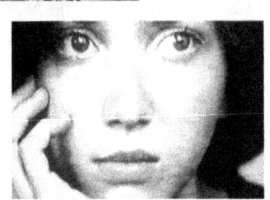

The Light Eternal is a model monograph, an exemplary job. The subject matter of the book is beautifully organised and dead on beam. (Lawrence Durrell)

It is amazing for me to see my work treated with such passion and respect. (Andrea Dworkin)

Sex-Magic-Poetry-Cornwall is a very rich essay... It is like a brightly-lighted box. (Peter Redgrove)

CRESCENT MOON PUBLISHING P.O. Box 1312, Maidstone, Kent, ME14 5XU, England
0044-1622-729593   cresmopub@yahoo.co.uk   www.crmoon.com

www.ingramcontent.com/pod-product-compliance
Lightning Source LLC
Chambersburg PA
CBHW032150080426
42735CB00008B/649